THE
MAGIC
OF
Pathworking

About the Author

Simon Court began his magical training with **AMORC** by correspondence as a teenager in 1958. He also began reading some of the very few books on magic that were around at the time, those in particular of W. E. Butler and Dion Fortune.

Soon afterwards he joined the **Society of the Inner Light** and studied with that group for a year until pressure of schoolwork won the battle for his time. After a break in studies to complete his education and get settled into a career, he again began his daily exercises and soon came into contact with the Helios course, later to become the **Servants of the Light** (SOL), in which he enrolled.

He studied for some years and took the role of administrator and senior supervisor for the Australian students of the SOL under the guidance of Dolores Ashcroft-Nowicki. In the 1970s he was the President of the **Canberra Lodge of the Theosophical Society** for two years. He was also invested as a Leading Knight in that organization's **International Order of the Round Table,** a medium for teaching ethical values to children of members through principles cast in the form of a chivalry structure. In addition, he actively supported the **Liberal Catholic Church** in that city.

During that decade he also ran a number of ritual magical training circles, notably **OORIMBA** in Canberra and the **Rainbow Serpent Lodge** in Sydney. He ran eclectic magical gatherings in Melbourne, styled the **Agathodaimon Cult,** and conducted discussion groups in Brisbane through to the end of the 1980s.

He then went on to travel and work extensively through Europe and England between 1991 and 2001, meeting with many representatives of magical and pagan groups and orders and working with some.

He now resides back in Australia and spends his time between collating his written material and acting as an elder at various pagan gatherings in Queensland and New South Wales.

He was at one time a member of the **Glen Innes Celtic Festival Players** and took the part of Merlin at each summer and winter solstice, when the battle between the Holly and Oak Kings was publicly enacted at the Glen Innes Standing Stones.

THE
MAGIC
OF
Pathworking

A
MEDITATION
GUIDE FOR
YOUR INNER
VISION

Simon Court

Llewellyn Publications
Woodbury, Minnesota

FIRST EDITION
First Printing, 2020

Cover design by Shira Atakpu
Cover image by veneratio/stock.adobe.com
Editing by Marjorie Otto

Llewellyn Publications is a registered trademark of Llewellyn Worldwide Ltd.

Library of Congress Cataloging-in-Publication Data (Pending)
ISBN: 978-0-7387-6541-9

Llewellyn Publications
A Division of Llewellyn Worldwide Ltd.
2143 Wooddale Drive
Woodbury, MN 55125-2989
www.llewellyn.com

Printed in the United States of America

Other Books by Simon Court

The Meditator's Manual: A Practical Introduction to the Art of Meditation
(The Aquarian Press)

Discover Meditation
(Sterling Press)

To the memory of Olive Ashcroft of the Servants of the Light,
who selflessly supervised my studies and guided me for many years.

Acknowledgments

There are many people who have passed on their knowledge to me or from whom I have learned. I particularly owe thanks to Dolores Ashcroft-Nowicki, one-time Director of Studies for the Servants of the Light. It was she who taught me the methods and theory of pathworkings and kindled the fire of my enthusiasm for this way of working.

In my travels in the United Kingdom I also had an opportunity to meet up with Marian Green and work with one of her groups. It is she who gave me the occasional prod to actually set things down.

Special thanks must go to all of those who have worked with me in various ritual groups, whether participating, supporting, or establishing.

I also thank the students, too numerous to name individually, who have used some of my earlier pathworkings in the past and whose feedback has been very helpful to me.

Contents

✣

Introduction
✠

This is a book presenting an integrated set of what are called "pathworkings," which I created within the Western Mystery Tradition. Pathworkings can be described as visual meditations used to create inner change to influence outside actions.

But it is not a book just for members of magical groups. Anyone can use these techniques, and I have prepared them in a style that does not rely on any specific magical, Wiccan or spiritual way, although I draw on many sources to fill out and explain the different themes and processes. Traditional symbols and myths from different cultures have been drawn upon in the construction of the workings, and their practice and study can be of value to traditional and nontraditional students alike.

I was introduced to this magical technique by one of my teachers, a person well established in the Western Tradition. I simply fell in love with the method right away and it has been my friend ever since. If I need access to some information, I set up a pathworking to get that access. What is done in mind with intent will pop up in everyday reality in the most unspectacular ways. Some say that what we call reality is a joint projection of everyone's inner processes, in awareness or not. There is no direct proof that this is so, but many people I know and many reports I have seen mention methods of manifestation using the creative imagination to manifest desired results.

As a long-time practitioner of Western magical techniques, I view things slightly differently. That is, in my experience people sometimes attract to themselves items, events, or situations that an outsider can see is the result more of what they *are* than what they *do*. When I found earlier in life some practitioners of Western magical systems who claimed this was so and that the best magic was to work on yourself so that what came to you continued, as always, to match what you are, I decided to join them and learn more. These magicians of the Western ways were saying that there is no magic that influences things, but there is a magic that changes oneself so that things come to you by natural attraction. This works, whether you want it or not, so work on oneself is primary. I have found this so in both mistake and success and the work continues. I am passing on a tried and tested technique using my own discovered symbols and themes.

The book is organized into two parts. Part 1 presents, by way of preparation and introduction to the method, a set of pathworkings based upon the five elements—earth, air, fire, water, and spirit or quintessence. These serve to lead the reader-student to their inner working place. They create a balanced foundation for a balanced life and a base upon which to build further.

There then follows part 2, the main work, which is a set of thirteen workings based on lunar and astrological themes as these are taught within the Western Mystery Tradition. Each working has the pathworking itself and a description of the themes and symbols used. The pathworkings lead the practitioner to become familiar with the archetypal parts of their inner nature via the features of a consistent inner landscape. The discussion of themes provides a supporting analysis of the symbols used with their meanings.

But before we can dive into this we need to know several things. We need to know more of the what, the why, and the methodology, for a start.

What Are "Pathworkings"?

Within the organizations where I trained, the term "pathworkings" has quite a specific meaning: a fantasy journey, a journey in the imagination that has been crafted along archetypal themes to achieve specific result. Although the term is often used interchangeably with "fantasy journey," I am using it here for a specific form of fantasy journey.

When I think of describing the difference between pathworking and a fantasy journey, I think of a saying from late-nineteenth-century writer G. K. Chesterton, "The traveller [sic] sees what he sees; the tripper sees what he has come to see."[1]

---

1. G. K. Chesterton, *The Autobiography of G. K. Chesterton*, eds. George J. Marlin, Richard P. Rabatin, John L. Swan, Joseph Sobran, Patricia Azar, Randall Paine, and Barbara D. Marlin (San Francisco: Ignatius Press, 2006), 306.

From my point of view, fantasy journeys are set up to lead you to an inner place where you can unlock experiences related to you yourself. Pathworkings, on the other hand, lead to specific inner places created by magic workers and storytellers where you can experience your relationship with a collective archetype.

These are not universal set-in-concrete definitions. They are just descriptions of how I am using the terms in this particular book. My use is based upon what I was taught in the Western Mystery Tradition.

Fantasy Journeys

If someone asks you for directions to a place and you run through the route in your mind's eye while giving directions, this is a form of fantasy journey. If you relive the events of a particularly pleasurable holiday, this too is a form of fantasy journey.

Fantasy journeys take place in the imagination. The imagination is the stimulation of the senses by internal means, rather than external. The same senses are used in a fantasy journey as in an outer world journey. The difference is only in where the stimulus comes from: "outside" or "inside."

For most people, the visual sense is dominant with the other senses in a sort of ranking or hierarchy of importance. The same occurs in a fantasy journey. Usually, it is the visual imagination that is dominant and texts of fantasy journeys and pathworkings rely on this in their descriptions of the journey. But, the other senses are really just as important and the more the whole range of sense can be brought into play, the fuller the experience will be.

The fantasy journey follows a predetermined route. In this it differs from daydreaming and reverie. Though the journey itself is laid out beforehand, the experiences that a participant might have are personal.

If a number of people take a fantasy journey together, their experiences will be individual, yes. But it may turn out that some have similar experiences and responses to the events or details of the journey. This is the same as when people react to events in the outer world. Some experience it the same way and some do not. There is not much difference on the inner levels of the senses.

The Origins of Pathworkings

The term "pathworking" is derived from the magical lodges of the past, such as those of the Order of the Golden Dawn. The use of the word "path" indicated a line on the Qabalistic Tree of Life that joined two of the spheres (Sephiroth) of that diagram. The paths in those systems had particular attributions and correspondences, and these were built into the images of the fantasy journey created to tread that path in the mind's eye. The workings had a particular place within a magical framework. They were used for training magicians in the use of magical faculties and to open up access to different levels of thinking and experiencing in a structured, predetermined way. The workings of the program I have created here contain similar themes drawn from Celtic, Grail, and English mythology.

An important difference between fantasy journeys and structured pathworkings is the degree of undirected versus directed thought and feeling. A fantasy journey may take you to a place and invite you to note what feelings and thoughts arise. A pathworking, on the other hand, may take you to a place and invite you to create the thoughts and feelings that relate to the working. This is not to say that you will not also have your own reactions, but the invitations are for you to align the talents of your incarnate self with archetypal themes.

Are Pathworkings Only for Members of Magical Groups?

Put simply, yes, but not only for such.

These workings draw on magical symbolism common to a wide variety of magical work. They also are woven through with myth and legend that I have found in common use in both Wiccan and Neo-Pagan groups. In fact, I have led pathworkings similar to these in presentation to both formal magical groups and various nature and wild magic groups, an unusual combination.

These workings draw on my own experience, study, and practice.

Why Do Pathworkings?

Again, put simply, discovery and integration.

Let us suppose we are each a charioteer trundling along. Say we have a chariot and two horses and that the chariot and charioteer represent the physical and energy bodies. Now suppose that one horse is Reason and one horse is Feeling. It makes more sense to train both horses rather than focus on just one. It will give a smoother and more directed ride when required.

Can we train the feelings? Of course we can. Actors have been portraying feelings on demand and getting into character for centuries. We can all do it, but commonly we do not. To work on training those feelings, in some workings you will be invited not only to note and react in thought to features, but also to allow suggested associated feelings to arise, or to generate such feelings. This is, of course, in addition to those that arise in you at the time.

The Western tradition teaches that our everyday world is in the outer plane of manifestation. It also teaches there are inner planes and that a given plane is causal to that next outermost to it. A given plane is a plane of effects for those planes that are inner to it.

Because our physical existence is the outermost plane, then all other planes are inner to this one and causal. It follows that anything undertaken on the inner planes can, under the right condition, produce effects in our outer physical plane. So, you should understand that work done on an inner plane can, under the right conditions, produce changes in an outer plane, like this physical one we know so well.

However, inner plane changes can also come through in changes in consciousness too, and it is this aspect that is the primary reason for performing pathworkings. We place an archetypal impulse on the inner planes and it works out into either everyday physical life or, more usually, into consciousness.

This is the true meaning of magic—to produce changes in consciousness in accordance with will. These workings are deliberately constructed and crafted by the author with the acquisition of this skill in readers and practitioners as the primary goal.

The Structure Behind the Workings

Now to an overview of how the workings are presented.

There is first a set of elemental workings in part 1 where you get to know the elemental realms and experience their nature, linking it with the resonant parts in your own nature. It is normal for one or other elemental force to predominate in a given individual and to some extent this can be related to the features of their astrological birth chart. Undertaking these elemental pathworkings helps the practitioner achieve a more balanced nature, a nature more suitable to take on further journeys into the inner realms.

Having created the groundwork and location for inner work, you are then presented with the main work in Part 2, which is a set of thirteen workings.

These further establish the locations, geography, and relationships for the inner landscape within which all work is performed.

The symbol system used for this main section is based upon the operation of the astrological moon through the twelve astrological signs. Because this is "inner" work, the symbolism of the moon as "new" is used. This does not mean that the workings have to be performed to synchronize with the actual physical and astrological New Moon in a sign. This will be explained further in the next section.

What's Special about These Pathworkings?

Rather than being a mere collection of pathworkings addressing different aspects of the incarnate nature, I've deliberately crafted these workings to form an integrated journey to self discovery on multiple levels. Every working in this book has not only a specific job, as many do, but also a specific place in a journey of unfoldment and discovery.

This approach is rare, but it has been put together for you and it is here. It is very unusual to find a set of pathworkings as the actual training. Normally, pathworkings are used as an adjunct to a training course using other methods such as reading, ritual, energy work, and other techniques.

Here, right here, is an effective training course based solely upon the ordered presentation of pathworkings, crafted by an experienced student and practitioner of the arts. Each has a specific task in the process of ordered self-unfoldment.

The Method of Working

In magical ritual teaching, the principle of "intention" is extremely important. I was taught that intention is paramount in ritual work. Ritual work can be performed "on the inner," non-physically. In such cases, anyone anywhere in the world may join in and clock time is not a factor. Intent is the key to synchronization on the inner levels of group consciousness. I was taught this and have found it to be so through experience.

These workings are designed around the symbolism of each of thirteen New Moons and their style, content, and intended effect in each case to one of the twelve astrological signs. Although the signs are organized around the cycle of the sun at each New Moon, sun and moon are in conjunction and in the same astrological sign. Each working has a description and the material in that description should be used for daily meditation subjects in the time between one working and another.

Although the workings are designed around the thirteen New Moons of a year, they do not have to be done on the days of those specific matching New Moons. They do not even have to be done at the New Moon at all.

On the outer plane, synchronization is by clock and calendar. On the plane of imagination and dreams where we will be working, synchronization is by intent. All that is necessary is that the workings are done four weeks apart with the *intent* that they match with the corresponding physical event. The other days of those four weeks should be spent on meditation on items within the discussion that accompanies the working, or the elements of the working itself, or your responses and realizations during the working.

Why the New Moon Symbolism?

The phases of the Moon are often used to symbolize plans and their unfolding. The New Moon represents inception of an idea. By the First Quarter we have gathered our resources, planned our method, and put it into effect. By the Full Moon the plans reach fruition. During the waning phase, we enter the wind down of the project to its end at the Third Quarter. During the dark Fourth Quarter, we review the project and prepare for the next project or next phase. And so it continues.

These moon phases are not actual timings but ways to help us understand the symbolic meanings of the moon phases as we might view them operating through the signs in an astrological chart. Doing pathworkings at the New Moon sets the ball rolling and floats an "intent" for the next cycle.

The Additional Working

Normally there are twelve complete lunar cycles in a year, but this is not an exact match. In everyday life we often note Full Moons and there is normally one per calendar month. There is an effective creep due to the different times of the cycles and every three of four years we get two Full Moons in the same month. We call this a "Blue Moon" in English-speaking countries. I have also seen the term "Black Moon" used in the United States and Australia for the second New Moon in the same month. Because of our time zones the naming does not coincide around the world. The term "once in a blue moon" is not universal. I resided and worked for a couple of years in Belgium. The French speakers there said *tous les trente-six du mois,* or "every thirty-sixth of the month." Not quite as interesting.

For those ritual workings performed by my group and myself, I coined the term "Rose Moon" for the second New Moon in an astrological sign, not month. This was relevant to our workings.

Therefore, I have included a thirteenth working to include the associated symbolism I associate with this event. The second New Moon in a sign does in fact occur in all of the signs some year or other, so in a sense it participates in symbolism with all others and can therefore have symbolic qualities of integration.

The Method and Timings

These workings can be done at any time. It is not essential that they be synchronized with external events. The only proviso is that sometimes the effects of a pathworking take time to be consolidated into consciousness. To make sure the pathworkings have time to consolidate, I suggest working with one particular working within a four-week period. This gives a full lunar cycle for all the effects to work through into everyday realizations. If you wish, match the workings to a New Moon as the schedule to follow. It does not have to be in the astrological sign of the working. Just the next New Moon when you are ready to start.

A Daily Habit

After performing the working on the day of the New Moon, make notes of your experiences. Over the next four weeks, perform a relaxation and meditation each day, taking one topic each session from your realizations, experiences, or from the discussion notes on the working. This relaxation and meditation should become a daily habit.

A suitable meditation method to enhance pathworking experiences is the "Seed Thought" method. This is described in appendix A along with preliminary relaxation and breathing, to "set the scene."

There is a trick to establishing a daily habit. We already have daily habits: regular meals, shower, dress, undress, go out, return, and so on. The trick to establish a new habit is to insert it between two existing adjacent ones, such as get up—meditate—shower, or put dinner on—meditate—have dinner, or get dressed—meditate—have breakfast. There will be sequences of regularity in most of your days and the two you pick to sandwich your new meditation habit will be whichever two suit your lifestyle best.

The Diary

Use a notebook to record your progress and experiences. Why not make it a bit special? Find one with or add a mystical design on the cover. Or find one contained within a leather outer cover, decorated in a way that has meaning for you; something about the notebook that is special to you and linked to the inner work you are going to undertake.

In this book you should record for each session:

- The date and time
- The name of the current working
- Then for the day of the actual working record:
    - Your first thoughts after performing the working
    - Any notes of realizations after the working
- For days of the remainder of the four-week period:
    - The seed thought or idea chosen for meditation from the working, your experience, or the discussion text
- For all days:
    - Optionally any other factors that you would like to monitor—weather, state of mind, moon phase, season of the year—things that are important to you already

This is your foundation.

The Pathworking Method

Each chapter opens with a brief summary of what the path is about. To the extent that our natures are universal, a short description of aims and direction will be provided and can be useful. On the other hand, to the extent that we are individual this header is brief, as it would not be helpful to state a possible realization before the traveler has encountered it for themselves. There is some guidance for you to build on and extend in ways unique to yourself and your own development. Sometimes we go boldly and sometimes we do not put our arm in a hole unless we know what critter may be down there.

Each working has a preamble that provides links with workings already performed and a reference to the intent of the working. It is intended just for continuity and advance information and is not part of the working itself. If you prefer to do the working with no preliminary information, feel free to skip it. It can, however, be useful to provide structure. The choice is yours.

The next step is to review the text of the working itself. Have a brief look through the details and decide how you would like to deal with it. Some people like to read the text and get the feel of what is going on. Then they remember the essential details and later do the working from memory of the text. Although relying on memory can be tricky, this is probably the easiest way.

Others like to record the working onto a media player, phone, or tablet, and then play it back to do the working while listening to it. When making the recording, you will need to pace the speaking to allow time to visualize the images during playback. This can be a bit tricky and if you want to dwell a little longer on some aspect, you will not be able to do so unless you risk breaking your concentration by pausing the playback. But for a hand-held device, "Pause" and "Play" switching may be simple and nonintrusive. Those who taught me this method, and other creators of pathworkings, usually recorded their working to run, with pauses, for about twenty minutes.

There are some people who can use what I call "dual consciousness." Although this is a natural talent, its deliberate use is quite rare. But it does occur. Such people sometimes prefer to read the working while doing it. This is probably the most difficult method as it is too easy to let the events in the outer world overshadow the events of the inner working, which is the opposite of what is intended. However, care in setting up the place and time of working can prevent these distractions. There are many ways that human beings use the faculty of attention and so some are more able to easily use this last method than other people. Indeed, some people read novels in this way, reading and experiencing at once.

Another way of working is for someone to read the working while another person, or members of a group, tread that working. This works best if the reader can also do the working at the same time and so be sensitive enough to others to know where to pause for longer and where to move the action along a bit quicker. In other words, the reader should preferably have the dual consciousness type of attention.

Given the above background, I strongly advise that you read the working to get some understanding of what it is about and then memorize the key points, locations, scenery, feelings, and such. You could make your own bullet point list of the key features beforehand and this will aid remembering the working.

When the time comes to do the working, assign about forty-five minutes at a time and location where you will not be disturbed by any of the usual events or commitments of your everyday life. You should also minimize the unexpected as well. Turn off the cell phone and other electronic prompters and advisors. You can collect any messages later. You could even put a note on the door in case people call around.

A very useful psychological device to keep the inner and outer realities compartmentalized is to decide on a signal or set of signals to tell yourself that you are beginning or ending a session. I strongly advise that you use such signals. This could be a mime of opening curtains at the start and closing them at the end. It could be lighting a candle and dowsing it. It could be a mime of graspingly entering a darkened room at the start and of reminding yourself to remain silent about the work at the end, finger to lips. It could be the casting and taking up of a circle. It could be the lesser banishing ritual of the pentagram at start and end. And it could be as simple as snapping your fingers before and after. Choose whatever signal or set of signals makes most sense for you and the magical work that you might already do.

With that all taken care of, the next step will be to find a relaxed position to do the working in. Personally, I favor a straight-backed chair. The reason is that after a busy day I might relax a bit too much in a very comfortable chair or sprawled out on a bed. The ideal we are heading for is a pleasantly relaxed body with a mind expectantly alert. There is a knack worth learning, which I refer to as the seesaw. When the body is active, the mind is relaxed, and when the body is relaxed the mind is active. The inner and outer can complement each other.

You may have relaxation and breathing exercises already to take you to such a state. By all means use them. If not, relax by gradually working your way down your body, head to toe, letting go of any tensions in the muscles on the way and allowing your body to "settle" into place.

A regular breathing pattern using the four-fold method may help relax you further. This method has you breathing in for a count of four, holding for two, breathing out for four and holding again for two. By holding I do not mean closing the throat, but rather just a cessation of breathing. It's not quite the same as holding your breath while underwater or tantrums. If you would like to use a short mantra to focus the mind, by all means do so. Once you're relaxed and focused, you'll be ready to begin the working.

At the end of the working, reverse the initial process. Use a simple mantra such as "I awake to the body." Use some regulation of the breathing, which could have become quite shallow during the working, and a general physical stretch to wake up the muscles and nerves again.

Finish this with your closing signal, such as drawing the curtains, or dowsing the candle, or a ritual closing of the circle; whatever combination of things you have chosen for this purpose. Finally—not tomorrow, not after a coffee or other refreshment—but immediately and *as part of the working*, write up your journal entry.

Then it only remains to take the note off the door, switch on the phone, unless you were using it for the recording, check messages, and you are back into everyday outer living. Have a snack as well. This helps close down the inner levels. This is not so much because having them near to outer levels of thinking is dangerous, but more because you have made them do some work and they need to close off to consolidate what has been done.

That is the method of the pathworking as used in many groups, training circles, and orders.

Part One

The pathworkings in this book are separated into two groups. The first group introduces the method of pathworking and simple element workings to promote an initial balance within the practitioner as a sound and firm basis on which to build the main pathworking program.

Part 1 of this book first introduces a set of pathworkings based upon the five elements—earth, air, fire, water, and spirit or quintessence. The purpose of these workings is to create a balanced foundation that will flow into everyday life and provide a base upon which to build further. This first part provides an introduction to the method of working.

Like any structure, a proper foundation is needed before further building proper can proceed. Leaving aside the quintessence for the moment, the Four Elements of the Wise are the mystical foundation of all things and this four-fold division can be applied to categorize things in any area of study.

We can look at the structure of a living physical person as earth (flesh and bone), air (the operation of the lungs), fire (the operation of the nervous system), and water (the circulation of the blood).

A Jungian view of the personality might provide us with sensation, thought, intuition, and emotion, these relating to earth, water, air, and fire respectively.

These four divisions can and have been used to structure and make sense of a range of different areas of study. Whether used deliberately or not, the four-fold elemental structure is fundamental to the way we humans in incarnation make sense of things. Tibetan mandalas frequently show a four-fold layout. It is fundamental to human understanding.

The four-element division of any topic of study forms the basis for understanding and for seeing the relationships between parts, the relationships that make the whole thing work.

But over and above this, there is a fifth principle in the background. It represents the meaning or the essence of the subject being studied.

In this section we will tread the four paths, of each of the elements, one after the other, to create our inner plane basis. We will finally tread the fifth path to bring life or reality into this initial basis for future work.

Once we have established this basis, the real work can begin. It is not a separate part, however, as during part 2 there will be a connection back to the part 1 set.

Part 2 is the yearlong set of exercises. This part provides a set of pathworkings and extends the initial foothold on the inner planes by introducing additional elements within the broader inner landscape. This leads the reader to tread these ways and discover additional locations, taking one working every four weeks, preferably at or near the time of the New Moon in that month. These pathworkings will firmly establish the practitioner as the ruler of their inner kingdom. This can flow through to normal outer existence, providing benefits in everyday life.

But first, we will create an inner plane setting for these part 2 workings. This setting is the first part of an established inner plane landscape and your familiarity with the landscape will grow as you continue to tread these and other paths. It represents "clearing the decks," similar to getting everything ready, tools laid out, space prepared before any other work begins.

Introductory Path:
The Garden

—————— ✟ ——————

As mentioned earlier, if you do not want foreknowledge to color your experiences, skip the introductory paragraph and go straight to the pathworking. You can do this for any of the workings.

In this working, we will establish a starting point within the inner realms that is your very own. This will be your entry point. You will then find a second location that will both serve as your work area and will function as the entry point for the remainder of the workings in this group. The entry point is yours; it's private. The work area is shared, like a public park is shared.

Pathworking

Begin by settling into your seat and relaxing. Breathe deeply and as you breathe out let all your cares and tensions wash away. Close your eyes.

Relax, sink down, and draw apart. As your body relaxes, your mind becomes clear and sharp. You are alert and ready to build the images as they are described.

In the place where you are sitting there is a doorway, a doorway that is not normally seen, a doorway into the inner realms. In the mind's eye, rise up and approach that doorway.

You stand before the door between the realms. Study it. As you study it, an image you create to represent this chapter appears on the door. The image first becomes lighter and then fades. As it does the door opens to admit you into the main street of a historically early village or small settlement. You know somehow that this is your village in the inner realms.

Look down at your feet, your hands, your clothing. Make a note of how you are dressed.

You hear the sound of the door closing and, looking back, you see that you have come through a solid wooden door set in the wall of a hut. This is your hut. You turn back to look around.

The street running past the front of your hut leads to the right and left. To the left the road becomes narrower and rougher and leads out of the village to a dark forest and in the distance you see a range of mountains beyond. You seem to know that no one goes into the forest.

To the right the street leads out of the village toward pasture and farmland. You turn right and walk in that direction. You pass a few huts, but few, if any, people are around.

As you come to the edge of the village, there is on the right of the street a high wall of stone with a tall iron gate. This is the local park. Turn, go through the gate and into the park.

The park is surrounded by the stone wall. Most of the park is filled with grass and a few trees around the edges. There is a sense of peace and serenity. You see that the path by which you entered leads to a central rose garden. You walk toward it.

The rose garden is laid out in a square. The path you are on leads to the center where there is a smaller circular garden bed of roses, with benches to sit on. You make your way there, passing through an arched trellis twined all over with wild rose. You sit on one of the benches. It is peaceful and the warm breezes release the scent of roses around you.

When you are using this place as the starting point for your pathworkings in this series, you would now close your eyes and let the images arise for your working itself. This bench in the rose garden will be your starting and ending point for the following five workings of this section.

On this occasion, just close your eyes and experience being present in the park among the trellises of wild roses and the beds of cultivars of various colors. Take a few moments to pause here ...

Open your eyes and reconnect with the garden setting. Feel the bench on which you sit.

It is time to return. Retrace your steps out of the central garden and out of the park.

On the street once more, turn left and walk back to the door by which you entered this realm.

Stand for a moment before the door, the door to your hut. Then open it and pass through. Return to your place in the physical realm as the door closes solidly behind you.

After a moment or two you become aware of your position and the place where you are sitting. Take in once more the sounds and scents of your surroundings in the physical plane. When you are ready, open your eyes, breathe deeply, and stretch cramped limbs. Brothers and sisters, awake to the body!

Discussion

There are several significant symbols built into this working. These are described here.

The Door: This is a common device used in pathworkings and other methods of inner plane working. It signals to your inner self that we are marking a distinct division between the normal consciousness realm of everyday life and the inner realm of realities that are reflections and precursors of events in the outer world. This is important to guard against "leakage" between the planes. It is not the way of magical training in the Western tradition to blend the realities or allow the planes to infiltrate each other unless specifically under our control. The person trained in the Western tradition might be perceiving other psychic realities when they want to be but not at other times.

The Village: This device places us in a context or community. It indicates that there are lives and events other than our own that are going on in the inner realms. These planes are not our personal play areas to act in however we wish, but exist in a context that is available to all. Consequently, there are expectations of appropriate and responsible behavior to take into account. We wish to delve into and work within the global, archetypal inner realm and not just within our own personal unconscious. The idea of us having a place within a community signals this.

The Hut: This is our own place within the community that is the village. It signals that we belong here and we are not just a random traveler.

The Park: This is a further aspect of the community idea. A park within a village or small town is an area in common for all. It is a place where any may wander, play, meet, and participate in arranged or regular events, such as a farmers' market, a fête, or a festival. It is also a place where people can go to be alone with their own personal thoughts.

The Rose Garden: The symbol of the rose has been used for centuries as a symbol of the mysteries, of that which is spiritual in our lives and of that expression of spiritual realities in the outer world—love. The Rosicrucians used the symbol of the rose upon an equal-armed golden cross. This indicated spirit embedded within the four-fold expression of matter. The rose is an outer expression of the inner life that will give meaning to our workings.

These are the essential elements of our setting: the door as marker of division between the realms; the village as a signal that we are working in the Collective Unconscious; the hut to signal our own place within that collective; the park to signal that we are participating in shared experiences, allowing our realizations to pass to others and for the realizations of others to be available to us as appropriate; and the rose to bring the higher forces into our work.

We are now ready to tread the first set of paths.

Path 1: Earth
✢

In this path, you will enter as before through your own hut and then proceed to the park. From there you will meet the monarch of the earth elementals, make any private conversation, and receive a gift. Each elemental leader focuses on the quality of their element, and the intention is that through this meeting you may strengthen the earth qualities, listed below, in yourself. In being with the elemental leader, you have an opportunity to feel corresponding parts of yourself being noted or activated.

Preliminary

In these workings we will be entering the elemental realms. Each preliminary will only deal with general indications of the nature for that element. The purpose of these workings is to come to appreciate how these forces react within yourself. We focus on each element in turn and use it as one of five points around which those qualities in ourselves can gather and be more easily identified and used in everyday life.

The elementals are the inhabitants of these realms. These are real entities but of a different order of existence to we humans. They dwell within their own elemental realm and they exert their influence in all matters that relate to their element. It is their nature that gives character to the element with which they are associated and meaning to those forces operating in our own selves.

The elementals have a more or less loose hierarchy depending on the element concerned. There is, however, in all cases a monarch or leader of those elementals. In the Western Tradition, we always approach the element and the elementals of the realm through their monarch. To do otherwise is not correct protocol and could be considered rude. On your journeys into the elemental realms, you will meet with the monarch for that elemental and it is customary to offer a gift.

The gift offered should really be something of yourself or a symbolic object representing something of yourself. You are enlisting the assistance of the elementals and getting to know them. It is a two-way street.

Before you start each of the workings, decide on what you will offer and what symbolic form it will take within the inner realms. This will be your gift. Here are a few keywords relating to the element of earth that may guide you: positives to develop—steadfastness, dedication, stability, silence; negatives to diminish—stubbornness, acquisitiveness, lack of commitment. Potential gifts might include a pebble or rock for steadfastness, or a ring for commitment. Your choice will depend on how it relates to you or how you would like it to relate. It could also be something that represents a personal earth quality that you would like to increase or know better.

The elementals of earth are called gnomes and their monarch is Ghob.

In the workings to follow, the preliminary information will be in the following form:

Element: Earth

Elementals: Gnomes

Elemental Monarch: Ghob

Qualities: Steadfastness, dedication, stability, silence

The Working

This time, create an image to represent this chapter and place it on the door that leads into the inner realms. Then make your way to the park setting to begin your working.

You are sitting on the bench with the gift for the leader of the earth elementals in your pocket.

You hear a rumbling sound to your right. You look in that direction and see that a large hole has appeared in the ground. You stand up and move to the rim of the hole. Looking down into the hole, you see a set of rough-hewn stone steps leading down into a darkness that is pinpointed with small bright lights.

Begin your descent of the steps. They lead down and down into what first seems to be darkness. Above you is the hole framing the blue sky. The steps take a turn to the right and the view from above is now no longer visible. You pause for a moment in the darkness and let your eyes grow accustomed to the lack of light.

You now can see that there are pinpoints of light coming from the walls. With this light you are now able to see that the steps continue downwards. Continue on your descent and realize that the light from the walls comes from countless gems and crystals set in the walls.

As you descend, the passageway gets wider. After a while, it opens out into a large cavern with a level floor. This space too is lit by untold numbers of gems and crystals set in the walls of the cavern.

At the far end of the cavern there stands a solid stone throne. Upon the throne sits the short-statured monarch of the earth elementals. Make your way across the cavern to come closer for an audience.

Elemental beings do not have gender in the human sense. We might *see them as* or we might not. Since gender does not apply, they may appear to our sight as one or other or both or neither. Ghob appears, dressed in robes of blood red, yellow ochre, and burnt umber, colors of the earth. He is short and stocky with darkly tanned skin, looking as ageless as rock and just as immovable. He wears a heavy gold chain and has a gem-studded golden crown upon his head. It looks heavy but he carries it lightly.

"Welcome, Child of Earth," Ghob says with a smile of greeting. "What brings you to my realm?"

You tell him *in your own words* that you wish to meet and know him and to learn how you may work with the elementals of his realm. You then present him with your gift.

"Thank you for your gift," says Ghob. "Know that those of my realm will be ready to help you in your work when they are invited." He reaches out to the side and you suddenly notice a large sack there that you had not seen before. It does not appear out of nowhere. It was always there and you realize you just did not notice it. He reaches into the sack and brings out a small raw nugget of gold. This he hands to you.

"Take this as a token of the cooperation that exists between us," Ghob says. "Keep it with you in your travels. Go now and let there be ever peace between us."

Thank him, take the token, and place it in your pocket or pouch. Take your leave and return across the cavern to the stone steps that led you here.

Mount the steps until you reach the turn where your eyes are dazzled by the unaccustomed brightness of the circle of blue above. Your eyes adjust and you finally reach the surface. Stepping out of the hole, you return to the park bench and sit for a moment, closing your eyes. A rumbling sound tells you that the hole has now closed. You look to the right and see the grass on the ground as normal.

Stand and return to your hut as in the previous pathworking. Go through the door, closing it firmly behind you, and return to your seat. Pause for a moment getting your bearings. Awake to the body.

Discussion

When we work magic, in physical reality or on the inner planes, we also work with beings of other types of existence. The elementals are just one group of these. The goal or dreaming of the elementals is to more purely embody the essence of their elemental type. By working with them, we assist them in achieving this just as they also assist us in furthering our own evolution. It is a cooperative effort and although their evolutionary position could be esoterically considered as "lower" than our human one, this should never be a factor. They willingly work with us and assist us, but it is a work of cooperation for mutual benefit, not the relation of master to servant.

The earth elementals bring to our work their qualities of solidity, steadfastness, duration, endurance, and patience. They are miners of precious things hidden within the earth. As such, they can show us how to find in ourselves and in our lives the precious among the dross. They show us in part how to turn the alchemical earth into gold or the Stone of the Ancients. They can remind us that within the darkness, light may be found; that in fact darkness is what keeps the light safe and waiting until found or needed.

In the working, your way is lit by small lights coming from the dark earth around you. This reminds you that the dark is not an evil but a place in which the seeds of light may take root. And you descend into the darkness to discover this principle. It is this light that guides you on your way to your destination.

The earth elementals—Ghob is one of these—are called gnomes. We also know them through the idea of the dwarves of fairy stories, myths, and legends. They are traditionally miners and earth dwellers. The idea of dwarves as beings who share our existence is firmly rooted in our racial and evolutionary consciousness. The other realms are real and they find their expression in our lives in various ways, often through fairy tales, myths, and legends.

It is possible, and not uncommon, to actually see the earth elementals, the gnomes, in our normal existence. The veils between the realms are more or less thin at various times and places. Under such conditions, an earth elemental can appear sort of like a dark elongated cone on its side. This has given rise to the idea of the gnome's cowl streaming out behind as the gnome moves or runs. I have heard this described by three different people independently as "the rear half of a black cat running around a corner." This is a gnome.

If you have cats, they can see them and the playful gnomes will often dash straight at a wall and then either go through it or head at right angles straight up to the ceiling. Of course the cat tries to follow and smashes straight into the wall or tries to follow the gnome straight up the wall. This is great fun for the gnomes. Humor is a factor.

Gnomes usually attach to a particular house. You know when you have a resident gnome because things tend to go missing. Eventually, you find them exactly where they were supposed to be. The gnomes do not take them as such. They have the gift of casting a "glamour" so that things in plain view still cannot be seen. It is their way of acquiring an item not for self but for safekeeping. With their cooperation, you can learn this skill. But beware: You might glamour something and temporarily fool yourself.

It is not so much that they actually remove things and put them back. They are using the "silent secret" power of earth to cloud your perceptions so that you do not see what is in front of you. While it is hidden from you, it is theirs. Later, they remove the "cloud" and it is yours again. In this way they study objects and the stresses that have been stored in them. This is how they come to know us.

This is the "glamour" that you experienced with the sack of trinkets at the side of Ghob's throne.

The exchange of gifts is a physical representation of a more general mystical principle, called "exchange." It is a far-reaching principle and it is not appropriate to delve into it at this point. In this working, it is a symbol of the cooperation that now exists between you and the elementals of earth.

All of the elements—air, fire, water—are elements of power. The element of earth is more silent.

Yes, there is a power that we see in landslides and earthquakes. But of all the movements of elements, the earth is the slowest, the most inert, the most difficult to change. Fire burns, air blasts, water overcomes, but earth resists.

This resistance is essential to us. It gives us a solid base on which to stand. When we work our magic, it is on the solid earth that we stand. Without this resistance we would succumb to the universal law—all action has an equal and opposite reaction. We might start a force in one direction and it would drive us off in the opposite direction. With the earth as our footstool, this effect does not occur.

The earth absorbs. It is totally receptive. Whatever is given to the earth, it accepts. It does not judge, it just accepts. We can push against it and in pushing we progress. With the solidity of earth we can reach even the stars.

The earth is silent and dark. When a dark age comes in our history, knowledge and wisdom are lost. When the period comes to an end, that knowledge and the wisdom that goes with it are slowly but surely restored.

It is the earth that guards our knowledge. It is the earth that guards our traditions. Practitioners of psychometrics can read objects. They can tell the history and the nature of the owners of those objects. These stresses are stored and held in objects and objects are of the earth.

The history of the earth is stored in the earth itself and is accessible should we know how. In the earth there are crystalline objects, precious or not, and these are perfections of stress storage. They concentrate the memories and stresses within their crystalline structure. Such is the huge storage capacity of these gems and crystals that the stresses act as an energy source.

Many people like to use crystals in their work. There is nothing wrong in this, but we have to consider the energy we are taking and how this is powered by the memories of the earth. No power source is limitless. If we do not put in as much as we take out, the crystal will lose all that it had.

The memories the earth holds and the concentration of those memories in gems and crystals are important. We may take crystals out of the earth and use them. If we use them in our magic, we charge them up with more knowledge and memories. They become batteries for our magical work. Ideally, we should use crystals for a while and then rebury them in the earth and get a new one. This is another aspect of the principle of exchange.

In this way we guarantee that our traditions will live on in the care of the dark silent earth until such time as they are needed again. I personally know of magicians who make this a regular part of their practice.

When we see a tree, we know that the trees roots extend beneath the ground at least as far as the spread of its branches. The ground holds the tree, protects it. This is part of its power.

Elementals are not the same creatures as fairies and elves. These belong to a different order of existence, although they too have their place. Sometimes it is easy to confuse the two as the elementals can often be seen in places that match their nature. This is why gnomes are very often seen in our homes, for these after all are merely modern-day extensions of the cave in the earth of our ancestors.

It is very important to work with the elementals because in being with us they evolve. They move more and more to greater individualization, so that when you know one, there is a chance that the one you know will remain differentiated from the elemental essence of which they all partake.

Because of the nature of earth itself, its inertia and solidity, the Gnomes are much more individually separate than the other elementals. The others drift much more easily between form and formlessness.

Whenever you need the qualities of the earth element, you can mentally reach into your pocket or pouch and hold the gift that Ghob gave to you.

Path 2: Water

—————— ✢ ——————

In this path we meet the leader, the focus point, of elemental water. Your conversation is private and you have an opportunity to feel matching qualities within yourself. And if you try this, you will receive a gift.

Preliminary

Element: Water

Elementals: Undines

Elemental Monarch: Nicksa

Qualities: Fluid, powerful, yielding, rhythmic, life-giving, exchange

Decide upon your gift and its symbolic form before you start—a small glass, flask of water, or a soft foam ball for yielding-ness. Let the qualities speak to you.

The Working

Create an image for this chapter that you will use to represent it on the door into the inner realms. Then make your way as usual to the park and the park bench. Settle, close your eyes, and prepare to take the pathworking.

You feel a gentle and varying pressure on your left side. You feel a coolness brushing past your face. Yield to this pressure and let it carry you away.

Open your eyes. You are under the water of a stream, a river, and the current is carrying you along its course. You are somehow able to breathe normally.

Your eyes seem to adjust slightly and you can see the separate flows that make up the current, running swiftly and straight at the center, slowing, eddying, swirling in little circles near the banks. Surrender to the flow and let the river carry you on its course.

The banks get farther away and soon you can no longer see them. At the same time the current slows little by little. Soon you are making your way through the river's estuary, almost lazily, toward what you know must be the sea.

Sure enough, the movement of the water carrying you changes. You are carried forward for a while and then backward for a little before being carried forward again. You are now subject to the tidal motion of the ocean. Give yourself up to this motion and feel yourself as part of the ocean, of all oceans, of the life-blood of this planet.

You are being carried gradually toward a pale blue light. As you get closer, you can make out the distinct yet fluid shape of a being more or less stationary, yet who is also gently moving with the pulls of the tide. This is Nicksa. You approach Nicksa and he says, "Welcome, Child of Earth." The greeting is delivered with a smile. "What brings you to my realm?"

Tell Nicksa in your own words that you wish to meet and know the essence of elemental water and to learn how you may work with the elementals of this realm. You then present your gift.

"Thank you for your gift," Nicksa says. "Know that those of my realm will be ready to help you in your work when they are invited." Nicksa's hands are then cupped and within that shape there forms a chalice. It is made of water and yet retains its shape. This is presented to you as Nicksa says, "Take this as a token of the cooperation that exists between us. Keep it with you in your travels. Go now and let there be ever peace between us."

You give your thanks, take the token, which retains its shape and even feels solid to your touch. You place it in your pocket or pouch.

Now the tide is changing and you are being drawn with the backward and forward flow toward the shore. Soon the water is swirling into energetic waves and you are borne along, close to the surface by their power and energy.

You break the surface in the spray of a wave and this bears you easily and somehow gently onto the sandy beach. Walk a little way up the beach, turn to face the ocean and sit down on the fine white sand. Look out over the incoming waves with their horse's mane spray. After a while, close your eyes and listen to the thundering sound for a time.

Gradually, the sound recedes into silence. When you open your eyes again you are sitting once more on the bench in the park. Relax for a moment. Then stand up and return by the usual route to your hut and the door between the realms. Pass through as usual and relax back into position. Awake to the body.

Discussion

Water is fluid. The late Melbourne astrologer and theosophist John Farquharson, who had spent time in China, once said of the presence of the British in China that they were like a hand in a bucket of water. Put the hand in and the water moves aside to make room. Take it out and you cannot see where it has been.

The *I Ching* has a lot to say about water in its various commentaries. For example, it flows and fills every hollow. Though fluid, nothing can stand against its massed force. When deep it is dark and dangerous. In a lake it is reflective or shows the effects of wind, which cannot be seen directly.

The way that water flows on, fast or slow, direct or in eddies, provides for some mystics a metaphor for living the mystic life. It is as though we are leaves upon a river, sometimes in the center, moving swiftly on, and sometimes at the edges, staying in one spot for a while in turning eddies. All of these qualities tell us something of its magical power and purposes.

But there is one other quality of water that I want to concentrate on here, and for me this is an important quality. When gathered into the large body of an ocean, it has tides. It is pulled by the moon around the earth and heaves up and down in a regular pattern. This movement is the foundation of rhythm, of cycles, of flow.

And when we come to deal with energies, our relationship with nature, our relationship with others and relationships generally, the sense of flow and rhythm is very important.

Violet Mary Firth, who wrote and is known as Dion Fortune, was the founder of the Society of the Inner Light. She wrote a number of books on magic, several unpublished pathworkings and rituals, and some occult novels.

Two of these novels, *The Sea Priestess* and *Moon Magic*, contain enough information to construct several rituals, all based around the principle of polarity and in particular, sexual polarity.

Polarity is a fundamental principle of creation, whether we look at the straight flow between two "poles" or the cyclic nature of outward flow and return flow. Polarity was the first principle to come into existence after the arising of Being/Existence itself.

For our purposes at the moment we can take the cycle of high tide to low tide and back again as our flow between two poles or extremes. And it is important to note that the talk of poles is only an abstract marking of agreed borders for the discussion to come. What is always of interest is what are the possibilities that may exist within this defined space.

Dion Fortune has her priestess say:

"I am the eternal woman—I am She!
The tides of all men's souls belong to me
The tides that ebb and flow and ebb again
The silent inward tides that govern men
These are my secret—these belong to me." [2]

The cycle of tides between two points is shown in the Taiji symbol, sometimes called the Yin-Yang symbol. The idea of tides stands behind the teaching of the arising and passing away of existence and of thought in Buddhism. Tides and cycles are used to recognize cyclic events and these are important to us in our magic. Each day we have sunrise, noon, sunset and midnight. Each month we have new moon, waxing moon, full moon, and waning moon. Each year we have the cycle from midwinter through to midsummer and back again.

All of these cycles cause tides in the energies that surround us and exist within us. These have their effects on us. The understanding of the nature of the water element is fundamental to our understanding of tides in all manifestations and forms. It may be thought that the breath, the action of breathing in and out, is related to the element of air. And in a sense it is. But when air moves in a regular and controlled fashion, it acts in the nature of a tide, and tides are the province of the element of water.

Arising and Passing Away
Some cosmologies, like those of certain Buddhist Schools, teach that existence is constantly arising and passing away as a function of consciousness. Thought also arises and passes away and students are encouraged to become aware

---

2. Dion Fortune, *The Sea Priestess* (London: The Aquarian Press, 1957), 167–168.

of this in their meditations. And behind all of this is the tide of the four-fold breathing exercise, which gives a direct experience of the tidal flow in the arising and passing away of all existence.

This is not mere mysticism. Our Western view is clouded. When the Australian Aboriginal legends speak of the "Dreamtime," some people have treated it as solely a kind of creation time, a one-off. This is not so. Some stories are of this creation form, but others relate to an ongoing process within which all things, animate and inanimate, have their own "dreaming," their becomingness. For example, the dreaming of a rock may be sand. In a similar way, we may view the Big Bang as an ongoing process, not as just a one-off event.

When we study magic, and by this I mean the science behind our devotional and celebratory practices, we may follow the path laid down over centuries by various schools and traditions. Generally, the first level of teaching is to know the self. The second is then to work from the basis of that refined self to the relationship with others and with nature. The third stage takes us from this harmony within and without to knowledge of and cooperation with the divine powers behind all existence.

We often first work on gaining knowledge and developing our own powers through meditation and energy work. There is a tidal element to this. Later, our work in circle becomes more important and we come to see our part in the patterns and the interflow of energies between others and ourselves. This has a tidal nature.

Water also makes a mirror. It was, in fact, our earliest mirror. This establishes a polarity between yourself and your image. We know that between two poles an energy or tide can flow. Water makes the very best reflector for mirror magic.

The essence of healing is mirroring—whether we mirror the person, heal the problem within ourselves and then reflect it back, or merely mirror the person so that they may truly see themselves and thereby heal themselves.

Water is also the universal solvent. From its use in homeopathy or religious practice as a container of the minute essence of "a potency," or non-physical ingredient, to its value for ordinary use such as cooking, it is the medium for holding other things and making them easily available to do their work upon and within us.

Path 3: Air

—————————— ✛ ——————————

Following on in sequence you will next meet the elementals of air on their own terms. As before, you will need to take a gift for the ruler of the element and you will again receive one in return. The intent again is to awaken in yourself the qualities associated with the element.

Preliminary

Element: Air

Elementals: Sylphs

Elemental Monarch: Paralda

Qualities: Variable, changeable, vitalizing, flexible, uncooperative, individualism

Decide upon your gift and its symbolic form before you start.

The Working

Open the door into the inner realms. Then make your way as usual to the park and the park bench. Settle, close your eyes, and prepare to take the pathworking.

You feel buffeted, pushed lightly from side to side. When you open your eyes, you see you are high in the air, moving this way and that as the winds blow in ever-changing directions.

Looking up you see a bright light and you know this is your destination. Head in that direction, moving your body while being buoyed up by the moving air.

But the winds keep moving you, changing your direction. It is hard to keep heading toward your destination. You are blown off-course, first one way and then another. No matter how you try, you cannot move in the direction you wish. You can make out figures within the wind, the sylphs, light blue and wraith like. Some seem playful, yet mischievous. Some seem to have no knowledge of your presence at all.

You relax and stop struggling. The winds carry you off, changing direction now and then, backtracking, ever varying. You remain relaxed, enjoying the sensation of being carried along effortlessly. Even though your direction is ever changing, you notice that you are being brought closer and closer to the bright point in the sky.

Soon you are proceeding more directly to your destination. You see a shining blue throne in the air and sitting upon it is Paralda the monarch of the sylphs. This being appears tall and slim, wavering slightly, his robes moving in the air.

"Welcome, Child of Earth," Paralda says and you hear the words floating through the air. They are delivered with a smile of greeting. "What brings you to my realm?"

Say in your own words that you wish to meet and know the essence of the realm and to learn how you may work with its elementals. You then present your gift.

"Thank you for this gift," Paralda says. "Know that those of my realm will be ready to help you in your work when they are invited." One hand reaches out into the air and a feather is borne along a breeze, brought by a Sylph. Paralda gently takes the feather and hands it to you: "Take this as a token of the cooperation that exists between us. Keep it with you in your travels. Go now and let there be ever peace between us."

Give your thanks, take the token, and place it carefully in your pocket or pouch.

Relax and give yourself to the winds. They take you this way and that again, gradually bringing you closer to the ground. Below you see the park and the bench. After a short time, the winds lower you gently onto the bench.

Relax for a moment. Then stand up and return by the usual route to your hut and the door between the realms. Pass through as usual and relax back into position. Awake to the body.

Discussion

Air is fickle. It blows this way then that way. It varies in strength from gust to hurricane. Yes, we can track storms as a whole, but at a more detailed level, air can be going in any direction at any time.

There is a saying, "Tree that bends in the wind does not break." One of the things you learn from this working is that it is only when you surrender to the movements of air that you can then make your way in the direction you wish. The wind rustles the leaves and sways the branches of the trees, enabling them to breathe and, by transmission of the forces down the trunk, tries and strengthens their roots.

We can "taste" the wind and learn of coming weather conditions. Scents are borne on the wind and it is an excellent chemical communicator not only to animals but also to other trees and plants. Sit for a while among trees when a breeze is rustling their leaves. You will then know that the movement of air is how trees communicate with each other, sometimes across vast distances, spreading and modifying messages made of chemical and scent, and perhaps a little more besides. It was Dion Fortune who said that divination does not tell you what is going to happen. It tells you which way the wind is blowing so that you may trim your sails accordingly.[3]

I've attended a number of Pagan summer gathering events put on by the Church of All Worlds in Australia. It was common at those gatherings for attendees to gather in groups representing the four elements, according to star sign or inclination, in preparation for the main summer afternoon ritual. Incidentally, the children attending were assigned to the element of spirit with an adult fairy mentor.

I usually participated in the air group, by choice. While the people of the other three groups soon got into working out how they were going to represent their element in the ritual, the members of the air group seemed unable or unwilling to take a particular direction, so to speak. And this was precisely their quality. At the end of one conference, photographs were taken of the four groups. In three photographs, the subjects were all facing the camera. Not so the air group, they were all facing in different directions, heads at different

---

3. Dion Fortune, *Practical Occultism in Daily Life* (Wellingborough, UK: The Aquarian Press, 1935), 39.

angles. And this is exactly the quality. Incidentally, comparing the photographs later, you might conclude that the air example was more artistic. It is no accident—the word "inspiration" has its roots in "breath" and so relates well to the element of air.

As an aside, I have noticed that this quality also shows up in the whole air group of the signs of the zodiac—Gemini, Libra, and Aquarius.

In Gemini, air characteristics manifest as an issue with choosing one of two options. I have a daughter who is a Gemini native. When very young, she would play happily all day, but at the end of the day she would sometimes cry because the day was over and she had wanted to do something else. I suggested to her that at the start of the day she should decide on what to do, stand in front of the bathroom mirror, and say to her reflection, "This is what we have decided to do. Right? OK." This solved the problem for her.

In Libra, the quality manifests as a continual changing of decision between options. With Aquarius, the native will choose all options at once and very cleverly weave them into one single choice of action or decision.

There may be similar strands in the other groups of zodiacal signs, but my real-life experiences have not included such observations as yet.

The qualities of air can help you learn commitment, decision, and a wholeness, all-at-once approach to life, yet still permit you a freedom to decide your destination.

Yielding yourself to the varying quality of air does not mean an aimless "going with the flow." Rather, it means being flexible and using apparently antagonistic or contrary flows to still achieve your own course and direction. You will learn to "trim your sails accordingly." These are the lessons that the air elementals can teach you. These are the ways that they can help you in your inner plane work.

Path 4: Fire

_____ ✢ _____

During this pathworking, you will encounter the element of fire and the elemental leader. In the exchange with this leader, you will have an opportunity to link up the fiery qualities of your own nature with the element that enflames them.

Preliminary

Element: Fire

Elementals: Salamanders

Elemental Monarch: Djinn

Qualities: Burning, purifying, invigorating, transforming, removing imperfections

Decide upon your gift and its symbolic form before you start.

The Working

Go through the door into the inner realms. Then make your way as usual to the park and the park bench. Settle, close your eyes, and prepare to take the pathworking.

You open your eyes and you are on a mountain pathway. Behind you the way leads down to the valley below. Ahead of you, the path winds off upwards toward the cloud-covered summit. To your left, the ground drops away, gently at first and then steeper toward an edge on the side of the mountain.

Watch the clouds for a while and notice that they are coming up out of the mountain itself. Within them you see occasional flecks of dark red.

Take the path upwards. It is narrow but not dangerously so. Ahead, the path turns around to the right as it follows the contours of the mountain. Follow the path and come to the point where the path turns. Continue on for a little way until you come to a cave mouth set into the side of the mountain.

Look inside. It is dark. There is a faint smell of sulfur and you can feel some heat coming from within. This is the way that you must take. Enter the cave mouth.

At first it is dark, but as your eyes adjust you see that the way is lit by a dull red glow from somewhere ahead. Continue on, toward the red glow. The passageway gets wider and is now lit on each side by burning torches on the wall. The flames dance, ever changing, alive.

After a short time, you enter a larger cave with a pool of fire at its center. You feel the heat from this living flame. Move closer to the edge of this fiery pit. Some flames leap upward from the pool and you see the forms of the salamanders that give them shape. They fall away back into the pool of flame again and all is quiet for a moment.

A large flame begins to form in the center of the pool. It rises up, its base still merged with the pool's surface. As you watch it changing, it takes the shape of a person. This is Djinn, the ruler of the fire elementals.

"Welcome, Child of Earth," says Djinn and a smile of greeting comes with the words. "What brings you to my realm?"

Say in your own words that you wish to meet and know this realm and its ruler and to learn how you may work with the elementals of his realm. You then offer your gift. It is borne away from you and toward this figure on a river of fire.

"Thank you for your gift," Djinn says. "Know that those of my realm will be ready to help you in your work when they are invited."

One of Djinn's hands reaches down into the pool and lifts up a burning sphere. As it leaves the pool, it cools in Djinn's hand and becomes a pure black sphere of obsidian. Djinn's fiery hand extends and the sphere floats toward you, "Take this as a token of the cooperation that exists between us." Djinn says. "Keep it with you in your travels. Go now and let there be ever peace between us."

You give a thank you and take the token, now cool to the touch. You place it in your pocket or pouch.

You turn away from the fiery heart of this volcano and make your way back through the passage. After a while you emerge once more on the mountain's slope. Follow the path back the way you came and around to the left, to your initial starting point. Sit down on the path and close your eyes. The scents of sulfur and the hot breezes gradually pass away.

Open your eyes and you are once more sitting on the park bench. Relax for a moment. Then stand up and return by the usual route to your hut and the door between the realms. Pass through as usual and relax back into position. Awake to the body.

Discussion

Fire is the element of transformation. It has the quality of burning and burning transforms one thing into another. It can be destructive, from one point of view, but destruction is necessary for a change of state to take place. Destruction is one side of the coin of transformation.

In some cases, the fire is purifying. It is used to heat ores and from the molten result we can separate out and extract the metals within. It is used to heat metal and shape it into a sword, or a plowshare, as the need requires.

The same fire will rage through the Australian bush where the seeds of the native plants require intense heat for their germination. Out of the destruction of the old arises the new as in the story of the phoenix.

In the human personality, it relates to the emotions. I say "emotions" as opposed to feelings. Feelings are more fluid in my view, more watery. Emotions can be driving forces as the derivation of the word implies. They can enflame us. It is these that transform our lives. It is these that can overpower and destroy. It is these that can empower us to new ventures and new ways of being.

All of the elementals are part of the whole element even though we may chose to see them as individuals—gnomes, sylphs, undines, and salamanders. In the element of fire it is the easiest to see this quality.

We look at a fire, a campfire, say, and we can see at one and the same time the fire itself and the individual flames that make up that fire. In this way, observing fire can teach us about the nature of all the elemental kingdoms.

Unlike the creatures of our everyday world, the elementals can appear separate to us and yet be still one with the totality.

In fact, it is we who impart the illusion of individuality to these beings. They do not have it in the same way as we know it for ourselves, dogs, cats, trees, ants. This is part of the contract we have with the elementals, experiencing individuation.

Fire as emotion can also be passion, in all its forms. However logical and thought-dominated our work or projects may be, we still need passion behind them to bring them to fruition. Passion can drive you through the all-nighter you pull to complete a job. Passion can bring your poetry, your writing, your music, your artwork to enhanced life. Passion can lift your relationships with others to more meaningful heights. And so it is when we come to our magical workings that we need the element of fire to empower them, to give them the force of accomplishment and transformation.

Fire in its purifying form burns away the dross, the unwanted, to leave us with the pure essence we seek. A fire is also a metaphor for our own nature. We are each beings that exist within the One Life, as flames within one fire.

Fire uses earth for its fuel, it is fanned by air and it can drive off water. But of course, from another point of view, earth, water, and sufficient air may dowse fire. Emotion (fire) may be enhanced by thought (air) and yet thought may kill desire. There is no single circular rock-paper-scissors game for the elements.

This working is set in the active area of a volcano. The dynamics of a volcano rely upon the fires within the earth, the magma. While molten materials can be influenced by gravitational forces and flow dynamics, fire itself, the flames, are not.[4]

But fire has its rules. It needs fuel to burn. Within that restriction, it follows its path as though with a life of its own, appearing to make choices in direction and intensity.[5] Just as the fire of burning generates heat, so the fire of transformation generates energy. This can also be personal energy generated as a psychological "complex" is transformed.

---

4. The particles in a flame can, of course, be influenced by physical forces.

5. You can see an excellent example of this in the movie *Backdraft* (1991). Donald Rimgale, Robert de Niro's character, illustrates the notion that fire has a life of its own.

The fires of passion within us follow similar rules. When we construct our rituals and invite the element of fire into our circle, we need to provide the fuel for the fire, which is the structure of what we are doing, the direction of flow at full power, and the conditions under which it is diminished.

Path 5: Spirit

✣

In this working, you will encounter the representative of spirit. You will be given a drink of this essence and feel it interacting with the four previous elemental experiences. This working will bring a cohesion and wholeness to the prior elemental path experiences.

Preliminary

Element: Spirit, the quintessence

Elementals: None; spirit ensouls

Elemental Monarch: Its order of existence is higher than the elemental kingdoms

Qualities: Ensouling, enlivening, empowering, bestowing meaning

Decide upon your gift and its symbolic form before you start.

The Working

In the mind's eye, pass through the door into the inner realms. Then make your way as usual to the park and the park bench. Settle, close your eyes, and prepare to take the pathworking,

In your inner vision, the scene of a park with a large misty lake arises. In the mind's eye, stand up. Walk along the grass and walk down to the water's edge. As you do so, you become very aware of yourself in this working.

Stop just before the water's edge and feel the grass, the earth, or the sand between your toes. Feel the wind upon your face and hear it rustle in the trees and leaves. Hear the lapping of the water at the shore's edge. Feel the heat of the sun upon your face.

Walk into the water a little ways and feel it around your feet and ankles. Look out over the water and see the mist that sits upon it. As you watch, the mist begins to roll away. This reveals a pathway leading out into the water. You cannot quite tell whether the pathway is of earth or solidified water or some other substance, but you walk along it with the water lapping at each side, right and left.

At the end of the pathway, which extends some way into the water, you see a stone pedestal, behind which there is a beautiful person, somewhat elven in appearance, facing you across the pedestal. This person is dressed in robes of ethereal silver.

"Welcome, Child of Earth," the person says and you hear the words and see a smile of greeting, "What brings you to this realm?"

Explain in your own words that you wish to meet and know the powers of this realm and to learn how you may work with them. You then present your gift.

Your gift is received by one hand and the other hand indicates the top of the pedestal where you see a pool, making the whole thing akin to an elegant stone birdbath.

The water seems liquid, but it is misty and burns with an inner fire. It swirls and moves like the breezes and smells of earth. It moves with some secret inner tide. It exudes beautiful scents of flowers and trees.

This is the quintessence beyond the four elements at the shore, yet feeding each of these elements with life. Your host takes a silver shallow cup, immerses it in the water and takes a drink. It is passed to you and you also drink from it.

The liquid runs through you like fire to the tips of your fingers, the tips of your toes, the top of your head. Your lips and fingers tingle. Your heart leaps and opens. Your brain is alive with thought and your whole body sings with vitality.

Feel the inner spirit of yourself quicken each of the four parts of your nature, body for being, mind for knowing, emotion for feeling, imagination for sensing.

The elven one speaks: "Thank you for your gift. Know that those of my realm will be ready to help you in your work when so invited."

"Take what you have experienced here as a token of the cooperation that exists between us. Keep it in your memory on the travels that will open up to you. You are now prepared for the next stage of your quest. Go now and let there be ever peace between us."

You say your thanks and return along the narrow path to the shore. When you look back, the path and pedestal have all gone. The lake is clear of mists.

Feel your vitality, dance with the wind, frolic in the water, scintillate in the sun's rays, vibrate in the earth. Relax for a moment and let the inner scene fade from your inner vision, but yet its sense remains. Then open your eyes, look around, stand up, and leave the park.

In the street there are some village folk, watching you, smiling. Some may shake your hand, some may embrace you in passing. The greetings you receive will be in the usual form in which you normally experience these in life—a hug, kiss on cheek, or a handshake, for example. The number of people will neither be too many nor too few. There will be nothing in this to cause any discomfort. Pass unimpeded through the smiling friendly people to your hut and the door between the realms. Pass through as usual and relax back into position. Awake to the body.

Discussion

The four elements are balanced as an equal-armed cross. The fifth element is called quintessence because it is the fifth essence and this fifth element represents spirit. Spirit is something other, extra dimensional to the four elements. It cannot enter existence except within a vehicle of the four elements.

Our physical self is created from the four elements—earth for bone, water for blood and muscles, air for the lungs and organs, fire for the nervous system and brain. All kept together in a bag of skin.

A fragment of a ritual I once performed within a group asked, "How do we serve?" The response was "Brain, muscle, and nerve." And, unsaid, the frame that holds it all together.

This building process starts at conception. When the elements are present and balanced, at a certain time, spirit can attach and begin to express itself. This is called the quickening. This idea can be seen in the Jewish story of the creation of a golem.

The Rabbi of Prague, Rabbi Loew, created a golem. He went to the mud flats at the banks of the Vltava River. There he fashioned with the wet mud the shape of a prone body, lying on its back. These are the elements of earth and water.

Then he built a fire and took the clay-mud figure to be dried by that fire. This is the element of fire. Once the figure dried, he leaned over the body and breathed into its mouth. This is the element of air.

This was the creation of a vehicle out of the four elements. But it still needed the vital fifth essence—spirit, or in this case life. He wrote upon its forehead the word "emeth," which means God's Truth, or "strewth" in older English parlance. The creature then came to life, just as in the derivative story of Dr. Frankenstein when lightning was added to the body he created. To destroy the golem when it went off wreaking havoc, the rabbi removed one letter from the word on its forehead, changing it to "meth," which means death.

And so the fifth essence—spirit—is the life force that animates the four physical elements. It animates them and finds its expression, in this plane, through the combination of those four elements. Its true essence, however, is not of this plane.

The four elements and spirit have been symbolized different ways at different times and by different groups. The most common one is the pentagram, which shows the point of spirit at its top-most point, ascendant over the four elements.

The reverse pentagram represents matter ascendant over spirit. It is often used as a symbol of evil. Ironically, some police forces in different parts of the world use a reverse pentagram in their logo. However, in this case it means the ascendance of the word of the law over the intent of the law, or, as we say, the letter rather than the spirit. The spirit is a matter for the court system.

The word "spirit" comes from the Latin word *spiritus* meaning something that comes in and/or out, hence respiration, perspiration, inspiration, and so on. The spirit, or essence of light comes in and out of collections of the four elements in a series of lives in incarnation. It enters at the quickening and leaves at death. It is not created and not destroyed. Rather it is eternal among that which is transient, living, growing, learning, and evolving.

Spirit as we know it in the form of our own life force can be likened to an individual flame in the single fire that is Divinity, the Supreme Being, the Great

Architect, The Mother, God, Allah, Yahweh, or whatever we wish to call that which is behind everything. As is said in the Western Mysteries, all gods and goddesses are one and there is but one initiator.

Another symbol of the five elements in balance is the rose-cross. This shows a bloodred rose in the center of a cross, sometimes equal-armed and sometimes not. It is also sometimes represented as a circle-cross. This is to represent the spirit completely encompassing the four elements.

If we take the pentagram and fold one point down into the center, we will have pretty close to what the rose-cross represents. In that symbol, the cross represents the four elements balanced and the rose represents the spirit that takes residence or incarnates into the balanced form.

This rose-cross symbol was used and still is used by the Rosicrucians, of all types, and is also used by some magical orders. Magical orders and other groups of the Western Mystery tradition are external representations of one or other inner or withdrawn orders.

One of these is the Order of the Rose. This order is withdrawn and like spirit, finds its expression within the "body" of an outer order, such as the Order of the Golden Dawn and others of the Western Esoteric Tradition.

What is true of the spirit entering and leaving a physical body is also true of an inner order being linked or not with a physical order or group. In the Western Esoteric Tradition, outer orders "hive" and the link goes with them. After a while the parent order winds down on the outer, its experiences resuming into the inner order, which was its spirit, so to speak. There have been examples of orders that have continued to operate even after the inner contact withdrew.

Talking with my eldest son, he asked if I thought that businesses and companies should go through this same evolutionary process. After discussion, we both decided that it should work that way for a healthy business line. At some time or other, key and/or original people would move on and hive off a new business in the same "tradition," leaving caretaker people to see the business through the second part of its life, from height to memory.

Spirit can be transferred physically through any of the elements. It can reside without animating. This is the case with sacred stones in nature religions, relics of saints in Christianity, talismans in magic. It is the case with the practice of a priest or elder breathing into the ear of a newborn and of pagan and shamanic practices of using incense, smoking, and smudging.

It is the case with water that is blessed and used for purification, sometimes with the addition of salt, an earth element component. And sometimes it is the case with sacred fire passed from a central candle to others that are lit from it. But over and above all of these it is best represented as light. When light is crucified upon the cross of the four elements, it is extended into those elements-in-balance. It then becomes "Light in Extension"—Lux vel eXtensis, LVX.

Part two

The pathworkings in this second part are constructed from symbols drawn from astrological and Qabalistic sources.

The workings first start with a principle and this principle is based on the symbolism of the New Moon in an astrological sign. From this principle the working is then constructed using the meanings of astrological symbols and matching symbolism selected from a number of sources, Greek, Celtic, English, and more. In a discussion following each working, the meanings behind the elements are given and expanded upon.

It is intended that the workings be performed once in each four-week lunar period with the remaining days of the period being used for meditation on the topics given in the discussion or upon the personal realization while doing the working.

The set of pathworkings falls into three series. These are:

Journeys to Realms Within

This series introduces the style of the pathworkings to come and creates a set of anchor points upon which the further pathworkings stand and through which they mediate their influences into your life and being.

Journeys to Realms Between

In this second series of workings, you will be moving into another level of the inner realms. This new level contains adventures that work more subtly upon the psyche. They deal with broader issues and need to come through in a staged way, via a point of contact that has already been established. This makes them more effective than if they were worked directly.

Journeys to Realms Beyond

In this third series of pathworkings, we pass beyond the self and the deeper self and enter into the paths of the great myths and legends of an earlier time. In our quest to delve deeper and deeper into our own inner natures, we have progressed through two levels already to reach this deepest level that borders upon the Collective Unconscious.

In addition to the paths that make up these groups, there is one additional path that stands alone and is different. It is placed between the second and third groups and this pseudo-group is called "The Interlude." The group sequence is therefore: Journeys to Realms Within, Journeys to Realms Between, The Interlude, Journeys to Realms Beyond. The name of this path is "The Nameless Path."

Pathworking Programs

As already mentioned in this book, there is no need to synchronize your workings so that they begin on the New Moon in Aquarius, the basis for the symbols in the first path of part 2. It is not even necessary to pay any attention at all to the moon phases, but to just do the workings in order—one every four weeks as previously mentioned. The pairing of paths with moon phases in signs is meant to relate the workings to the meanings of the signs. Just as the lunar year unfolds from a New Moon starting point in the real world, so too can the series of journeys unfold in the inner realm from their chosen starting point, whenever that happens to be.

Preparations for Working

The paths that follow are more fully involved with the inner realms and the inner nature of the practitioner. I will here remind you that you need a technique to provide a psychological boundary between these realms. Without such a technique, the inner and outer worlds can interfere with each other, cross over into each other, in the form of what is called "leakage" in the Western Esoteric Tradition.

Journeys to Realms Within

———— ✛ ————

This first series of pathworkings, "Realms Within," introduces you to the key features of the inner landscape where all takes place. It gives you a foothold in your own inner realm. Each of the locations examined here provides an anchor point for various key energies that come into play during these workings.

There are four workings in this series:

- "The Dark Wood," in which you will find your special place within the inner landscape of these paths.
- "The Crystal Cave," a place where you may see shadows of things that have been or things yet to come.
- "Town and Tower," where mind, thought, and philosophy present their wares.
- "The Sacred Grove," a natural meeting point with nature and the powers behind nature.

With these four anchor points in place, your later experiences on these paths will more easily find their way into your everyday consciousness.

Let us begin with the Dark Wood.

Path 1: The Dark Wood

—————— ✢ ——————

I remind you that each path will have a brief preview and indication of the purpose of the working. If you are the type of person who prefers raw experience first and extracting or discovering meaning afterward for yourself, just skip the paragraph before the pathworking itself. If you prefer to know what is coming before experiencing it, then feel free to read that information in the first paragraph under the path heading.

The purpose of this first working is to find your next place of working within the realm. Up until now you have worked in a garden attached to the edge of your place of residence in this realm. However, greater destinies call and in this path you will leave the known behind and enter the unknown, the forest. As in all true quests, you, the potential hero, have no idea what is to come or how things fit together. This is an adventure of discovery, the discovery of a special place of significance to your quest. It is an awakening to the inner worlds.

Like many heroes in legends, you will head out into the unknown to find a place that has more meaning for you and opens more possibilities. But to do that, you must enter the unknown. If it were known, there would be no mystery to unravel. You will enter the dark wood that the villagers avoid because it is only here where one may find a castle of marvels. Every journey outside current knowledge is always a journey into the unknown. If it were known, there is no adventure and no achievement. You will enter the dark wood to find what you need to continue.

Preamble

To begin this path, you will find your place to work and make your opening or beginning signs. Settle down, make yourself comfortable and begin to relax and breathe rhythmically.

With your eyes closed, let your mind become alert and prepare to allow the images of the working to arise in your mind's eye.

You see the room that you are in. Everything is normal including the extra door in the room that you have been using already. Create an image of this chapter to put on your door into the inner realms.

Reach out and open the door. It swings open easily and you step through. There is a soft sound that tells you the door has closed behind you and a "click" sound suggests it is now locked.

———————— THE PATHWORKING ————————

At first it is too misty for you to see anything. There is no hint of your usual hut. In fact, you are pretty certain you are outside. You strain to see but cannot make out any shapes except for slight, vertical differences of shades of gray. You hear the sound of distant sweet music. The volume ebbs and flows as the mist swirls around you. Your vision clears and you are in a dark forest.

Suddenly you feel tired and confused and you sit down on the ground.

How did you come to be here, in this dark forest? You seem to remember a village, with friends and family. There was something about a journey, or quest, and some fond farewells. After that, the memories are hazy.

You check what you have with you and find that you are carrying your four elemental tokens in your pockets or pouch. It seems you prepared for something, but you can't quite remember any details. And now you seem to have lost your way.

The ground is cold and you shiver involuntarily. Whatever seasons may exist in the outer world, this inner realm is deep in the throes of winter.

As you feel the cold seeping into your bones, you notice that the music has stopped. You find yourself sitting on the ground beside a tree in a silent, misty trackless forest.

You look around. The trees are bereft of leaves. The mist is cold and damp as it drifts lazily through the skeletal branches and curls its wisps around the solid trunks.

Standing up, you look down at your clothes and take careful note of what you are wearing.

On the ground, you see leaves dusted with the white of frost and the cold of it bites through. As you stand there, you feel that the silent cold is gradually sapping your energy and will.

There is a sound over to the right, the sound of an animal, perhaps. It could have been some sort of small woodland creature. You decide that activity is better than gradually freezing over, and you head cautiously off in the direction of the sound.

The rustling sound comes again and you follow. It seems to be an animal heading off to your right in short bursts. Perhaps it is foraging as it goes. You follow, stop and listen, and follow again, in a repeating sequence.

You do not seem to be gaining on the animal, whatever it is. Neither does it seem to be getting farther away. And still it keeps heading in the same direction, more or less, as though it had some destination in mind or trail to follow.

Your curiosity is aroused and you feel a burning urge to find the source of the noises that you are following. Soon you come to a narrow track. It is exactly the sort of track that would be worn by a variety of animals over time as they made their way to the various waterholes at dawn or dusk.

It is now clear from the sounds that come back to you that the creature is following this track some way ahead of you. You continue on.

The way becomes a little easier now and the effort of reaching this clearer track has increased your circulation and warmed you up a bit.

Suddenly you emerge in a clearing. There, at the other side of the clearing stands a large stag, having huge antlers like two human hands with delicate fingers waiting in supplication to receive benefits from above.

The stag turns its head to face toward you and its brow shines with a strange bright light straight into your eyes. You shield your dazzled eyes from the blaze of light. You blink. In the afterimage you see a violet pentagram in a circle superimposed upon the trees across the clearing. The stag has gone. The afterimage fades and you cross the clearing, listening for any sound. You hear nothing. The wood is silent.

At the other side of the clearing, there is a track and you follow it into the forest again.

You notice that the mist has all but gone. Somewhere a weak winter sun is clambering arduously into the sky. But you do not see it. The branches of the trees now meet overhead and form a ragged tunnel for your journey.

You begin to feel an inevitable necessity to your presence on this track, as though the whole journey had been planned long ago. It takes on the feel of a holiday long looked forward to. You become more excited at the hint of wonder yet to come. In fact, the feeling gradually grows that something quite spectacular is waiting ahead. But there is as yet no indication of what that spectacular thing may be other than a dark wood in the winter. Suddenly, the thought "the dark wood beyond the village" comes to you, but there are no other clear memories with it.

The track veers sharply right and you follow it, continuing on. You find yourself suddenly in another clearing. In the middle of the clearing are four marble pillars around a large marble block. The block is placed upon a marble base made of three disks decreasing in size so that from all sides there are three marble steps leading up to the block.

Resting upon the capitals of the columns is a circular piece of marble that forms a canopy over the whole arrangement. A large sarcophagus of some sort is resting on the block.

Your curiosity is really humming now and you quickly cross the intervening space to examine your find more closely.

Upon the marble block there rests what looks like a coffin made of ground glass. You peer through the top to try to see what is inside. The frosting of the glass makes it hard to see, but it seems to contain a person of indeterminate sex, strangely dressed.

You walk around the open mausoleum to view the coffin from all sides. You find that there is indeed someone silently resting inside, dressed as from a long-gone age of magic and fantasy. You make out elf-like boots and a dark blue robe. The lid is tightly fastened. You make a half-hearted attempt to shift it, but it does not move at all.

The marble block upon which the coffin rests has an inscription in strange runes on one of the two long sides. You lean down to study it. There is a stirring in your mind as of a long-lost memory. The mystic runes slowly seem to form words that you can read:

Your inner name is sprung
Whence Will and Power are one.

After a moment's thought, you decide to press on. You go to the edge of the clearing opposite the spot where you entered. Just as you might have expected, the track continues.

The track winds in and out of the silent trees, always keeping more or less to the same direction as far as you can tell. It is clearly marked and you know that you would have no trouble finding your way back to the tomb.

The track leads straight out of the forest onto a narrow road. The ground falls away slightly to each side and the road runs directly ahead to a distant mound. Upon that mound there stands an ancient castle.

You head straight toward the castle. The trip is uneventful. Close to the castle you pass a crossroads. One road leads off to the right and farther in that direction you can see the wooded foothills leading to a high mountain. The other road leads off to the left. In that direction you can see rolling hills and a distant town nestling in a valley. The way to the castle is ahead and you stride out in that direction.

The castle stands upon a mound and the road ahead rises up to enter the gate in the castle walls. The walls are high and solid and appear to completely enclose the castle.

You make your way along the road. The gates stand open and there is not a sign of life anywhere at all. After a brief hesitation, you walk on and enter the courtyard.

Around the walls of the courtyard are a number of small constructions that probably served once as stables, servants' quarters, and storerooms. At the back of the courtyard stands the castle proper and you examine it from your standpoint just within the gates.

It is a solid square construction with a single tall tower at one corner. There is a broad ramp leading up to the pair of large doors, doors that serve as the entrance to the castle.

Quickly, you walk up the ramp and pause at the top. There is a creaking sound from behind you and you turn to look back at the courtyard. The gates through which you entered have closed, apparently of their own volition. Here is a mystery that you will leave for the moment. You turn again and enter the cold dark interior of the castle building.

You find yourself in a large entrance hall. To the right and left are small doors set in the walls. Ahead are two large wooden doors that stand open. You walk on through these open doors and find yourself in what must have been the great hall of the castle. There is dust everywhere. This place has not been used for years. It would take time to clean it up and bring it back into proper shape again.

Within the hall are some tattered tapestries hanging upon the wall. In the center of the room is a large round table with twelve seats arranged evenly around it. Cross the floor to the table. Examine it closely. It is circular and has a dark wooden surface, about hip height. There is a gold inlaid circle in the center, the size of a large dinner plate. Radiating outward from this are twelve gold inlaid lines joining with a large gold inlaid circle just in from the table's edge.

You see that each chair around the table has an inscription in strange runes upon it. Somehow you know that on one of these chairs you will be able to read the inscription and that it will be your own name, your outer name or your secret inner name. You know that you will not be able to read the names on any of the other seats.

Begin looking at the chairs in turn, seeing if your name forms out of the runic script. It might be the first you check, it might be the last. But it will surely be one. And if you do not spot it the first time around, you will on a subsequent search.

You find the chair whose runes resolve into a name for you. Pull the chair out and see that there is a small rock on the seat. Pick this up, put it on the table at this spot and sit upon the seat: your seat. Remember this seat and where you have placed the rock.

A thought occurs to you out of nowhere. Take out the four gifts of the elementals and place them in the central circle of the table. Place the gold nugget closest to where you are sitting. Place the obsidian sphere opposite that, farthest away from you. Place the feather to the left side of the central circle, and place the watery chalice to the right. These are now in the center of the table equally spaced and forming a cross.

For the first time in this working, you no longer feel the cold. You now feel a warm glow to this room that seems to keep the outer cold at bay.

Relax for a while and ponder the nature of this castle. You remember that the seat in which you sit has your name on it. Perhaps this is your castle. Perhaps it is a heritage of which you were previously not aware. It is certainly deserted and perhaps available.

Close your eyes. After a moment you hear quiet murmuring and the sounds of people. You open your eyes and briefly see shadowy shapes sitting in the other chairs around the table. Then they slowly fade.

Look around and study the floor, walls, and ceiling of the great hall. Notice that there are wooden doors set into several places in the walls. Look at the wall that was to the left as you entered the hall. In the center of that wall you now notice a golden curtain on a rail, probably covering a doorway.

Get up from the chair and go to the curtain, leaving the rock and other treasures on the table. Draw the curtain aside and see a wooden door behind it. When you try the handle, it swings open and away from you easily and silently. There is a short corridor beyond, which ends as it joins a corridor crossing from right to left. You walk up to the junction.

Looking to the left you see the corridor leads to a door on the right side of the corridor, a short distance down the corridor before it rounds a corner to the left. To the right you see the corridor leads to a door on the left side of the passage before it comes to an end.

You turn left into the first corridor. Walking along, you come to the door on your right. This door is unnamed. You try to open the door and find it's unlocked. It leads into a room set up for use in a manner appropriate to the practices of your preferred religious or magical way. Look around and take careful note of what is seen. You catch sight of a large iron key. It may be useful so you take it with you.

You leave the room and turn left into the corridor, going back the way you came, back to the short corridor that leads back into the great hall. You walk past this to the door on the left. It is unlocked and opens easily into a dusty room.

The room is bare but for a comfortable chair just inside the door facing the far wall, a tall holder with a large unlit candle in each of the four corners, and a plain curtain hanging on the far wall. You go over and examine the curtain, but there is no door behind it, just the wall. There is nothing else in the room.

You leave the room and turn right into the corridor, making your way back to the junction and turning left to return to the great hall. You close the door and draw the curtain behind you. Return to the seat that is yours and sit on it again. Relax and allow thoughts and impressions about this place to arise.

After a while, stand up, have a last look around, and begin your return.

Go back through the large doors and walk outside. There is now a bleak sunlight showing in a watery blue sky and the edge has gone from the cold.

You notice that the gates of the courtyard are still closed but there is a small door to the right of the gates. Walking over to it to, you try the door but find it is locked. Perhaps the key you found will fit this lock. You put the key in the lock and turn it. A sharp *click* tells you that the door is unlocked. Take the key out of the lock and keep it with you as you open the door and peer into the darkness beyond.

Postamble

Step through and find yourself back in the room from which you began this working. There in front of you is the spot where you relaxed during the preliminaries.

Turn and look through the door seeing only a gray mist. The scene of the courtyard is no longer there. Close and lock the door, and then return to your seat. It's clear you have the key to this castle realm. And you now know for certain that the castle is yours.

Gradually, bring your attention back to where you are sitting, to your body, and its limbs. When you are ready, open your eyes, stand, and make your finishing or closing signs, gestures, or actions. You have awoken in the physical.

When you have some free time, make a rough sketch map of your adventure so far. At this stage, you could put the forest, the road, the crossroad, and the castle on the map. This will be an interesting journey and you will be able to add more to the map as you proceed on your quest. You could also make a sketch of the castle layout.

Discussion

The workings of this series always begin with a starting point in your physical environment. The continued use of the "extra door" serves to provide a definite and distinctive entry point to the inner realms. I'll explain here a little more about this technique.

What we are doing in the imagination is also occurring in the various levels of our psyche, described in different ways depending on your choice of psycho-spiritual discipline. This includes the discussion of "planes," such as "inner planes" used in some schools of thought.

We are integrated beings, and we often refer to different "functions," such as mind, emotion, and so on, as though they were separate things. It is sometimes useful to refer to different functions in this way. It is a handy device, but nonetheless a fiction. Sometimes we refer to apparent things called the mind and the emotions and I will do the same, but I want to make it clear that these are handy symbolic constructions to help us talk about different functions that make up the whole being.

"The mind" finds it easier to operate with known and fixed parameters. By using a standard method to enter the inner planes, which is to say become aware on other levels, we are setting up a reliable access point. To this end, we use an unvarying setting for the start and end of the workings. This also helps us to keep the actions and events in one plane separate from those in another.

As previously mentioned, there is a technical term in the Western Esoteric Tradition, "leakage," referring to cases where the planes flow into each other. We would find it difficult to function in the everyday world if we were encountering events and situations from the inner levels as though they were physical events and situations. This is why much early magical training in the Lodges of these traditions deals with setting up boundaries and signals, so that the transitions between the planes, or between different modes of awareness, can take place voluntarily and at will. Indeed, Dion Fortune, a noted magical worker of the last century, often stated the standard definition of magic as "the ability to cause changes in consciousness according to will."[6]

---

6. Dion Fortune was associated with the Order of the Golden Dawn and wrote a large number of reference and fictional works on matters relating to the Western Esoteric Tradition. She founded the Society of the Inner Light, which trained students, many of whom went on to found their own training schools and to research and write within the Tradition. Although subsequent Wardens of the Society may seem to have distanced themselves from any association with Wicca, many practitioners of Wicca count Dion Fortune as a witch as well as a ceremonial magician. See "A Seashore Ritual," in *The Witches' Way: Principles, Rituals and Beliefs of Modern Witchcraft* by Janet and Stewart Farrar for a reference to this.

Aquarius

As described in the introduction to part 2, we assign the first working to the New Moon in Aquarius. According to the Western system of astrology that I use and was taught, we have already entered what is often called the "age of Aquarius." The way we are, the way we relate with each other, the way we see things, all of this and more is conditioned by the age in which we live. Many teach that whereas natal astrology relates to individuals and their tasks in incarnations, the Great Ages of the zodiac relate to tasks that must be learned by humanity as a whole.

It is said that Aquarius is the sign of working together, the power of the group over the individual, and such. We may appear to be working these paths in the manner of the Age of Pisces, where each worked as an individual. However, because many people are working together and their castles map, to a certain extent, one upon the other, this manner of working is in the Aquarian system.

In addition, the legend of King Arthur and the Knights of the Round Table gave us a prefigure of the workings of the Aquarian age—a round table at which all who sit are equals, bringing their individual and unique skills together to create a multiskilled team. Maybe they were not equals in rank or learning or status or a million other things, but equal by virtue of the fact that all humans are valued evenly, without prejudice—one person's opinion being as good as another's and all having a right to a say.

This may be controversial but I firmly believe that this is the learning for this age. And this is why the sign of Aquarius was chosen as the starting point. From here the other paths will unfold the path of the zodiac logically but in terms of an Aquarian starting point.

The Key

An important event of the first working of the New Moon paths is the finding and acquiring of the key to the door between the realms. This signals to "the mind" that you do in fact now have the key to those inner realms and can come and go, and more importantly, open up and close down as you choose.

You will use this key to enter and leave the inner realms of these workings for each of the following New Moon sessions, clearly unlocking and locking to signal the start and end of the work. In this way, you have further protected yourself against "leakage."

In later workings, you may find that you are almost doing a working within a working and at such times you will be operating on a new level of awareness. The same rules will apply at each transition, but the most important one is this first one because the awareness levels of everyday life are involved.

The Wood

There is a large number of examples in literature, in myth, and in legend where a series of adventures begin in a wood or forest. Many of the adventures in the extensive collection of legends of the Middle Ages—such as those of Arthur and the Knights of the Round Table, or of Charlemagne—take place in various settings within a vast and primeval forest.

A very famous allegory of the soul's journey is that of the *Divine Comedy* by Dante Alighieri. The story is told in the first person and the author writes that he came to himself, midway through life, in a dark wood. We may or may not be midway through life when we undertake these workings. At any stage of our lives we can become bogged down and lose sight of our spiritual purpose on this planet. And many times in our lives we might "come to our senses" and realize this and then take steps to get back on course again, so to speak.

However, it is certainly true that we can have a major spiritual crisis around midlife.

Charles Williams, in his commentary on the *Divine Comedy,* writes at length on the nature of this forest. He suggests that the inner realm of adventure is in part like one great forest of the unknown. Within this forest there are magical places and features, each with its own story. These features supply fixed and known starting points within the greater unknown of the forest.[7]

Taking this statement of the human condition symbolically, we use it in this working to indicate to ourselves that we are to "wake up," or "come to ourselves" on these inner levels, within these inner landscapes. Once awake and aware, we can begin to find our true path again.

---

7. Charles Williams. *The Figure of Beatrice* (Cambridge: D. S. Brewer, 1994), 107–108, 114, 175–176, 193.

The Stag

In such a vast bleak and dark forest, it would be useful to have a guide to show the way. And, since we are bound upon a spiritual quest, it would be better to find our guide under the blessings of divinity. Therefore, we find the stag, at one time an animal of the god (in the form of a stag, for Herne the Hunter) and of the goddess (in the form of the deer for Diana the Huntress).

The Pentagram

I thought to set a symbolic seal on this work overall and one which is in a sense least partisan. The pentagram represents the four elements with the quintessential spirit. It is used by magicians, Wiccans and Pagans alike, even by the Christian and Qabalistic magicians of the Middle Ages. Its color represents values of the spirit and the complementary color of yellow relates to mind and clear vision.

The Tomb

The first thing that you are led to is a tomb or open mausoleum. In fact, it is not exactly clear who resides within or even if they are alive or not. All of these questions are open.

In dream symbology, a tomb stands for a set of restrictions that surround the dreamer. Well, to be honest, there are many interpretations, but this is the one I am using for the working.

There are many legends and tales that tell of a sleeping person—the well-known *Sleeping Beauty* being just one of them. Numerous heroes are said to have not actually died but to have rather withdrawn to sleep until needed. There are legends of Bran the Blessed, of King Alfred, and of course of King Arthur. The theme is all but worldwide, especially when we view such legends as resurrection themes.

There are other heroes who remain locked up or in a form of retirement until needed, such as Merlin, for example. And there are other ways in which someone can be "locked away" from their usual pursuits. Examples include those set to wandering the earth, whether on a quest, under a curse or for some sort of eternity. Stories of these can be found everywhere in fairy tales, scriptures, and legend. They similarly are in an in-between state before coming to use their proper powers again. We can remember, too, the long quest of Isis in seeking the scattered and dismembered body parts of her husband-brother Osiris before being able to produce Horus, the Child of the Aeon.

The first email-based program for these workings started with the Dark Wood, titled *The Wood of Broceliande* on January 22, 2004. Interestingly enough, I later found this entry in the *Arthurian Book of Days* for that date: "Of all the places in the wide woodlands through which the Fellowship of the Round Table went on adventure, none had a more terrible reputation than the Chapel Perilous … Lancelot … saw the body of a knight lying under a cloth …"[8]

The runic saying on the tomb makes reference to Will and Power. These are two of the traditional three aspects of life, the universe, and everything as defined by many magicians. The third aspect is of course Love. I have found it useful to map these onto other trinities, such as Brahma, Shiva, Vishnu; Lower World, Upper World, Middle World; Lord, Lady, Child of Promise; and so on.

Such analogies of structure sometimes yield fruit, sometimes not. It can also be an individual thing, varying with prior studies and training. Not everyone sees analogies the same way and this is as it should be.

We can consider the two under discussion, Power and Will, in terms of actions. When the Will to act is at one with the Power to act, we get a pure action in the world. It is as though we might see at a lower level that we take responsibility as we exercise a balancing authority. A fundamental tenet of job specification in the Australian Public Service of the last century was that "there can be no responsibility without commensurate authority."

On a higher level, we are looking at the wielding of the will, which has been brought into line with the Divine Will, or the Will of the Universe, if you prefer. Spiritual writers and commentators tell us that when the personal will is so aligned, we will have the power of the divine, or the universe, behind us. In these cases, Will and Power are one.

There is a reference to "the place where will and power are one" in Dante's *Divine Comedy* and many researchers see this as the origin of St. Augustine's maxim, "Only love, and do what thou wilt"; the "do," or action, standing in place here of "power." This is then seen to have given rise to Aleister Crowley's "Do what thou wilt shall be the whole of the law," and the Wiccan rede, "In

---

8. John Matthews and Caitlín Matthews, *The Arthurian Book of Days* (Hemel Hempstead: Prentice Hall, 1990), 20.

seven words our law fulfill / In harming none do what thou wilt," and variants thereof. My own groups used, "Love all, harm none, do what thou wilt."

There is a mystery here and one that you will unravel for yourself. It is not possible for me to say much more at this stage about this symbol because it will come up again and I do not want to preempt your future impressions.

The Crossroads

The pathworkings we undertake involve the inner planes and I have said above that this might better be regarded as inner levels of awareness. What I have not yet said is that these inner levels of awareness—inner landscapes—map onto the physiology of the human brain, if they are to work at all well.

The castle, which we will discuss next, features as a central point or influence in our workings. But other workings within the landscape may take place to "right" or "left" of the castle, or "in front" or "behind." In fact, we already know that the wood is "behind" the castle in a sense, meaning that we were in the wood before we encountered the castle.

The directions of right and left can map onto the hemispheres of the brain and partake, to some extent, of their characteristics. To the left we would expect things relating to the so-called "logical" side of the brain. On the "left side" of the pathworking, you see the town, relating to the idea of imposing our structures upon the realm of nature. This theme fits well with this logical categorizing style of thinking.

The other side, the right side, leads to other things more closely related to the generalist, holistic, and so-called "emotional" side of the brain. We will see more how this works as we continue with the paths yet to come.

The Castle

Finally we reach the castle, our own castle. Dream interpretations and psychotherapeutic inner workings usually regard a structure, such as a house, a room, and of course a castle, as a symbol of the self. In keeping with the milieu of these workings occurring in a partly Dark Ages, partly mythological setting, I have chosen a castle to represent the presence of the self on the inner levels. The castle is, at one and the same time, a representation of yourself and your base in these pathworking realms.

Castles can be found in any size, shape, or form. If you read the Holy Grail legends, you will find a veritable treasure trove of occupied, unoccupied, and ghostly occupied castles. Some are safe, some mystical, some confusing, and some dangerous. Sometimes the perception of the castle changes for the same person at different times or for different people at the same time. People in everyday life present us with the same characteristics and behaviors.

When you settle into your castle, you are also settling into yourself. As you explore the castle, you are exploring yourself. When you go from certain parts of the castle into the surrounding landscape, you are activating skills and talents and functions that you will be able to use in the outside everyday world.

The Great Hall and Table Round

At the very heart of the castle and the self, we place a mandala, a pattern, a design, a pictogram, or a layout to represent the balanced inner nature. Your great hall has four walls to represent the four quarters, the four elements, four cities of Irish legends. Many designs, from some buffalo hide paintings to Tibetan artwork, show this basic four-fold system. Some do not, of course.

In our case, we have within the four-fold system a central circle, consisting of a round table. This is exactly as the round table of the grail legends—a place where each knight sits as an equal, with none greater or lesser than any other. Taking lines joining opposite walls, we get an equal-armed cross with a circle in the center, being the table. This is one design for a Celtic cross and this is our balancing mandala. In our case, each quarter of the table will have three segments, making twelve in all.

Once you are in the hall, you need to establish yourself as the owner of the castle. To be the owner you will have the right to sit at the table and this you will find by walking around the table until you find your name on a chair. As you saw in the pathworking, you may have to go around more than once to find this name, which is part of the mystery of the castle.

The castle in the working is each person's own castle. Yet, at the same time, all castles are the one castle. So, on the first circuit around the table, you might be looking at a parallel castle. Usually by the second circuit, if not before, the chair is found.

Now what of the other seats, the other eleven chairs around this segmented round table? These seats can be taken by others from the past, the present, or the future, incarnate or discarnate, human, or from other lines of evolution, such as elves, for example.

The seats may also be taken by aspects of your own self. In fact, even if you are having some sort of communication with beings other than yourself, it usually takes place via an internal representation of that being rather than directly. We can view all who may appear at the table as aspects of ourselves, even if there is more to that behind-the-scenes, so to speak. Because of this "internal virtual entity" quirk of the human nervous system, you can be assured that nothing will come to you that does not have a resonance in your own nature.

The hall and round table are the heart of the castle and so by analogy the heart or center of your own self. It is to this center that you can marshal your resources, in a manner of speaking. Here all aspects may appear and have a voice.

This ability to bring your inner resources together for some piece of work is very important. Indeed, there are some "positive thought" schools that recommend using the imagination to personify a group of "experts" to assist you in your ambitions and desires. This is little other than using symbolic forms to encourage you to bring your inner resources to bear.

The Rock or Stone

In each pathworking there will be an object of some sort that you will find and bring back to the table. There are twelve segments on the table and twelve standard pathworkings. There is also a thirteenth pathworking for the second New Moon within a sign. This second New Moon happens every two to three years, so it is taken into account in the series of workings.

The gift from this thirteenth working will go in the center of the table. Where you place the other twelve gifts is entirely up to you. I will remind you later, though, to keep a record of your placements.

After placing your "gift" of this path, you set up the elemental gifts you have already received while treading the paths of Earth, as previously described in the working. This symbolically brings into this set of workings the experiences you have already had and the realizations you have already attained. It provides a link of continuity.

The first gift of the New Moon series is the stone or rock, which goes at your own place. It can appear in many forms—raw to ornate—and many sizes—pebble to chunk, but never too small or large to place on the table. In a sense, this is an anchor point for all the rest. The discussion for the final working of the series will have more to add on the subject of the objects found.

The Unnamed Rooms

The castle of the self has other rooms and chambers and these are symbolic of different parts of your own inner life.

Usually, religious and magical practices are a very personal and private affair, even though one may join with others for gatherings and celebrations. The first room is your own inner holy of holies. Here you will find that you can have the *exact* working space you need, and this space will overshadow your actual physical workspace, enriching it. This inner version of your working space may also change with time.

It is, of course, your indoor working place. You will probably have needs for outdoor working at times. Never fear. You can rest assured that later pathworkings will suggest places on the inner levels where you can conduct your outside circles and practices. These too can be set up so that they can "stand behind" the actual places you work in out in the everyday world. The second room, on the other hand, is concerned with inner workings and you will see how this works later in the series.

———

This working is intended to establish a starting point and a foothold in one aspect of what has been called the "inner planes."

The inner planes can just as easily be viewed as aspects of consciousness. As such, they have been built by the evolution of mankind, the storytellers and word-weavers, and all creative inner activity into the rich form that we know them today.

I told my children that the inner realm is the place where all stories are true. These levels of awareness are at one and the same time the source of our creativity and a response to our creations. Once a foothold has been gained, we have a starting point for other adventures to come. We are taking a journey together in this series. May our adventures be wonderful, challenging, and rewarding.

Path 2: The Crystal Cave

✢

Now that you have established a new reference point, it is time to find the other magical places within your realm. In this path, you will make your first journey out from the castle and find a magical cave. The purpose of the working is for you to realize symbolically that the inner world is causal to the outer world. As always with pathworkings, this idea is not stated but presented in symbol forms.

This is an important place because you will come here more than once. Like the different rooms of the castle, it will feature later as a starting point for adventures leading deeper within the fabric of this realm. Pay attention to the way that you come to the cave, as you will use that same way to return to it later. These steps will not be repeated later, but you can refer back to this working for the information on the steps needed to get here if necessary. The way to the cave will seem somehow shorter each time you travel to it.

The zodiac association for this path is Pisces.

Preamble

Relax and breathe rhythmically in your work place exactly as in the previous working. The scene of your work area arises before your eyes. Once more there is one extra door, just like the previous pathworking. Rise up in your mind's eye, approach the door and, using the key you obtained in the last working, unlock and open it.

There is a swirling mist beyond the door. You step through and immediately find yourself in the castle courtyard. The door between the realms closes behind you.

The Setting

Once more you cross to the main doors of the castle itself and pass through the entryway into the great hall.

There, as before, is the round table with the stone or rock from the last working upon it exactly as you left it, together with the central elemental gifts. The chairs are all in place, but this time you will not be seated because you are going to go beyond this hall on your pathworking.

Look around the hall. There are a number of doors other than the one through which you entered. One of these doors has upon it a design that looks like a crystal. Your first task is to find that door and stand before it.

Examine the location and the nature of this door and then open it and step through into the scene beyond. You find yourself outside the castle on the grass of the mound where the castle was built. Do not at this stage wonder at how such geometry may come about. Just accept the position you are in.

You close the door behind you, noting that it blends in with the wall around the castle. Unless one knew it was there it would indeed be hard to find. Yet you know its location and there is a form to the apparently random scratches and markings of the wall that hints at the design of the crystal symbol.

———————————— THE PATHWORKING ————————————

From where you stand, the ground slopes gently downward. Behind you there stands a castle wall and set into it is the door through which you have entered this realm. It is a warm day in early spring and the scents of many flowers are upon the air. You begin to make your way down the hill away from the castle, following a faint track in the grass. A little distance away you see that the ground rises again and is densely wooded. And although you cannot see it from this angle, you somehow know that further beyond stands a high mountain.

At the bottom of the incline there is a small stream, rapidly flowing as though fed somewhere by melting mountain snows. It has a laughing, joyful sound. Not far away from where you stand you will find a place where you may easily cross this stream. It might be a shallow ford and it might be stepping-stones. No matter how it appears to you, you cross over the water at this point and as you do so, you see two fish swim past heading downstream. Once on the other bank, you continue on your way following a path that leads up into the wood ahead.

The path is narrow at first and the trees grow thickly forming a dense canopy overhead. As you walk on, the road climbs higher and the way opens out into a broader track. Sunlight now filters through the leafy cover, dancing and sparkling.

Many smaller tracks lead off to the right and left, and it may be that someday you will explore these. At the entrance to one of these narrow overgrown tracks, one of the saplings has a few streamers of tattered red and white ribbons fluttering from it. Perhaps it marks the way to something. Today, however, you must continue along the broader track, striding through the peaceful forest.

As you go on, the trees thin out even more, and soon you see ahead a steep rocky cliff face. The path leads you to the base of this and stops. Somehow you must find a way to the top of this cliff. You survey the possibilities—firm earth and rock here, loose shale and rubble there. Perhaps if you are very lucky there is even the beginning of a path already. In any case, you must find some way to reach the top. If you are not able to do this, do not despair but return from the pathworking by retracing your steps and you can try again another day. Eventually you will find a way if you persist.

When you have decided how to ascend the face, you continue on your way. The climb seems long and hard, but you persevere and eventually you reach the top of the cliff. There is a plateau here and a lake, still and clear. Beyond the lake the single peak of the mountain rises high into the clear sky, reflected in the still water of the lake. You rest for a few moments, taking in the scene and all its details. You hear the distant sound of a waterfall and realize that somewhere the lake is spilling off the cliff to the land down below. A track leads around the plateau's lake to the foot of the renewed rise of the mountain. It is this track that you now follow.

The air is crisp and clear. It refreshes you as you breathe. Colors look bright and full of life. Soon you come to the base of the mountain. Here stands an olive tree with widely spreading branches. It grows very closely to the rock face of the mountain. There is also a spring that bubbles forth from the rock and fills a small rock pool. The overflow from this pool runs into the lake itself. Near the pool is a rough niche in the rock face where a small wooden goblet stands. You pick up this goblet and fill it from the pool. You take a sip of its clear cold contents. Then, following age-old tradition, you let a few drops fall upon the ground…

You find you are thirsty after your long walk and hard climb. You drink your fill of the refreshing water and then replace the goblet in its niche.

Look again at the olive tree. Somehow the drink has altered your sight, for now you see a dark cave mouth in the rock behind the tree. Why did you not see it until you had drunk of the spring?

You pass behind the tree and enter the cave. Ahead is darkness. You stop. An old woman, the guardian of this place, blocks your path. There is no menace in this. You sense a question asked of you, "By what code do you enter this place?"

To this you must reply, "Under Love, let Will and Power be one."

If you do not give this exact reply, whatever you experience will not be a part of this pathworking. It may seem that you complete the journey as described. Yet without the correct reply, all that you will experience will be delusion, not the realities linked into this working. This is one way that the guardian works to ensure that the code is upheld.

She hands you a lantern that springs to light, and by its light you can peer farther into the cave. Beyond where the woman stands, you see there are two tunnels, one heading straight ahead and one branching off to the left. The woman moves to block the entrance to the left-hand tunnel leaving the way straight ahead clear. You walk in that direction, past the woman.

The air is cool. A straight passageway lies before you. You walk along it into the heart of the mountain. As you walk, you observe the texture and formation of the walls, the floor, the ceiling above you. Is this passageway natural, or constructed?

Looking ahead you see that the passageway will soon take you into a larger cavern, which glows with some hidden light. The light in this cavern seems to ooze from the walls themselves. The cavern is large and in its center stands a dark pool, roughly circular.

You go to the pool and look into its inky blackness. Thought alone may not plumb its darkly depths, nor knowledge say all that dwells therein. Its surface is best left unruffled, mirror-like, yet more than mere reflections may be seen within it. This cave and its lake contain many wonderful and mysterious treasures. Now it is time to explore one of these.

In a place where the cavern wall comes close to the edge of the pool there is a small opening. You make your way over to it. You have to bend low to look into its dark interior. Within the interior is a small cave. You put the lantern through the opening and its light is reflected from bright crystal walls. You hear a soft, chime-like sound. If you squeezed you could crawl through the opening and into this cave. You do so. The cave is too small to stand up in, but you can sit with your back against the wall in a half-reclining position, the lantern by your side on the ground. The walls, floor, and ceiling are crystalline and multifaceted. In one part of the wall there is set a very large crystal. It is like a mirror, yet all it shows now is a bright light. It is the Crystal of Vision.

You sit and gaze at it. Perhaps the light in it is the reflection of the light of your lantern. Slowly the light dims to a pearly gray iridescence. It begins to cloud within its interior. You continue to watch. The pale light of your lantern is now no longer relevant. Here and there patches of darkness appear among the clouds within the crystal. The patches increase in number and last longer. The cloudiness is dispersing, leaving a blackness within the crystal. Soon it is totally jet black. Yet still you watch, and, as you do, images begin to appear in the crystal. Keep watching and the images will appear. This is the start of the vision for which you journeyed here. Relax and observe; pause for a moment.

A pure point of light appears in the crystal. As this light grows, the images within the crystal fade. Soon all is engulfed in the bright light of the crystal. The vision is over. You now see that the light within the crystal is but a reflection of the light of your lantern. It is time to leave. You will have other opportunities to come here again and to explore the treasure house of images that may be found here.

You pick up your lantern and squeeze through the entrance-way back into the main cavern to stand for a moment, taking in the details once more. There is a shard of dark crystal on the ground and you bend to pick it up. It is rough, flat and circular; not a lot to really interest you, but you put it in your pocket or pouch anyway.

You make your way to the passageway by which you entered the inner cavern. Soon you come to the mouth of the cave and again you pass by the guardian. It may be that some special sign of recognition is given to you or a greeting for your future use. This is, of course, in addition to the statement of the code that is required to gain access to this realm. You should always encounter the guardian upon this path. If at any time the guardian is not present then your work for that time will have to be postponed.

Passing around the olive tree you are once more in the open. You look back but no longer see the cave's mouth except perhaps for a dim outline superimposed upon the blank rock face. Turning, you once more skirt the edge of the lake and come to the top of the cliff face. Here you descend by the same way that you originally used in making the climb. Now, it seems a little shorter and easier than before. At the bottom, you once more find the track that leads into the forest.

You take this track, again entering the cool peace of the ancient forest. The track narrows as the trees crowd thickly together, but soon you emerge from among these trees and stand before the small creek or brook. From the other bank, the ground rises to form a small hill, atop which stands your castle and starting point.

You cross the creek and ascend the track that takes you to the door in the castle wall, the door by which you left the great hall. A last look around and you pass through the door, closing it firmly behind you.

Postamble

Once again you are in the great hall of the castle with its round table. Your rock or stone is in its place in front of your chair. Take out the shard of crystal from your pocket and place it on another segment of the table. It is your choice where you place it, but remember the position.

Make your way to your seat and sit upon it. Relax and spend a few moments reviewing your experiences. At this time further thoughts and realizations may come to mind.

Look around at the other seats. Some may be occupied by shadowy indistinct shapes; some may not. Whatever the situation, mentally share your experiences with any who seem to be present, seen or unseen. It may be that you receive some impressions from them in return.

After a few moments, leave your seat and make your way out into the courtyard again. From here you will use your key to return through the small door in the castle wall to your original working place, completing your working exactly as before.

When you write in your journal, and if you have not already done so, draw a twelve-segment circle with a center to represent the table. Make a note on the drawing of the location of your rock or stone and of your crystal shard.

It is time now to start your inner realm map, if you have not already done so. Mark on your map the castle and the dark wood of your first working. Also mark the stream, the lake, the cave, and the mountain. Put in as many notes as you need. You will return later to the crystal cave.

Discussion

In the last working you established a place for yourself on the inner levels, a place to work from. In this working, you enter the inner realms and find yourself already at this new place, the castle, which will be your jumping off point for this and further adventures. In this way, a thread is maintained between your physical working place on the one hand and the castle on the other.

Your physical working place is the center around which your day-to-day events occur and the common starting point for inner workings. To balance this, you now have the other end of the thread, the castle on the other side of the door. This point acts as a center or, if you prefer, a gateway between all that occurs on the inner levels and this level. It is as though you have inner experiences and then bring them back into your inner self or inner base before returning to the physical realm.

This method of establishing one thing before moving on to the next gives us a logic pattern, an Ariadne thread, through the maze of inner psychological experiences and a way to bring them out into the light of day.

Pisces

This path takes place with the New Moon in Pisces, this being the next sign in sequence after our Aquarius starting point. What do we know of Pisces?

Among the suggestions of various astrologers, we continually return to the ideas of things hidden when tracking down the attributions of Pisces. All things withdrawn, not in plain view, unknown—these belong to the realm of Pisces.

This path has a lot to do with building a bridge between those things of which we are aware and those things of which we are not aware. In fact, the two fish seen in the stream can be taken as the two sides of a coin. In many diagrams these are linked together by a chord, and this might remind us of the "silver chord" that is said to join the astral body to the physical body—the body of the world of dreams to the body of the world of sense.

The point is that the hallmark of this path is the nature of things hidden and the means of access to them is by way of a mirror or mirror-like surface.

The Stream

The pathworkings in this series fall into groups within the series. The first working is in a group of its own, a group of one. This working is in the second group of the first series. When in a working you pass from aspects of the landscape of one group into aspects of the landscape of another group, you will find some sort of symbolic barrier or demarcation. In this case, you cross a stream.

The crossing of water has potent magical significance in this regard. In the Greek legends, for example, the way to the underworld of Hades required the crossing of a mighty river, named "Styx." This threshold effect of running water can also be seen in the notion that a witch cannot cross running water.

The Fish

Are we dealing with one fish or two? The idea of one fish being the mirror of the other is not new.

In the alchemical work by Abraham Lambspring, the first step of the process states:

> "The Sages will tell you
> That two fishes are swimming in our sea
>
> Moreover, the Sages say
>
> That the two fishes are only one, not two;
> They are two, and nevertheless they are one ..."[9]

The astrologer Richard Allen in *Star Names and Their Meanings*, states that in ancient times there was only one fish.[10] However, Greek mythology tells of Venus and her son Cupid being on the banks of a river when confronted by the monster Typhon. To escape, they plunged into the river and escaped with the aid of two fish. These fish were then put into the heavens as a constellation by

---

9. Arthur Edward Waite, *The Hermetic Museum Volumes 1 and 2* (Loschberg 9, Germany: Jazzybee Verlag Jürgen Beck, 2017), 159.

10. Richard Hinckley Allen, *Star Names and Their Meanings* (Mineola, NY: Dover Publications, 2000), 338.

Venus in thanks for their help. Later Venus and Cupid were regarded as the two fish of the constellation.

The Slope

The paths within the inner realms, and within ourselves, are largely untrodden, especially in any orderly and intentional way. Many paths will appear to present obstacles that must be overcome. How you do this will be your own choice arising out of your own nature.

In this path, there is a rise in level and this signals a change in consciousness. We are rising above the usual level where the castle resides and where other things reside as well.

We have to make this change because we are going to create images that will start to build a link between those aspects of the inner levels, of which we are not aware, and our normal inner consciousness as it exists at the level of the castle.

Once you have solved this problem of mounting the slope—and it will be more of a problem to some than to others—the ground levels out. You find a large lake on a plateau and then the ground rises sharply again becoming a mountain.

The Lake

All elements on the plateau then relate to the same levels of consciousness. This lake is the second introduction of a water motif, the first being the stream that you crossed.

Water is a major factor in this working. It is reflective, like a mirror, and indeed our first mirrors were pools and bowls of water. Some scryers use mirrors these days and yet there are still some around who prefer a bowl or dish of water for such work.

In earlier times, quartz crystal was thought to be a form of ice, and so the crystal element itself has an association with water.

This lake, should you one day explore it, is fed by the spring near the mouth of the cave, and at one point of its perimeter spills over the edge of the plateau to the land below in a magnificent waterfall. This water joins that of the stream that you crossed.

There are many tales and legends that feature lakes and other water features, like fountains and wells. These often have a keeper, guardian, or denizen associated with them. Many of the Holy Grail legends mention the Lady of the Lake and the knights of those tales sometimes met various ladies and clerics that lived in or near a lake.

The spring at the base of the mountain is, in magical terms, water coming forth from the earth. Drinking from magical pools, wells, or springs will often clear the sight—both physically and symbolically. Here, again, water is associated with things normally unseen. This brings us to the cave, an important feature of this working.

The Cave Entrance

At first, an olive tree obscures the entrance to the cave. In Greek mythology, this tree is sacred to Athena. It was Athena who sprang fully armed from the brow of Zeus and she has an aspect of a warrior goddess. But, she is also a goddess of wisdom. This should alert us to the idea that she is probably more like the "Scholar Warrior" of Chinese and Japanese martial traditions.

This guardian challenges us. There are many challenges in as many traditions of myth and legend. At heart, the keeper of the way needs to know who we are and where we are from. It is like being asked for ID or for a membership card: we only get in if we are one of the group, whatever that may mean, depending on the gateway we are confronting.

In Orphic tablets found deposited in ancient Greek graves, we find this particular poem between the Underworld and one of its new arrivals:

I am parched with thirst and perishing!

Then come drink of me, the ever--flowing spring [sic].
On the right is a bright cypress. Who are you?
Where are you from?

I am the son of Earth and starry heaven.
But my race is heavenly.[11]

---

11. Roy Kotansky, trans., *Lamella Orphica*, mid-fourth century BCE, gold, 2.2 x 3.7 x 0.1 cm (⅞ x 1 ⁷⁄₁₆ x ¹⁄₁₆ in), The J. Paul Getty Museum, Los Angeles, http://www.getty.edu/art/collection/objects/7194/unknown-maker-lamella-orphica-greek-mid-fourth-century-bc/.

This small poem deals with a tree, the question, an answer, the spring, and the deep well of memory, which we later find within the cave in the form of the dark central pool.

The cave is a very potent symbol. Access to other realms is often via caves in many tales and legends. In her series of pathworkings based upon the paths of the Qabalistic Tree of Life, Dolores Ashcroft-Nowicki has a cave as the entry point for the first working, that of the thirty-second path on the Tree. In this case, the path leads to the underworld realm of Queen Persephone and the Lord Hades. The guardian here is Hecate—the crone aspect of the Persephone-Demeter-Hecate triune goddess.

When the journey is to the land of the dead, this is the appropriate guardian. When the cave is used to lead to knowledge of the self, you will find Athena as the guardian. In this way, the pathworkings link the broad meanings of their archetypal symbols to more specific aspects.

Caves were once our homes and have been used for burial purposes. When we wander the trackless wastes for the wise hermit, we find them at the mouth of their cave.[12]

Jules Verne had his intrepid explorers enter a cave to journey to the center of the earth. Old tales tell of travelers who enter a cave and find treasures and sleeping warriors there, who must not be fully awakened. It was in a cave that Aladdin found the lamp, and in a refreshing change, C. S. Lewis had his heroes enter another realm through the back of a wardrobe.

Lest you think this association fanciful, did your play as a child ever include a wardrobe full of hanging clothes? If so, you would know the womb-like experience of such a place and caves themselves are wombs in the earth, places of safety. In many a film of the horror and thriller genres, a potential victim hides in a clothes closet, but not always successfully!

---

12. The older singular "they" of the English language will occur in these essays. It was once standardly used for cases where the sex or gender of the subject is not specified, is indeterminate or irrelevant. Some modern grammarians have tried to remove it but it clings on. And anyway I prefer it to the cumbersome and unnecessary "he/she" or "s/he" devices common among those who have forgotten what is already in the language for the situation.

No discussion of caves could ignore the Cave of the Nymphs. In the thirteenth book of *The Odyssey*,[13] Homer describes a mysterious and unusual cave. The description begins as follows:

> High at the head, a branching olive grows
> And crowns the pointed cliffs with shady boughs
> A cavern pleasant, though involved in night
> Beneath it lies, the Naiades delight.

A little later he says:

> Perpetual waters through the grotto glide,
> A lofty gate unfolds on either side
> That to the north is pervious to mankind
> The sacred south t'immortals is consign'd.

This idea of the cave having more than one use or more than one "plane" associated with it will be important to us later. Suffice it to say that our journey on this occasion took us via a way open to mortals.

This passage from Homer is not the source of the pathworking, which existed before I was aware of the reference. It should come as no surprise that all humans find similar things on the inner levels, which after all reflect the inner nature of human beings. The details will vary but the essentials will be the same. Those who explore the inner realms will encounter similar things, events, inhabitants, and adventures purely because we share our humanity across all cultures.

Your pass-phrase for this path continues the theme of the previous one. The permutations of this phrase would make good topics for meditation. Many of the meanings in these workings will become clearer as we proceed. Sometimes this can creep up gradually. Sometimes an insight occurs all-at-once.

In the Western Esoteric Tradition, different groups have different ways of referring to the fundamental principle of three. In the case of Aleister Crowley, we find in the Book of the Law "there are therein Three Grades, the Hermit, and the Lover, and the man of Earth."[14] At the time of writing, the class term

---

13. Homer, *The Odyssey*, trans. Alexander Pope (London: J. Walker and J. Harris, 1811), 213.
14. Aleister Crowley, *The Book of the Law* (York Beach, ME: Red Wheel/Weiser, 2004), 31 .

"man" was commonly used for people, humans. In today's world the sense is more preserved by using "person of earth."

In the case of W. E. Butler we find Power, Love, Wisdom, "These are usually thought of as the Paths of Power, Love and Wisdom, and all mankind evolves along one of these roads." [15] I personally equate these trinities to the three-fold goddess of Mother/Love/Lover, Maiden/Power/Person of earth, and Crone/Wisdom/Hermit.

The two strands differ more in appearance than in reality. There is a correspondence with Will and Wisdom. The second Sephirah on the Tree of Life of the Qabalists is named Chockmah—meaning Wisdom, and is to do with Will, among other things.

When Dante entered a cave mouth to begin his journey into the underworld, he was met with the motto "abandon hope all ye who enter herein." [16] Hope is only our refuge when we do not *know*, and when we have not *faith*. If we have either knowledge or faith, or even belief, then hope is not required. Knowledge and faith are like two sides of the same coin. On the one hand, we know with certainty. On the other we have faith, which is belief without support. That is the case of faith, as I am using the term, there is no supporting knowledge whatsoever. From my point of view, "belief" partakes of both aspects, taking us from one to the other, but being neither. With "belief" there is some evidence known to suggest what is believed.

As two sides of the same coin, faith and knowledge spring from Wisdom. And this linking of Wisdom with Will reminds us again of Athena, the scholar-warrior.

The Romans called Athena "Minerva," and the Romans built a temple to Minerva in Bath, England, around a sacred pool. In Romano-Celtic times, the British goddess Brigantia (Brighid, Bride) was shown with the attributes of Minerva.

---

15. Walter Ernest Butler, "Esoteric Government," Servants of the Light, accessed December 10, 2019, https://www.servantsofthelight.org/knowledge/esoteric-government/.

16. "Lasciate ogni speranza, voi ch'entrate:" This could be read more as "leave all (mere) hope behind," a deliberate act. The sense usually associated with the English version of the phrase is that there is now "no hope." This is quite different.

The Central Cavern

The main feature in this cavern at this time is the large central pool or well. If the crystal in the small cave that you use can be thought of as a window on your own inner nature, this large dark pool would represent a window upon the inner nature of the world. It is akin to the Well of Mimir of Norse mythology.

It is this central feature that joins us all together, linking our individual inner, hidden natures into the collective inner hidden nature of all humanity, and, beyond, that of all life.

The Crystal Cave

Finally you enter the small crystal cave, your own individual place to look deep into yourself and to scry for visions of past or future relevant to you.

This pathworking takes its name from the book *The Crystal Cave* by Mary Stewart. In the prologue of that book, the character Merlin says, "What I cannot see in dreams I see in the flames, the red heart of the fire or the countless mirrors of the crystal cave."[17]

In your crystal cave you have a crystal mirror. Both crystal balls and mirrors are used for scrying. The examples range from the stereotypical fortune-teller with crystal ball to Dr. John Dee and Edward Kelly, conjuring magical visions in a mirror in Elizabethan times.

Scrying is carried out with all manner of shapes and sizes of mirror, water-dish, crystal, and basically any reflective surface. Some people use the hinged three-mirror that shows front face and each side, sometimes seen in the dressing rooms of actors and presenters.

The interesting thing about crystals is that they are said to retain images and energies impressed upon them. They reside in the earth and so contain in this way the memory of the earth herself, together with all that has occurred thereon.

While the experiences with the crystal cave are personal, they can come up from a very deep and archetypal level of consciousness.

———

17. Mary Stewart, *The Crystal Cave* (Hachette, UK: Hodder & Stoughton, 1970), 1.

This working can release hidden things, things from the depths of the self. But these workings are constructed so that realizations will come through the events of everyday life after the working itself.

The experience in the working can be powerful and vivid. However, the fuller meanings of those experiences will work themselves out in the week or two that follows the working. It is as though the working itself was a request to the deeper personal levels, and via them to the universe itself. This request will be answered in ways that are appropriate to you and to your present life. Although this holds true of the pathworking process generally, this particular path is designed to activate knowledge of the relationship between inner requests or visions and everyday consciousness and understanding.

Path 3: Town and Tower

—————— ✛ ——————

In a sense the castle is a correlate of the physical self. It has many rooms yes, but it is solid, stone on stone. In the crystal cave we tapped into the sense of looking within and connecting with inner forces. This path will lead us to a town, which is a symbol of knowledge of result brought about by thought and intelligence. It will represent aspects of knowledge and knowing. We know from experience of course, but we can also know from the experience of others through their writings. The purpose of this working, then, is to gain an appreciation that communication of inner realities requires an outer form. As you travel this path, keep in mind that Aries is the zodiac representation for this working.

In this working, you will seek and find the repository of knowledge within yourself. When it comes down to it, we know an awful lot. We know facts and methods taught at school. We know things from books we read and we know things we have been told. Our range of knowing can stretch from before we were born through the work of others. This working symbolically takes you to your own center of knowing and communication. Finding this within yourself may open access to memory, to things once told by others, to previously lost memories. It is always personal. But, symbolically you are here finding the core of knowledge within yourself. You know things that you do not know you know. It is all here in this library.

Preamble

Relax and breathe rhythmically in your work place just as you have in the previous workings.

The scene of your work area arises before your eyes. As before, you rise up in your mind's eye, approach the door, unlock it, and open it.

There is a swirling mist beyond the door. You step through and immediately find yourself, as usual, in the castle courtyard. The door between the realms closes behind you. Once more you cross the courtyard to the main doors of the castle itself and pass through the entryway into the great hall.

There, as before, is the table, the stone and crystal shard from the last workings, together with the elemental gifts, and the seats. But, as in the previous working, you will not be seated.

Look around the hall. There are a number of doors other than the one through which you entered. One you know has the design of a crystal upon it. Another one has upon it a design that looks like an old book. Your first task is to find that door and stand before it. Examine the location and the nature of this door and then open it and step through into the scene beyond.

You find yourself outside the castle with open country around you. Behind you there is no castle to be seen, but it appears that you have just emerged from a tent. Do not, at this stage, wonder at how such geometry may come about. Just accept the position you are in.

You allow the tent flap to close behind you. This flap bears a design just like an old book. There are no other tents in sight. You turn and look around.

——————————— THE PATHWORKING ———————————

You find yourself in open country. It is rocky and barren as far as the eye can see. To the left, the ground rises slightly and gradually, and, as you look in that direction, you see a rider-less horse heading toward you. You wait, and the beautiful horse comes closer and closer until it is standing right in front of you. It tosses its mane once then stands still. It has deep brown eyes, which seem to brim with love and compassion.

Somehow you know that this horse will take you to your destination. You mount the horse easily and it gracefully turns to head back the way it came. The ride is fast, yet smooth and flowing as you and your steed glide up the hill. If this working is being taken as a group, it is at this time that you will become aware of your companions.

You reach the top of the rise and the horse comes to a stop. You see spread below you a fertile valley with a patchwork of fields—green here, yellow there, brown here, flower-filled there. A broad river meanders through the valley and on the other side of that river there is an ancient walled town standing four-square amid the fields and farms. Close to the town there is a single high hill topped by a tower of some sort. A road proceeds from each of the town's four main gates. One of these roads crosses the river over a stone bridge and angles up the hill to pass close to where you are waiting.

As though understanding your wishes, the horse starts forward toward the town below. As you approach, you pass fields where farmers toil, some of whom stop and passively observe your swift passage. Finally, your mount begins to slow as you reach the stone bridge. A ram stands at the side of the road and watches you without interest. You cross and the warm sunlight strikes the river to one side, seeming to turn it briefly into a river of quicksilver.

Ahead of you looms the town gate, but as it is daytime it is open and travelers are free to pass in and out with only a cursory glance from the guards. You ride through the arch of the gate and along the streets of this town. You move at a slow, steady trot now as the road becomes busier. People walking, people on horseback, people standing at the doors of the buildings that crowd along the edge of the narrow street.

Look at the buildings and the townsfolk. What period are you in? What year do you think it might be and what country?

You continue on your way along the street, knowing that you are moving right to the center of this town. Your movement slows its pace to a careful walk, as the streets become even more crowded. Finally, you enter the thronging town square. Here you must dismount and lead your horse. There are gaily colored stalls around the edges of the square offering a wide profusion of wares. They attract merchants and townsfolk alike giving an impression of bees around a honey pot.

In the center of the square there stands a wooden platform. A crowd is gathering around the platform watching a juggler and two tumblers. You move closer to watch, still leading your horse. You see equipment for making up simple stage sets at the side of this platform and realize that sometimes plays are performed here. The juggling and tumbling comes to an end and a robed figure, tall, lean, and ascetic mounts the platform. He addresses the crowd.

"What is knowledge? Knowledge is defined as the knowing of or about something. The only way that knowledge may be gained is through a life of selfless devotion to its pursuit. But not all things that can be known about are equal. Indeed, some things are worth knowing about and some are not. It is quite an ordinary thing to know about the times for planting crops. How much greater it is to know of the words of the famous philosophers of the Golden Age.

"In order to have knowledge, one must first know about what to know about. Otherwise one could spend one's life knowing about worthless and quite ordinary everyday things rather than the higher mysteries of the mind. Only great and unrelenting dedication to the works of the Ancient Ones, together with many hours of meditation, thereon, will bring one to the exalted level of teacher. Only then can one speak or write truly and critically of the works of the ancient philosophers, thereby taking one's place in the unbroken line of philosophical tradition. Only through the lives of such dedicated people can knowledge be passed from generation to generation."

He pauses briefly before continuing.

"Next market day I will speak to you of one of the greatest tools in the gaining of knowledge—logical syllogism. For the moment I remind you that we teachers among men must feed our poor frail bodies if we are to continue our studies."

He passes among the crowd collecting money and skillfully answering questions. The towns-folk seem happy about what was said, yet you feel somewhat dissatisfied. Surely there is more to it than this?

Looking up over the heads of the crowd, you see in the distance the hill with its tower that you noticed from the rise earlier. The sun glints from a small crystal dome at its top. Your horse shuffles expectantly. Perhaps what you seek is there. The horse shuffles again and tosses its mane.

You begin walking away, leading your mount, toward that side of the square which will lead you to the tower on the hill. As you leave the square and enter the streets once more, the press of people begins to diminish. Soon you are able to remount your horse and ride, slowly at first, then ever more rapidly until you pass through the arched gate at the outer wall and onto the open road.

This road leads past the base of the hill, but there is a well-worn track leading upwards and you take this. You ride higher up the hill and, looking off to the side, you see the town and fields spread below. You come closer to the tower. It is of old stone with a carved wooden door at its base. It is quite a large tower. You dismount. Around the outer wall at chest height are a number of iron rings. If your horse has a bridle and reins, you fasten them to one of these. Otherwise the horse will wait patiently for your return. You approach the door.

It opens to your touch revealing a small bare foyer. The door opposite is open and through it you can see a book-lined wall. It is very quiet. You cross the tiled floor of the foyer to the open door. The room is quite large and almost every part of the walls is covered with books, from the polished wooden floor to the ceiling high overhead. In one wall there is a fireplace and on the floor in front of this is a thick rug. To one side are a table and a number of wooden chairs.

Pick a section of the bookshelves and peruse the titles there, but do not as yet touch any of the books.

You pause for a second, hearing a sound behind you. Turning, you see a smiling man standing in the doorway. He speaks to you.

"Welcome to the library. Many books are kept here on many different topics. Look around you and feast your eyes upon this dazzling display of knowledge. And not a fraction of all our books are on show here, for mark you well, that in this library we keep every book that has ever been written. There is no exception to this. Every book we have is translated into every tongue, past and present, known and lost. Doubt not that this is the library of libraries and that all knowledge is held here."

You remember the speaker in the town square. Is knowledge to be truly found in dusty ancient tomes? Or in the bright sunlight of a flower-filled field? The man speaks again, amusement in his eyes, "This library has two types of books—ones which move and ones which stay still. I shall tell you first about the ones that stay still. These are of three kinds.

"First, there are books written by those who have merely read other books but who have neither experienced the subject matter at first hand nor originated anything new themselves. These are 999 of each 1000 books. Copies of these we give away to philosophers and commentators.

"The second group is written by those who write from their own direct experience or who set forth completely new ideas that have never been on the earth before. And 999 out of every 1000 remaining books are of this type whether so-called fiction or non-fiction. We display many of these in this room and care for them for they are an inspiration and a guide to all those who read them.

"The third set are not about anything in particular, but the reading of them produces predictable experiences in the reader—experiences that change the reader irrevocably. And 999 of each remaining 1000 books are of this type and the one thousandth one is so constructed that it presents these experiences precisely, invariably, and in a certain order. All of these we keep in a safe place, for they are the treasures of our species."

The man crosses to one of the shelves where a clay jug and two clay goblets stands. He pours wine, mead, or juice from the jug into the goblets and offers you one of them saying, "Drink."

You take the proffered cup and taste the liquid. It is exactly to your taste. The man continues talking, "And so to the books that move. These we call teachers. There are three types of these too. The first type are those that know about. These may be found everywhere. They are like signposts and they represent 'truth.'

"Then there are books that know. These are usually found at special places. They are like the horse or carriage that takes you on your road and they represent 'life.'

"Finally, there are books that can cause you to know. These are like the road itself and represent 'the way.' They may be found anywhere at all—a king here, a servant there, a farmer, a merchant, an innkeeper, a carpenter. Once in an age there comes a book that is all of these things.

"Now I shall leave you to study one of the books here at your leisure. You may come here at any time to study. If you come with a question pertaining to knowledge, the answer will be found here, either through a book that stays still or one that moves, for others use this place too. For the moment, the third category of book is not available to you, but in a while you will find these for yourself. If you need any assistance, call on me and I shall be there. I am known by many names to many people, but for now I am the librarian. Ask now any question you have about knowledge or about this place."

You ask your question if you have one and listen closely with the inner ear for the reply. Then you thank the librarian.

"When you come to this place again you may be challenged by a doorkeeper," the librarian says. "If that happens you will uses this phrase as your pass: 'Drink ye deep of the wine of knowledge or drink not at all.'"

He leaves. You search the shelves until a book attracts you. You take it over to the table intending to read it. You sit with the book and open it. An old, partially rusted flat piece of metal falls onto the floor. Perhaps it was a kind of bookmark. You pick it up and examine it. Somehow you know that this is the gift the path intended for you. You put the piece of metal in your pocket and begin reading the book.

After a while, you replace the book on the shelf. It is time to go.

You leave the room and cross the foyer once more. Passing through the carved wooden door you are once more outside the tower.

It is getting late in the day. You greet your horse and mount up once again. The horse turns its head to the downhill track and takes you with it on the return journey.

Soon you join the main road again and head back toward the town. Ahead is the gate, but you do not go through this time. There is a track which leads around the outer wall and it is this you take, making your way around the outside edge of the town until you come back once again to the road that crosses the bridge.

Once more you cross the river and head off along the road, back past the quiet evening fields and up the rise. Looking ahead where the road leads, you see a misty shape in the distance. It looks vaguely like a castle, but it seems to be winking rapidly in and out of existence, appearing hazy and ephemeral, like a distant galaxy. But, you turn off the road at the place where you first joined it. Looking back you see, one-by-one, lights appearing in the windows of the farmhouses and the houses in the town. A steady light burns in the tower too.

Your mount takes you over the ridge and the town is lost to view. Rapidly you descend the slope until you come once more to your starting point. You dismount. You look again into the deep round eyes of the horse. Somehow it tells you that it will be there again when you need it. Then it turns and gallops off into the distance and out of sight. You lift the flap of the tent and pass through into the great hall.

Postamble

Make your way to your seat at the table and sit upon it. Take the piece of metal out of your pocket and choose a segment of the table and place it there. Relax and spend a few moments reviewing your experiences. At this time, further thoughts and realizations may come to mind. If you feel that others are present, you might care to tell them of your experiences and listen for their comments.

After a few moments, leave your seat and make your way out into the courtyard again. From here you will return through the small door in the castle wall to your original working place, lock the door, and complete your working exactly as in the last two paths.

When you are once more fully awake from your adventure, write in your journal, update your table diagram, and add the town, the tower, and your path there, to your map of your personal inner realm.

Discussion

There was a great interest in magic from the end of the nineteenth century and into the first half of the twentieth. Many organizations sprang up—some secret and some public—like the Order of the Golden Dawn, the Society of the Inner Light, the Golden Triangle Fellowship, the Fellowship of the Rosy Cross, and many more besides.

All of these organizations offered a graded series of teachings on the nature of the universe and the inner nature of humans. In this they accorded well with the Third Object of the Theosophical Society, founded by Madame Blavatsky and Colonel H. S. Olcott in November 1875, which states:

"To investigate the unexplained laws of nature and the powers latent in man."

Mediation

Giving expression to these ideas, the organizations gathered and collated documents and holy books from as many religions, regions, and time periods that they could. To these sources they added additional information gathered from the inner planes by the use of their own magical methods. These methods usually involved a form of dual consciousness where the operator raised their levels of awareness to make contact with the teacher behind the school, while at the same time staying aware of the physical surroundings.

This was quite a different process to that used by a medium in a Spiritualist circle of the time. In those cases, the personality of the medium was displaced so that other entities could "talk" through them. Dion Fortune makes much of this difference in approach in a monograph originally circulated privately but now published as *Spiritualism in the Light of Occult Science*.

Planes of Existence

From all this material the various schools and orders produced a variety of plans of the structure of the universe and of humans in outer and inner realities. These maps attempted to show how existence could be categorized, stretching from the mundane plane of everyday life to the unknowable, ineffable ground of existence, the true reality if we could experience it directly.

These plans varied, but they could, rather unsurprisingly, be cross-related with each other. Some divided humanity and the universe according to seven levels or planes, some according to four, some according to ten.

In essence it did not matter which system was used. None are actually true. They are constructs to help us better understand how things are and how things work. But, they have a power and that power is the way they enable us to make things happen. In this it can be said that knowledge is power.

Science

The simplest way to see this is to think of science. From a long study of the world, the universe, people, and more, we have a vast body of research material in which the greats of the past have been able to see patterns. Once a pattern is seen, then it can be checked. If it is found to pass the checks on its usefulness and extendibility, then it becomes part of the laws of nature, as we understand them at a given time.

Sometimes we see what we already thought we knew overthrown by increasing incidents of things that do not fit in any more. We refine, discard, or adapt and move on.

But this corpus of knowledge that is based on a particular belief system finds its expression in technology. What we have today would seem magic to those of earlier ages. This knowledge, even given that it is derived from a self-contained value system, enables us to produce results, marvels at times.

We tend to separate religion and science, but within the magical philosophy as taught in the West in those earlier days, religion, science, mysticism, and magic itself were treated as co-existing and differing belief systems, internally consistent to greater or lesser degrees.

Because we use our nervous system to study the universe, we frequently develop theories more about how we perceive and think of things than about the reality itself. The magicians of the Golden Dawn used the Tree of Life of the Qabala of the Hebrews as a map of both the universe and the human inner nature.

It should be no great leap then to consider the map of our internal landscape in general and of these pathworkings in particular as being also a map of realities relating to the universe at large and to ourselves.

Force and Form

In the cosmological principle of the various magics, two important realities emerge again and again. These are Force and Form. They are often seen as opposite sides of the frame upon which the weave of consciousness appears.

In these workings we move around the landscape going up or down to right or to left. We see different things in one place than in another. Similarly, we have different functions in the two halves of the brain. In popular parlance, the left side is the logical and analytical side and the right is the intuitive and artistic side. The reality is very much more complex than this but it is a useful simplification.

In this working, we went predominantly to the left to find the town. Now just what is this town?

Robert Benchley said, "There may be said to be two classes of people in the world; those who constantly divide the people of the world into two classes, and those who do not."[18] In the song cycle of Hugh Lupton and Liz McGowan based upon the ancient track in Norfolk known as Peddars Way, there is a recurrent theme of the original peoples being displaced by the invading peoples. This theme is worked out through the differences between those people who hold land in common as a trust and those who measure up and divide the land.[19]

Measure and Regulation

With the measuring up and dividing of land, there follows the need to register the land. From this follows the need to register people so that ownership can be established. And from this follows all manner of measures increasingly governing and restricting people's lives, movements, and activities. In the case of the history of the United Kingdom, one group is sometimes seen as Celtic and

18. Robert Benchley, "The Most Popular Book of the Month," in *Of All Things* (New York: Henry Holt and Company, 1921), 187.

19. Hugh Lupton and Liz McGowan, *A Norfolk Songline* (Norwich: Hickathrift Press, 2000).

the other as Anglo-Saxon. The previously mentioned song cycle bemoans the loss of the unfettered land and its replacement with stone walls and straight lines. Despite this being often regarded as a romantic simplification in the light of the known history of the region and peoples, the division is still valid and useful as an externalization of our own inner differences.

There is a hermetic axiom that states: "What is above is like unto what is below and what is below is like unto what is above, but after another fashion." This has in much more recent times been paraphrased as, "What is without is like what is within but after another fashion."

We can look at our inner faculties and place logic and analytical thinking on one side and emotional and intuitive thinking modes on the other. These we can see reflected in the "Celtic" style of people and the "Anglo-Saxon" type of people. This theme has run down through the history of the English-speaking peoples, which you can see more easily if you replace "Celtic" with "indigenous."

Now archaeological research on Norfolk has shown that the early stone walls that show today as marks on the land date back to well before the successive waves of Anglo-Saxon-Viking invasions. And evidence exists in Australia of a small number of non-nomadic indigenous groups in the past. But in general terms the Anglo-Saxon people are often seen as the "bad guys" and in parallel with this there are many who see the use of logical and analytical skills are somehow lesser or less desirable than more holistic approaches.

However, all of our skills are valuable skills, pretty much equally so. The trick we need is to know when to apply which one. When the analytical skill is required, it will not be useful to use our emotional powers. And where the emotional side of our nature is more appropriate to a situation, applying logic could be disastrous.

The Town

This pathworking takes us into a town. Towns are usually the assault upon the flowing nature of the land to bring an order, a structure, a stability that was not present before. Within a town comes a whole raft of other laws and regulations. The words *rule, ruler, regal, regulate, regular,* and others come from a common proto-Indo-European language root of *reg-* meaning to "move in a straight line."[20] These tight complexes of meanings are built into the English language. As we speak, so we think. As we think, so we act.

For our purposes then, the town represents the straight-line (ruled), formal (regulated) thought processes of which humans everywhere are capable. Within this we are confronted with one who conveys knowledge through speech. We are also told of those who convey knowledge through written words, those who convey knowledge by examples, and those who convey knowledge through actions.

Three Ways to Convey Knowledge

Let us look at the three ways to convey knowledge one by one.

The speaker in the town square prizes words and logic above the real life activities of clothing and feeding ourselves. In fact, he cannot do this for himself but relies on those who do to provide for him. Yet, he seems to place his own skills above those of his audience.

Those who write about facts, who draw arguments from facts and assumptions, are doing a similar thing as he is but in a written form. And I guess that includes me in what I am writing here.

The second group referred to by the librarian may give you some exercises or present you with a line that is not intended to tell you the fact, but is rather intended to lead you to realize that fact for yourself.

Finally, the third group includes those methods of communication where the message is not the main idea or subject text but is put across almost as a by-product. That is, the teaching to be communicated is not the subject of the writing. The words themselves taken alone convey a story or some tale. But in the reading of that tale, changes take place in the reader or listener and these changes are the object of the teaching intended by the writer.

The bards of old gathered and told tales; epic tales, cautionary tales, humorous tales, dramatic tales, tragic tales. Sometimes these tales had effects on the audience beyond the subject matter of the tale itself. The words of the tale

---

20. Online Etymology Dictionary, "Origin and Meaning of Root *reg-," Online Etymology Dictionary, accessed December 10, 2019, https://www.etymonline.com/word/*reg-.; The American Heritage Dictionary, "The American Heritage Dictionary Indo-European Roots Appendix," The American Heritage Dictionary of the English Language, accessed December, 10, 2019, https://www.ahdictionary.com/word/indoeurop.html#IR091000.

were intended to be the delivery system, so to speak, for the real and unsaid message.

Records

It is said by some that everything that happens is stored or leaves traces. In some occult circles you may come across the idea of the "Akashic Records," records that hold all these traces and which can be "read" by those suitably attuned.

I often suggest to colleagues and students of the Mysteries that these records can be "seen as" a vast library to which one can travel in the imagination and where one may refer to records there or confer with others found there. I have used this analogy in constructing this path because it works.

The Library

The idea of a library as a repository is not new. There was once a vast library of written knowledge at Alexandria, at the time a crossroads for travelers of knowledge and wisdom. The sacking of the city and burning of the books of the library is viewed by many as a dark spot on the history of the human race. Research shows us that about one third of the books were initially lost and many of those were replaced with copies. But the notion of the event as a disaster remains in the collective human psyche.

In more modern times, we can look at the library associated with the British Museum, for example. This library is a source of much reference material used by researchers in many disciplines.

Pathworkings take place in the imagination. The imagination uses the normal everyday senses, but constructs those experiences rather than experiencing them from the senses responding to outside stimuli. In this mode of thinking, which for most people is primarily visual, the brain patterns are usually quite different to those experienced in everyday life, and in particular quite different to those that occur when we think logically about a problem or some other issue.

Logic and Aries

This path intends for us to deal with the parts of our nature connected with logical thought, facts, categorizing, and analysis. It can be quite a difficult path at times, requiring as it does the pathworker to deal with conflicting brain patterns. When it comes to the crunch and we find ourselves in the library with a book that can tell us something, we frequently experience that knowledge in visions and symbols rather than words. This is because in a pathworking we are working with the brain in a different way compared to when we read or otherwise deal with words in our current plane.

Although the librarian presents these brain patterns as three paths, each one apparently better than the others, this is not strictly the case. The three ways are referred to by the librarian as "The Truth," "The Life," and "The Way."

When the signs of the zodiac are placed upon the human body, the sign of Aries is said to rule the top of the head. The top surface of the brain is referred to as the cortex and figures greatly in the way that we think logically. The connections of the cortex are just like the lines of logic followed in an example of careful reasoning.

Magical Diagrams and Paths

Magicians use a diagram that gives them a map of all of existence on all the various "planes." Many use the Qabalistic Tree of Life diagram for this purpose. In this diagram, we imagine ourselves at the base of the Tree in the sphere of physical reality as it appears to us, known as Malkuth. From that point we may ascend the Tree to more and more spiritual realms. There are three paths that lead out from Malkuth heading upwards. One of these on the left, and corresponding with the left side of our brains, leads to Hod. This sphere is concerned with the concrete mind and the logical and analytical modes of thinking. In this sphere the virtue is "Truth." It is the sphere of form.

On the right, a path leads up to the sphere of Netzach, concerned very much with the forces of nature. This direction takes us the way of "Life." It is the force aspect that counterbalances the form aspect of Hod.

The central path takes us first to Yesod, which has much to do with the other side of consciousness. The power it grants us is the "Vision" of the machinery of the universe. This is nothing more or less than the seeing of how everything works—how what is within becomes what is without, how the inner becomes the outer. To see this just once is to know the Way, which is the English translation of the Chinese word *tao*. It represents an acceptance of how things are and our own individual responsibility for how things are. Armed only with these we can tread the Way.

Each of these paths is but one of three ways to proceed and no one path is greater or lesser than the others; none is more right than the others. Some may prefer one way and practice their art as a ceremonial magician. Some may prefer to advance their spiritual understanding by Pagan rites under the power of the Full Moon. Yet others may take a mystical approach. Those who use the Tree of Life know that after Netzach, Hod, and Yesod, all three paths join up in Tiphereth, the sphere of consciousness in the evolving self, the self behind the mere incarnated personality. And of course, the Qabalistic Tree of Life is just one map among many covering the same realities.

———

Traveling to this library is like requesting the universe to supply you with a piece of information you require. Call there anytime to gain what facts and knowledge you may need. Of course, the way the information comes to you in everyday life might be quite ordinary. Or it could, at times, be spectacularly magical. The purpose of the working is to gain knowledge. Use it whenever you have need.

Path 4: The Sacred Grove

-+-

We have looked at the logic side of things; now in this working we travel to a natural location. Things developing by nature are developing in the opposite way to developments by the application of logical steps. Here we will locate in our landscape the less tame nature that represents this. Its intended purpose is to stimulate the balancing, non-measurable forces within you. If the previous path was thinking, this one is feeling. The experiences, therefore, take place in a natural setting. We find and face the reality of growth to an inner pattern, not to an outer regulation. In symbol we find nature within ourselves. As with the town and library, you will not return to this place as a step to others. These two you establish to visit when you have the need. Make careful note of the steps you take to get to this place and state.

Preamble

Relax and breathe rhythmically in your work place exactly as in the previous workings. The scene of your work area arises before your eyes. Once more there is one extra door just as before. As before, you rise up in your mind's eye, approach the door, and open it.

There is a swirling mist beyond the door. You step through and immediately find yourself, as usual, in the castle courtyard. The door between the realms closes behind you.

Make your way to the great hall and look around. There is the round table with its circle of seats. On the table are the things that you have already found from the various paths you have already trodden.

There are a number of doors other than the one through which you entered. Sometimes you may see these previous doors and sometimes not. One door you are now familiar with has the design of a crystal upon it. Another door you know has the design of an old book.

There is yet another one, which has upon it a design representing a large old tree. Your first task is to find that door and stand before it.

Examine the location and the nature of this door, then open it and step through into the scene beyond.

──────────────── THE PATHWORKING ────────────────

You find yourself surrounded by a dense gray mist. You see nothing at all except the mist around you. Behind you is the door by which you entered this realm, seemingly set into the trunk of a very large tree.

After a while, the mist begins to thin. Beyond the mist is darkness. The last wisps of grayness disappear to reveal the blackness of interstellar space all around you. You are not floating free, nor falling. You look down at your feet and see that you are standing upon a large circle of good, brown earth. All that exists right now is you standing upon a circle of earth in front of a large old tree in the cold infinite blackness of space.

Gradually the darkness begins to change, somehow forming patterns and shapes around you. The colors green and brown seem to separate out from the blackness. Slowly the scene you are in changes until you find yourself in a vast primeval forest of a kind not seen on earth since the dawn of time, since the earth was as young as mankind now is. The colors are rich and lush. There is a warm feeling to the atmosphere. The desire to join its lush naturalness surges within you. You feel the urge to remove all of your clothing and experience the freedom you feel in this most natural of settings. Do so if you wish.

You look around at the great trees, the ferns growing beneath them and the finer, small plants that form a carpet for all that live here. You see a path leading from your little glade and into the forest itself. This path goes off into the undergrowth, curving to the right as it does so. Follow the path, feeling the moist earth on your feet, the softness of the fine springy patches of fronds. A sense of lush rainforest, warm and moist, comes to you. The leaves of the trees form a canopy overhead and the sunlight, filtered green through this overhead canopy, makes speckled patterns on the tree trunks, on the path ahead, and on your own self.

Keep following the path.

After a while, the path opens out into a clearer area. Here there is only undergrowth as the trees you see have been cleared away long ago. On entering this cleared area, you see on your left the ruins of an ancient temple, its stone blocks standing in tumbled disarray. The bright sun beating on the vegetation-covered walls shows white where it strikes the stone beneath. It casts a golden beam into the dark shadows of the interior and this beam strikes something metallic and golden within. At first you cannot make out the shape but then you see that it is a huge bronze casting of an aurochs, the ancestor of modern cattle. The bronze detail now clearly shows the shaggy coat and the great curving horns.

How long ago was it that this temple was used for worship? What rites were celebrated here and to what ancient deities now long forgotten—or transformed by time and mind into forms more suitable for a changed culture? Does it all come to nothing in the end? Or is there some enduring theme that gives meaning to the great devotion of earlier worshipers?

Your path continues on into the forest at the other side of this clearing. You move on from this area into the coolness of the forest once more.

As you walk along this path you catch sight, out of the corners of your eyes, of small shapes moving among the trees on each side of the path. Part human, part animal, these joyous shapes dance on either side and the faint sound of tinkling bells and bamboo pipes comes to your ears.

You will, however, stay upon the path and ignore the creatures on each side, delightful though they may seem. For once you have stepped off the path into the undergrowth that surrounds it you will have lost your direction and you will then find yourself treading in many mysterious and perilous ways. For all those who enter this forest without direction emerge changed beyond recovery, and that which you seek here and which draws you this way, is only to be found in a *certain part* of this forest …

The path continues on curving to the right. After a short time you enter a glade that has a large rounded rock in the center, jutting from the very depths of the earth itself. You have reached your destination. Pause here for a while. Look around and take in your surroundings …

At the opposite side of the area there is a slight sound. Looking up you see two naked figures emerge from the forest, one a radiant woman carrying a crystal chalice of pure water, the other a tall shaggy-haired man with a bushy beard, even bushier eyebrows and carrying a flint spear. The two come toward you, their smiles radiating power and love.

They stop near to the central rock and beckon you to approach. You do so and as you draw close to them the woman steps slightly forward offering you the chalice of water. She speaks: "The chalice I bear contains the waters of Eternal Life. Remember that woman is the bearer of life to this planet and that the giver of life is also the giver of death, for in earthly existence the one gift cannot be given without the other.

"But those who come to know the life within need never fear death for the inner life is the true life, the unperishing life, the life of all time. Take then this chalice and drink deeply of its waters. Let the knowledge of the inner life flow deep inside you and course along your veins to take up residence within your heart."

Accept the chalice and take a drink from it. The water is cool yet vibrant with contained energy. Its power enters the very depths of your being, and from there radiates its living force around your whole body, flowing right to the very ends of your toes and fingers. When you have tasted this water, pour a small amount from the chalice onto the rock. It splashes on the rock and runs down in a rivulet to moisten the rich earth below. The woman accepts the chalice back from you and steps back a little.

Now it is the man's turn to come forward and he does so brandishing his spear. His eyes are wild and piercing. He beckons you to grasp the spear that is in his hand. You take the spear from him. It is vibrating with power, tingling in your hand. It is like it's alive. You see that drops of blood are appearing on the tip of the spear. The man speaks: "The spear you hold is the shaft of light of the heavens. Know that man is the sower of seed for this planet and that the scattered seeds rest in darkness like the stars of the Milky Way.

"The seeds of light are the inspirations of the high heavens and those who hold them and nurture them within their own breast take up the mystic quest whose prize is the heart. Strike then this spear into the rock as you wish the light from on high to strike into you, for in this light will be found your inner sight."

You walk closer to the rock with the vibrant spear, turning it point down. Three droplets of blood spill from its tip onto the stone as you raise it high.

Then you bring it down onto the stone, which it pierces easily, sinking deep within it.

You turn back to the couple again and they move gracefully apart revealing the forest behind them. From this patch of forest that you now can see comes a beautiful and radiant child carrying something on a serving tray. You cannot see what is on the tray for all is hidden by a cloth. The child is smiling and approaches you without any sign of shyness or embarrassment. A small hand removes the covering cloth and you are presented with a small acorn cup. This is your own special gift.

The child returns to stand between the two adults. The woman then steps forward toward you drawing you into her arms and embracing you. She says, "You are a child of earth. Return now and let there be nothing but peace and love between us."

She steps back and the man steps forward. He too draws you toward him and embraces you saying, "You are indeed a child of earth, but your race is of the starry heavens. Upon you now be the blessing of the mother, the father, and the child who is the fruit of both"

He steps back and the young child too comes forward, waiting to be embraced by you. Bend down and give a loving embrace, receiving the same in return.

The man, the woman, and the child turn and go back once more into the forest. Yet somehow their presence remains. Pause and contemplate for a moment all that you have experienced here ...

Turn around and follow the path back. It is starting to get dark quite rapidly. After a while, you come to the first glade again. It has grown very dark and it is the bright light of the moon that now makes fantastic geometrical shapes of light and dark against the tumbled masonry.

Pass by this temple of an earlier cult, knowing that each and every teaching is founded upon that which went before and that every extension of understanding depends upon the modification of what is already known. The process is organic.

You continue along the path, finally coming back to the bare circle of earth that was your starting point. Any clothes you left here you will find again and can put them on if you wish.

Even though you are now at your starting point, you notice that the path you had been following continues on. You walk off along the path once more and as you do the trees change in character. No longer the lush vegetation and giant trees of an ancient forest. There is now grass underfoot.

You soon find yourself in a park-like wood. The trees are well spaced and the grass is even and short. Shrubs and bushes are there but they stand separately rather than crowded together. As you continue on you see that the wood is coming to an end.

You emerge from the wood into pastureland, the cattle silent now in the moonlight. And there, standing ghostly in that moonlight, is your castle. You realize that the wood you have just left is also the wood by which you made your way to the crystal cave.

You continue on toward the castle. From here it is but a short way to a door in the castle wall bearing the tree design and by which you entered this working.

Postamble

Pass through this door, closing it behind you. You are back in the great hall.

Make your way to the table and place your acorn cup upon one of the free segments. Then, go to your own seat and sit upon it. Relax and spend a few moments reviewing your experiences. At this time further thoughts and realizations may come to mind. You may also see some other beings sitting at the table.

After a few moments, leave your seat and make your way out into the courtyard again. From here you will return through the small door in the castle wall to your original working place and complete your working exactly as in the last three paths.

Discussion

This is the last path of the first series called "Realms Within." Each of the four paths has dealt with a different aspect of consciousness, as we generally know it.

The first path created a basis, a foothold, in the inner realms. Thus, it formed an analogy for ordinary, everyday consciousness. The second path dealt with the workings of our consciousness that are normally below awareness. This is a form of thinking and feeling that goes on all the same whether we know of it or not.

The third path in the series dealt with the logical mind, the realm of thought and words, philosophy and knowledge.

This last path, the sacred grove, deals with what is sometimes referred to as our more emotional, or feeling, nature. This is just as much a method of thinking as is the more commonly recognized straight-line logical approach. The skills associated with this mode of thinking relate to wholeness and patterns, to seeing with the peripheral vision, rather than the central vision.

The logical and emotional forms of mentation, each having their own version of "intelligence," have often been likened to the different functions of the left and right hemispheres of the brain, and there is some fruitful learning that can come out of this analogy.

Sometimes these two methods of mentation are referred to as "male" and "female." Again, there is much that can be learned from looking at this suggestion, and, again it is far from the full story.

In fact, on this latter matter, it is now known that the hard wiring of the brain at a certain critical point in fetal development will depend on the amount of testosterone in the womb of the mother at that time. The developing fetus will build a brain with a combination of neural elements and balances that sits somewhere on a continuum of possibilities between a purely "male" brain and a purely "female" brain, regardless of the physical sex of the developing child. It just so happens that statistically males more often have a middling to high "testosterone" template and females more often a middling to high "non-testosterone" template. But crossovers occur. [21]

The Forest

It is useful to mention this point here because this pathworking has a number of sexual overtones. It does, in fact, approach the holistic mode of mentation from a setting of primordial nature. It does show the Lord and the Lady, the Horned God, and the Mother of All, as a dual-natured male-female divinity. The Child of Promise is shown as the fruit of their sexual union.

It is not so much that we are regarding the holistic type of mentation as more primitive. The logical mentation pathworking dealt, after all, with a

---

21. C. E. Roselli, "Neurobiology of Gender Identity and Sexual Orientation," *Journal of Neuroendocrinology* 30, no.7 (December 6, 2017), https://doi.org/10.1111/jne.12562.

town and the constructions of human beings. The purpose of the imagery of a primordial forest is to imply that which underlies all things.

Our present can only be truly understood in terms of our past. What we have is built on what has gone before. If we wish to see patterns and whole forms we have to look at the background against which the logical categories are made. For only in that way will we appreciate what the category making and classifying skills of the logical mind leave out. Only if we see what is included *and* what is not do we have any chance of appreciating the whole.

And so behind all that we may know or experience or make stands the primordial past. In our first moves away from that we begin to "leave things out." To get the whole picture, we need to return to that point. And "getting the whole picture" is what this mode of thinking is all about.

In keeping with the primordial theme, this is a path that can be taken naked. This puts you in touch with your own "original nature," unadorned by other overlays. We have a certain form. When we cover it, we are determining that those who see us will "leave things out" in the pattern they make of us. Of course, different people wear their clothes with different levels of comfort or naturalness, so this is left as a purely optional step in the working.

Finally, it should be said that the holistic mode of mentation is not contrary in any way to the logical mode, the everyday mode, or the modes that operate below awareness. All modes have their part to play in the totality of our existence, and each is equally important for the particular jobs at which it works best.

Why Taurus?

This path is related to Taurus in our continuing journey through the New Moons of the zodiacal year. Taurus is ruled by Venus and is also an Earth sign. It appears here as symbolizing the rich, sensuous Venus of a vibrant and verdant Earth.

It is said that we pass through great ages that correspond with the signs of the zodiac and the roughly two-thousand-year precession of the equinoxes. Much has been written about the end of the age of Pisces and the beginning of the age of Aquarius. When this age of Aquarius actually began, if it already has, is the subject of a lot of discussion.

Some place the beginning of the "new age" at the time of publication of Aleister Crowley's *The Book of the Law*, which heralded the beginning of the age of Horus. Some placed it at the time of publication of Robert Heinlein's *Stranger in a Strange Land*, seeing in that book's philosophy the basis for a new religion. Indeed, there was in fact a small planetary line-up at around that time.

There have been other line-ups and sets of measurements and calculations involving our galaxy's position in relation to the "Central Sun" giving dates ranging as far ahead as 2025 and as far as I know, probably beyond.

Suffice it to say that back in the 1970s some whose words I heard and read saw evidence of changes in religious patterns and philosophies every two-thousand years—more or less. Whether there is anything in this, I will leave to your own researches.

According to these ideas, in the supposed just-ending Age of Pisces, we had a religion that used the sign of a fish, involved fishermen as early disciples, and which featured a pivotal miracle involving fish and bread used to feed a multitude. The use and symbolism of the fish—ichthus—for that religion is based on the Greek word *ichthys*, meaning fish. This word is also made from the first letter of the words of a sentence in Greek that translates as "Jesus Christ, Son of God."

Following this once popular idea, prior to the age of Pisces there would have been then the age of Aries. The ages are reckoned to go the reverse direction through the zodiac because that is the direction taken in the precession of the equinoxes. During the age of Aries, the proponents of this theory expected to see a religion in force that was dominated by the symbols of Aries, such as a ram. There are many of my acquaintance that put forward good arguments for choosing Judaism as the candidate religion for the age of Aries.

This discussion brings us to the age of Taurus. According to this same theory, the best candidate for this age was taken as the religion of Mithras, the bull-god. However, known history timelines and closer analysis of roots of mythology just does not support this neat view.

In our pathworking sequence, we arrive at Taurus because it is the next sign in sequence. Taurus is an Earth sign and I have used the bull image because, for me, cattle are very much of the earth, in addition to being the symbol associated with the corresponding sign.

The Creatures

Along the pathway you were aware of other strange creatures. These beings are seen in different ways by different people in different cultures and in different ages of humanity. But throughout all this the reality remains that there are other orders of existence with which we share our lives and realities. Sometimes these can be seen with the physical eyes, but usually it is more often an *impression* at the physical level. When we open our inner sight we are often able to see creatures of a different type.

I am referring to several different types of creature. There are elementals of course. Each of the four elements has its own order of being, and, unlike us, it is made up solely of the nature of their own element, unmixed with any other quality. These are the gnomes of earth, the undines of water, the sylphs of air, and the salamanders of fire.

When we work magic, we come closer into touch with these entities. It seems they like to associate with those who are taking steps to develop themselves along the path of evolution in a deliberate rather than haphazard way. They will certainly assist those who perform regular magical rituals and such a bond can grow between humans and these beings that they will assist in everyday life as well. They seem happy to lend their qualities to your needs from time to time, whether you are trying to light a fire or trying to find lost objects. Indeed, there are many tales of objects lost far away in time or distance miraculously reappearing. This is often through the aid of these beings.

Other orders of being also exist. There are, for example, beings of light. These beings are often referred to as angels when we become aware of them and the lights around their bodies frequently give the suggestion of wings. Some call these beings "devas" and you may come across this term in your reading.

They seem to be able to act as some sort of intermediary between human existence and the divine. Whether mediating information and teachings or powers of healing and assistance, they seem ever-ready to dispassionately work with sensitive people of the human order of existence. Some regard these beings as akin to the elves of some tales. This is complex, as the term elf has at different times been associated with elementals and nature spirits, as well as devas.

This brings us to nature spirits. This order of existence includes all the beings that assist in the natural world of plants and animals. There are tree spirits and water spirits, spirits of place, spirits of animals, spirits of mountains, and spirits of the "vast deep."

When you work your magic in the open, in the wild, in the bush, in a natural setting, you will work with the spirits of that place. If you wish your magic to be effective, you will have to enter into a proper relationship with the spirits of the place where you work.

A proper relationship begins with acknowledging their presence. You will ask their permission, certainly in the early stages and certainly over any changes you might want to make to the environment, such as moving stones and rocks to make up a circle. You will invite them into the feasting parts of your ceremonies and provide them with food and drink from the feast. And after a time, some will establish themselves as your special helpers. They will sort out their own hierarchy and tasks so that all runs smoothly for you.

They have, for example, the power to hide your work place from the eyes of others. I have seen this in operation on more than one occasion and quite amusing it can be too. These creatures are very important to you and both they and humans benefit immensely from working together.

You do not have to be psychic in vision to do this. Once you start acknowledging the presence of the spirits of a place, you will soon come to know them. However, in some places, they are wary from past experience with humans and it takes awhile for mutual trust to build.

The creatures that you see in this working are intended to represent these spirits of place, plant, and animal. The Greeks saw them as fawns, satyrs, naiads, and many others. The music they make may be the little breezes around pieces of wood. Or it may be the crackle of living things expanding in the heat of the sun. It may be the tinkling of a small creek or brook. When you see a section of woodland suddenly spring into brighter color for no apparent reason, it means they smile at you.

The Clearing

The clearing is the central point of the action for this working. In the center is a rock emerging from the earth. This continues the theme of the primordial. The rock is more ancient than the soil and dirt that surround it. It is an earlier part of the formation of the planet. The fact that it protrudes from the earth is reminiscent of the birth process, the point when a child "crowns."

The birth process is appropriate to this path because this path represents the holistic mode of mentation and this is the only mode of mentation in which we can fully understand the human reproductive cycle. Logic and measurement just does not cut it here.

The Lord and Lady

Into the clearing come our divinities. That which we take for divinity is both our past, in the sense of the background of all our existence, and our future, in the sense that what we are now they once were, and what they are now, we will become. And so the cycle becomes complete as we return to our original nature and know it for the first time.

There are many ways in which humans have represented divinity. Sometimes predominantly god-oriented, sometimes goddess-oriented, sometimes as a pantheon of beings, each embodying specific powers, sometimes as a single being with many names, as in the Judaic Qabalah where one god has titles that vary among male, female, plural and singular forms.

I have put in this working my own personal preference. Whatever divinity might be, it certainly will partake of both male and female aspects. Probably more besides, but that "more" might be beyond human comprehension at this time. I like to see divinity as sometimes a god and sometimes a goddess. And sometimes my god is god of Earth and sometimes god of sky. Other times my goddess is of the Earth and sometimes of the stars.

But through all things, I see the Lady as an ever-present reality that has the three forms of Maiden, Mother, and Crone—separate and yet all at the same time.

I use these terms because those are the terms used in associated literature in mythology, in Witchcraft, in archetypal psychology, and more. They are terms for principles, not a proposed way of seeing real-world people. When writing in established fields, I try to use the terms already in use. I could separate the two poles of operation as action/support, foreground/background. And I could refer to the three ways of operation of these as beginner, expert, mentor, for both roles.

But, I wish to retain a nexus with other writings in the field, therefore I use Maiden, Mother, Crone, knowing that they are principles and not always linked hard and fast with genders and fixed modes of operation in the real world. In reality, we are all one or other at various times and in various degrees. Real life is far richer.

In the tales, the Lord mates with the Lady, becomes great and dies or is defeated or is sacrificed. Principles, not real-world genders. This sacrificed entity then returns to us as the Child of the opposite pole entity. But, in some cycles the hero is represented female and this hero also follows much the same hero pattern. It is a hero pattern, not a gender pattern.

It is that I describe these aspects of the One Divine Being as Lord, Lady, and Child, names for principles and degrees of operation. Different religions vary in the ways these basic principles appear, or not.

Their Messages

At the culmination of the working, the Lady and Lord each has something to say to us. The way the information is presented calls forth two fundamental principles—that of the sexuality between male and female polarities, and that of our unclaimed heritage.[22]

The important point is that there exists the reality of incarnation of our spiritual nature into matter and decisions we make to operate in that incarnation as some extent of sexual being: one pole, the other, neither, fluid. In this way we can function in polarity with others who have made their particular choice of manifestation. This working highlights these themes of polarity in the speeches of the Lord and Lady.

We are told of the tasks of the two sexes, taken in the abstract. This assists us in awakening deep powers relating to our sexual polarity, which is not necessarily the same as the sex of our physical body.

We are also reminded of the words taken from the Orphic tablets: "I am the son of Earth and starry heaven. But my race is heavenly."[23] This is intended to activate the knowledge that we have taken on self-imposed exile in matter.

---

22. References to gendered polarities do not necessarily refer only to a male person or to a female person. Any apparent value judgment relating to personal sexual preferences is unintended and accidental. The principles concerned are unrelated to the physical sexes of birth or choice. Your streaming subscription has a provider and a subscriber. It is in reality no more than that.

23. Roy Kotansky, trans., *Lamella Orphica*, mid-fourth century BCE, gold, 2.2 x 3.7 x 0.1 cm (7/8 x 1 7/16 x 1/16 in), The J. Paul Getty Museum, Los Angeles, http://www.getty.edu/art /collection/objects/7194/unknown-maker-lamella-orphica-greek-mid-fourth-century-bc/.

It is the choice we made to further evolution as a whole and we need to accept that it is a wholehearted choice.

Yet, we also know that it is a choice not in realities, but only in the manner in which we perceive things, in which we choose to perceive things. The exile is at once real and an illusion. We never left our primordial natural state. But we are "seeing reality" as the way that we see it. And thereby lies the secret of the self-imposed exile.

In some occult doctrines, "the fall" of Judaeo-Christian teachings is another view of this voluntary illusory exile into matter. Indeed, some commentators have pointed out that the sense of exile from homeland that is so strong in the Hebrew view is an outer reflection of the inner reality of the self-imposed exile of the Shekinah, or flame, from the fire that is god.

————

Whatever choices we have made upon our way in how we wish to present ourselves and interact with others, this working will activate those senses within and bring us to realizations in our everyday lives that are pertinent to the mystical concepts behind the scenes.

Journeys to Realms Between

In this second series of workings you will be using your anchor point of the crystal cave to move into another level of the inner realms. This new level contains adventures that work more subtly upon the psyche. They deal with broader issues and need to come through in a staged way, via a point of contact that has already been established. This makes them more effective than if they were worked directly.

The workings in this series are:

- "The Healing Temple," where you will contact the still center within from which flows all health and healing.
- "The Path of Adjustment," in which you will invite the inner world to show you how you deviate from your true path.
- "The Search for the School," where you will set in motion forces to lead you to make contact with the inner tradition that matches your own Way.
- "The World Between Worlds," where you will come to know the mysteries of inter-dimensional contact that is the key to creation and creativity.

Tread then these paths to follow deeper into the inner landscape, which is none other than your inner nature.

Path 5: The Healing Temple

--- ✛ ---

In this series, we move up a level and this is the first pathworking of the group. We have laid a four-fold foundation for what is to come. For this series, our starting point will be the crystal cave from path 2 in the Journeys to Realms Within series. We will be moving from the castle to the cave. You may need to refer to the notes you took back at that time because the way to the cave will not be repeated here. The idea is to now work from an established point that is already one level farther in than our castle starting point.

Just as you had the sense of leaving your physical body sitting in the chair while you went on your adventures, so you will now move in one level again, leaving a sleeping self in the cave as you explore these paths.

The first of these paths is the healing temple. Healing at this state, two levels in, is related to wholeness. I believe the words are related in derivation, whole and heal.

Here you begin with a trip to the crystal cave. However, the trip will be shorter this time. You know the way. Once in the cave, your finer self will move on to have a healing session. The intention of the working is to stimulate deep healing through an appreciation of balance, and to set in play conditions that will continue to heal at a deep level.

At the end of the working, you will not head straight back to the cave, but spend a little time in a garden. Relax there. Enjoy the place. Let the healing energy settle into your being. Your trip back will be a door in the wall of that garden into the crystal cave. You will bring back all that healing energy.

Preamble

Relax and breathe rhythmically in your work place just as you have in the previous workings.

119

Again, the scene of your work area arises before your eyes. Once more there is one extra door just as before. Rise up in your mind's eye, approach the door, and open it.

There is a swirling mist beyond the door. You step through and immediately find yourself, as usual, in the castle courtyard. The door between the realms closes behind you.

Make your way to the great hall and look around. There is the round table with its circle of seats. On the table are the things that you have already found from the various paths you have already trodden.

There are a number of doors other than the one through which you entered. You can clearly see these doors and there is one that you know has the design of a crystal upon it. Another you know has the design of an old book And another has upon it a design representing a large old tree. Locate the door with the crystal upon it and stand in front of it. You reach out, open this door and it opens into the crystal cave itself.

Take up your position in front of the crystal. As you gaze at it, the design for this working—a single serpent twined around a short staff—begins to appear upon it.

You keep gazing at the image until it takes on a three-dimensional quality. At this point it is a doorway through which you may step. However, it is only a finer essence of yourself that steps through, leaving the denser portions of your inner nature in a contemplative sleep within the cave.

─────────────── THE PATHWORKING ───────────────

It is a balmy Mediterranean evening and ahead of you a stone path winds through the trees of a cultivated garden. Some distance off to the left you hear the sound of waves beating upon a shore and the occasional sharp cry of a gull.

Looking behind, you see a crystal door set in a stone wall. Upon this door is the snake and staff design that you used as your key to enter this working. This is the door by which you will return to normal consciousness via the cave again.

You begin to follow the path. The scents of many flowers and trees come to you. Although night is falling, it is still pleasantly warm and there is yet enough light for you to find your way.

The path curves a little to the right and there are three stone steps where the way rises up to a higher level. You realize now that you have been walking gradually upwards.

Between the trees ahead, and to the left of the path, you see a building. It is made of stone and two-storied. Following the path, you come closer to it.

As you come level with the building, there steps from it a figure robed and hooded in soft gray. You notice that the astrological sign for Gemini is boldly embroidered in yellow-gold on the left breast of the robe. You see a warm smiling face and you hear friendly words: "Welcome, my friend, to the healing temple. Here all ailments can be helped and eased, for the center of all healing power and knowledge is here. Mind, soul, and body—all may here receive that which they need for wholeness-in-harmony. This path leads to the theater of operations. But it is not yet time for you to go there, for preparations must first be made. Come with me."

You walk with your guide and approach the great doorway of the building and again notice the sign for Gemini, carved on the lintel. You are led into the stone building and straight into a large tiled foyer that extends up to the roof like an inner courtyard. Numerous oil lamps set on shelves around the walls provide a soft, warm light. Arches and corridors lead off in all directions on this floor. Above, a balcony surrounds the foyer and, you presume, there are arches and corridors up there too.

Two people, attendants dressed in white tunics with gold edging, approach you. You turn to your guide who smiles and explains, "Go now with these two and prepare yourself. I shall await you here and then conduct you to the theater of operations."

You take your leave and follow the attendants along one of the corridors. Your way leads past many arches that give entry to different rooms. Some of these are empty. In some there is a glimpse of some healthful activity. Here...pause for a moment, for in this room there are a number of people performing a slow graceful series of movements, more like a dance than an exercise...

You continue and pass rooms set up for massage, rooms full of nutrition charts, rooms with shelves full of dried herbs and flowers.

Eventually your companions stop and indicate an archway. You enter and delicate, warm perfumed air caresses you. The room is large and the floor tiled. In the center is a large sunken bath, full now with hot, sweet-smelling water. Your attendants walk past you and move to the edge of the bath where they stop and beckon to you.

That bath looks so soothing and inviting. Come, set aside your clothes and give yourself up to that relaxing bath.

Your companions take your clothes as you divest yourself of them. You notice there are steps into the bath and these you take to enter the beautiful waters. Ah … so welcoming! The warm perfumed water caresses your body. As you relax you realize how tense you had been—a tension that had gone unnoticed.

Relax …

Relax …

Relax …

There is a touch upon your shoulder and there are your attendants—one carrying a large, soft, thick towel, the other holding a soft white robe. You have no idea how long you have been here. Yet the water is still comfortably warm.

You emerge from the bath and take the offered towel to dry yourself. Then you take the offered robe and dress yourself. The robe is warm and soft upon your skin. Here, too, are sandals of strong, yet soft leather for your feet. Try them—it is like stepping on air.

Now your friends lead you out of the bathroom and into the corridor again. You are retracing your steps to the foyer, passing all those other arches once more.

Here is the foyer. And here too is your first guide, ready to greet you with outstretched hands that hold a silver chalice. As you come closer, the cup is offered to you and your guide says, "Here, drink this. It will warm and relax your inner tensions as the bath did those of your body. It will help store and retain the healing powers that you will soon experience and it will make you more open to them."

You drink the golden liquid in the cup. It is strong, nectar-like, and warms you thoroughly inside, sending its fiery energy to the very ends of your limbs. Your senses become alert, your body alive. Colors look brighter, edges sharper and you feel a strong bond with your guide. A smile is returned and words of encouragement: "Come—it is time."

Your guide turns and moves toward the door, there taking up a lantern giving off a soft yellow light. With only a slight pause to look in your direction, your guide continues through the door to the outside. You follow.

It is now night outside. Your guide leads on along the path, the lantern casting a glowing circle to light your way. The moon is no longer in the sky and each side of the path is hidden in darkness.

The way curves to the right, climbing lightly. After a short time of walking in silence you come to three steps, which take the path up to a higher level. Ahead you can see many lights through the trees. You are approaching an open area. Closer and closer you come to this area in the wake of your guide.

All at once you find yourself in a large open space, brightly lit with the soft glow of hundreds of oil lamps. Ahead there is a stone block flanked by a man and a woman in priestly robes.

The block is about the height of the abdomen and the length and breadth of a mature adult. To the right is a huge semicircle of stone seats, row after row rising steeply one behind the other. Almost every available space is taken by white-robed figures so that very little of the silent gray stone shows.

Now, you see that the stone ahead is at the center of this semicircle and that paths and step-ways leading up into the seating area radiate out from the open space around the stone block.

What is this? Are you to be ritually sacrificed here in front of all these people? Is your life's blood to flow out over that stone and ebb away taking your consciousness with it? Have you been led here by the guile of your guide, your sense dulled and drugged? You turn to the one who brought you here. Again a warm smile of love and reassuring words: "This is the theater of operations. Each one here is a healer and the two you go to meet are master and mistress of all healing, from the twinned Priesthood of Atlantis. See, both wear the serpent staff emblem on their robes. This is a special place, made so that every ray of healing force mediated by those on the seats strikes exactly upon that stone. There the healer priest and priestess will direct the energies about you as you lie upon the stone.

"Fear not. This is no altar of sacrifice, though sacrifice is always needed to transmute force between the planes. Here we work with the healing power of divinity released by the ongoing sacrifice of spirit itself bound to the Cross of Matter. Come, step forward, and receive that which always awaits you."

You move to take your place. The priest and priestess help you onto the stone, which is surprisingly warm. You lie on your back. Feel the hard, yet somehow living stone beneath you. There is a power within this stone, stored here through many healing sessions such as this one.

The priest stands at your head and the priestess at your feet. Imperceptibly at first, but growing moment by moment, you feel a pressure, a definite pressure, coming down upon you from the gathered healers. With it comes the sound of a low note—sounded by all those present. The force plays about your head like a swirling sphere. The note rises in pitch and with it the pressure increases. Now the force concentrates in your throat. Feel its touch, delicate despite its great power.

Again the note rises in both pitch and volume. And again the power of the force at your throat increases. It plays in a radiant swirling ball. You feel incredibly warm and relaxed. This power has a loving quality. Surely all these here care very deeply for you to be doing this. Yet it is no more love than one person should have for another and no less than the love that exists between the gods and ourselves.

Once more the pitch and volume of the chant increases. You are surrounded by a sea of rich sound. It permeates you so that you no longer feel any boundaries between yourself and the universe around you. The pressure too increases and now plays in a sphere about your solar plexus. Fantastic colors swirl before your eyes making rich, ever-changing shapes.

The intensity increases. The force plays in a sphere about your genitals. All your senses are swamped with the healing life force.

Yet again the intensity increases. The force plays in a sphere about your feet. And still all your senses are swamped with the healing life force. Now you know it to be the One Force that permeates all and in which we live and move and have our being. This great force is gathered and concentrated at the center of the sphere at your feet. You feel its awesome and controlled energy swirling there, waiting.

The chant of voices changes now, dropping in pitch and volume with the grace of a swooping hawk. Then it slowly begins to rise again. As it rises, so does the One Force. It rises up your body in a living column, slowly, keeping pace with the voices. It reaches your knees and pauses there a moment. The voices increase their chant. Once more the energy rises and pauses at your abdomen. Again, the chant increases. Again the One Force rises and pauses now at your heart. The chant continues to increase and the One Force rises to pause now between your eyes. Your whole being is vibrating in harmony with the One Force, one with all of the universe, and one with your own self.

Again, the pitch rises. The column ascends to your head and pauses there as if gathering momentum. Then, on cue with the singing voices, the energy fountains out from your head in a burst of living light. Guided by the hands of the priest, it spills down in cooling, soothing strokes over your whole body. It enlivens every cell as it goes, taking away all tensions, all accumulated poisons and stresses, all that which dams up and obstructs your own life energy. Now this force gathers once more at your feet where it is purified by the gentle caresses of the priestess. Then, the cycle begins again, the gathered force rising and pausing, rising and pausing, rising and pausing, until it shoots out again as a fountain bringing its healing salve to shower down your body on its return. As it does this, the centers are activated, top of head, throat, stomach, genitals, on the down flow to the feet and knees, abdomen, heart, and brow on the up flow to the head, all of these centers are stimulated into more activity and vibration.

The up and around fountain effect continues around.

Then again …

And again …

You give yourself over utterly to this process. Time has ceased to have any meaning; all that exists is the sound, and the One Force. These two are your whole universe.

After a while, you notice that the sound has faded, and so has the feeling of the force. Yet, the effects are still with you. You open your eyes and see that the sky is getting lighter with the dawn. Have you really been here that long? Obviously, time in this realm is different to the time you usually know.

You look about you and see that you are alone. The sun's first rays now pour over the edge of the theater, warming your face. So welcome—it is like a lost friend. Bask for a moment in the warm radiance of the morning sun. How good to be alive this very moment, experiencing. No past. No future. Just this beautiful moment.

The past ties us down. The future fills us with fear. Yet the sun disappears each night and rises again with each dawn. Sometimes the nights are short and sometimes they are long. Yet the sun always returns, daily renewed. There is a lesson for us here.

You feel a slight touch at your elbow. It is your guide. Again the loving smile. Your guide shares some words of friendship: "You have now received the healing force mediated to you through the service of all healers of all times and of all places. Though you live life after life upon the earth, yet through this power you are truly made immortal. Though you stray from it into darkness and despair, it is always with you, always as close as your outstretched hand. Turn to it … and re-turn to it … any time that you wish."

Firm yet gentle hands assist you down from the stone. Your guide indicates the pathway by which you came to this place, and gives you directions: "Follow this path, but not back the way you came. It leads on into the gardens where you may walk at your leisure until you come eventually by that route to your door again. You will then return to your cave and from there to normal consciousness. This is the last and most important step of the healing process. Should you wish to visit these realms again, I shall be here to guide you once more. Remember though that I do not always appear as you now see me. Yet in your heart you will always know me. The healing is over. Go in peace and wholeness."

An embrace, a loving touch, and you leave. Walk now in the gardens. See the early morning wonder of the many flowers. Feel the freshness of the air. Smell the rich variety of perfumes. Hear the morning birdcalls and the busy flight of the bees. Walk along the paths, on the footbridges over the waterways. Stroll by the small lakes and ponds with wild fowl, fountains, and little islands. Enjoy these moments on your way back to the door.

Postamble

At some point you will find upon the path a short, gnarled, and twisted piece of a branch. Pick it up and take it with you

When you reach your door, the crystal door with the staff and serpent design shining within it, you will pass happily through to waken once more in your little crystal cave. The design will fade from the mirror and you will return to your castle.

Go to the great hall and sit at the table as usual. Place your twisted stick on a free segment and briefly review the events and feelings of the working. Then, still carrying the healing energies, return to the courtyard and so to normal consciousness.

Discussion

The journey to the healing temple is a journey that is made in order to contact the healing force within us and bring it into everyday life.

Now what is healing? Healing can be two things. From one point of view it is the correction of disorder. It is putting something right that is wrong, the healing of things that have already happened. I call this *curative* healing. But healing has another aspect and, I believe, a far more important one. I call this other aspect *preventive* healing.

Every one of us has our own state of health and of being in this realm. I do not want to suggest here some abstract universal ideal of health. On the contrary. Each one of us has our own situation within which we work. We can be "on form" or "off form" measured against our own best self, not someone else's, nor some mythical single ideal for all. That is not the reality of our existence. Healing in this regard is activating personal forces to keep us as much at or ahead of our norm as we can.

In this healing of prevention, we are concerned with "being" in such a way that further disorders do not occur. It is a way of life. The healthy life is one that is lived in harmony and order so that dis-order may not occur, always in terms of our own individual position in this. In practical terms, it is living this way as far as possible in a given situation so as to minimize the chance of unwanted disorder occurring.

But how are we going to live this way? What is it that leads us to live in harmony and what leads us to depart from it?

Life Force

We live in a sea of life force. We each use this force and express it in our own way. It is all around us but we are unaware of it. It is to us like water to a fish. Just so are we unaware of our immersion in that which sustains us. We use life force and give it expression. We ourselves are an expression of that life force in physical manifestation. There is, on the one hand, the force, and on the other our expression of it—our own use of it, our own personal choice of the uses to which it is put.

The extent that we cut ourselves off from this force is the same extent that we invite disorder. We become ill at ease or diseased within the context of our own personal norm.

In the curing of any problem, we must first look at the symptoms. We must look at whatever is causing the immediate distress and do what we can to alleviate it. This is very important. Once a problem has manifested, we must alleviate the symptoms first. Then we may address ourselves to the root causes.

While the alternative medical tradition disparages the orthodox tradition for its alleged failure to get to the inner causes, that same alternative has been accused of failing to alleviate the symptoms to give the patient *time* to alter the deep, inner conditions from which those symptoms spring.

A Complementary Method

Pathworkings, mental techniques, and such devices are all very well and superbly effective for some preventive aspects of healing. They are also excellent methods to use in conjunction with physical methods for the curative aspects. But only, very occasionally, will purely mental techniques totally replace physical attention to symptoms, at least at this stage in our human evolution.

What I am saying here is that a pathworking is no substitute for proper medical attention where symptoms are already present. Whether this medical attention is of the more orthodox style of Western medicine or one of the so-called alternative systems—such as naturopathy, acupuncture, and the like—is to my mind quite immaterial. The point is that a method must be found to treat the physical symptoms if they exist. This pathworking and others of its sort are no substitute for the necessary treatment itself.

But let us return to the idea of the healing source, the healing energy that is all around us. Occult mystics have taught that this life force is charged in the very air that we breathe and indeed many systems of meditation begin by teaching breathing exercises. These exercises regulate the breath and make breathing rhythmic, bringing the charged air deep within the body.

There are then other techniques, which remove the charge from the air and then circulate it around the body's energy channels. Suffice it to say that these methods exist without going into it any further at this stage. The important thing is that we are surrounded by this source of energy. We are immersed in it. Why then is it that we are not healthy all the time?

Each of us has our own usual state of health. Whatever that state is for us as an individual, we depart from it when we cut ourselves off from the healing energy by choices in the way that we live. Our thought habits and processes effectively shield us from the source of life itself.

The innocent is unafraid of life. The innocent greets each new situation face on. They have not yet learned to hold back. They have not yet learned to be rigid. I have seen a child burn a hand on something hot and yet reach out to touch the same thing again. Persistence in such a course would be downright foolishness. These cases, however, show an openness to life, a willingness to be hurt and to learn from those hurts.

Incidents

Here is the crux of the matter. We refer to such individual incidents as "hurts," and I mean incidents, not continuing conditions here. This is because we view it the wrong way. We should look upon these moments of hurt as learning. For when we open ourselves to life, the all-pervading life force is expressed through us, through our own uniqueness, through our own individuality. It thus brings experiences to us that we need in order to learn and thereby to grow. That is, we make a mistake, accidentally get hurt, and know not to do that again.

Again, I must emphasize I am talking here about incidents, not conditions that are ongoing for a person. Within the options that are available to us, some are healthy, some are not.

Healers

Every culture and religion has had its healing aspect. In earlier times within Western culture there was a "medicine woman," the old lady of the village who knew healing herbs and their proper preparation. A lot of that knowledge had been lost through the persecution of such people during the dark times of our history.

There have always been healers and in many cases they have been associated with the sun. Apollo, one of the Greek sun gods, was a healer.

The healer removes a condition, alleviates an ongoing condition, and supplies preventive skills and teachings. We all have different needs in this regard and at different times. The healer deals with the actual situation, not some fiction of how things "should be."

One of my younger daughter's primary schools had the motto "Je deviens ce que je suis": I become that which I am. This is healing.

Asclepius

The idea of a temple is that it should be a place dedicated to a deity operating in a particular aspect. The aspect we are here concerned with is that of healing. A good current example of a healing temple still exists at Epidaurus in Greece. This temple was dedicated to Asclepius, the son of the union between Apollo and a mortal woman. He partook of the nature of the gods and mortals within his own being. We are looking at a contact point here, a place where the normal round of existence may meet the life-force itself. One who partakes of two natures becomes in themselves a gateway between realms or levels of knowing and existence.

In exactly the same way, we each have our own point of contact as we have already seen and in this case the contact is with the healing energy that is all around us. Asclepius is for us a good representative of this point of contact between realms. He therefore mediates this meaning to us.

Now although part mortal, Asclepius was renowned for his excellent healing abilities. As a child, he was trained by a centaur. In psychological terms, the centaur is a symbol representing that process by which we become integrated. It is a step on the way.

The centaur was the teacher of Asclepius and under his tutelage the boy became very skilled in the healing arts. This was all very well until one day he was prevailed upon by Artemis to restore, with her help, the dead Hippolytus back to life. Aesculapius agreed and Hippolytus was resurrected. This angered Zeus and he struck Asclepius down. Raising from the dead, it seems, was only to be performed by the gods themselves.

Apollo was not too happy about this and brought pressure to bear upon Zeus to have his son Asclepius raised to the status of a god. Asclepius became one of the gods and in fact a god of healing, like his father, Apollo. Here we have the common theme of the redemption: recognition of the divine-human mixture; struck down or immolated by the divine; raised to the status of divinity. This has lessons for us in regard to the process of healing too.

The Serpent

Now the form in which Asclepius was often supposed to appear was that of a serpent or snake, and the symbol used to represent this was a single staff with a single snake twined about it. Even now this is used as a symbol for the medical profession in many parts of the world. It is interesting to note that this symbol has often been confused with the Caduceus of Hermes. This shows *two* snakes intertwined about a central staff. Hermes is not a healing god, but is concerned with the formal aspects of communication, such as words. In the light of this, we might understand why a lot of Western medicine is concerned with technique rather than with treating the ill person as a whole.

But apart from this, the symbol of the snake around the staff is important because we find the same motif appearing in other situations. For example, a similar symbol showing a serpent draped around a Calvary cross has been sometimes used in Christian mysticism to represent Christ, with a similar story of the sacrifice and deification of a healer. Reference to Christ here should be read as referring to the divine child. This child of divinity occurs in many religions other than Christianity and the mystical principles are not the sole domain of Christianity. This is quite distinct to the historical person of Jesus who in Christian teaching was the one and only instance of divine incarnation.

There are some parallels between Asclepius and Christ. For one thing, Christ as Jesus performed many noted acts of healing and healing miracles, including resurrection of the dead. Jesus was initially a semi-divine being born of God and a mortal woman. He was put to death by the patriarchs of the time. Zeus, remember, was the father of the Greek gods and represented the entrenched authority for the hierarchy of gods. Finally, Jesus was resurrected and became wholly divine in His own right.

A temple was erected to the worship of Asclepius at Epidaurus in Greece. Not much is left to be seen of the actual healing area today. There is, however, still an arena, an impressive semicircle of stone seats rising back from a central area. This arena is well noted for its excellent acoustic properties. No matter where you sit on those stone seats, the sound of a coin dropped on a certain spot in the central area can be heard distinctly and quite clearly. Nowadays, the acoustics are taken as evidence that plays were performed there due to the ability of the theater's structure to amplify the voices of the actors.

What is not so generally realized, though, is that this property works both ways, in a sense. Psychic energy can follow similar laws to that of sound in conditions like those found at Epidaurus. Properly formed and directed psychic energies, generated by people sitting in the stone seats would in effect concentrate at a central point of the arena.

The Arena

In our pathworking we consider this as a healing arena. On the seats in the arena are the people who could contact the divine source, the healing energy within themselves and who, channeling it through their own psychic energy, could direct it to the central point. Here the person needing the healing would take their place and this force generated by all the people present would be directed there, so focused and concentrated by the will and intention of all present that it could not fail to take effect.

At the site in Epidaurus there was an associated building, which stood to the side of the arena and was probably used for rest and recuperation between periods of treatment in the theater. Very little of this building remains now. As an aside, let us note that we still use the word "theater" both for places of play-acting and places of surgery.

Now let us return to the idea of energies circulating in the body. It is not sufficient to just tap this source of healing energy within. We must circulate its power through our very selves. We first re-establish contact with the source of life within ourselves and having contacted it we then put its energies to use in our subtler self, our psychic nature, in what is sometimes called our "etheric" body. We drive it along the meridians of our body where it may have its effect in curing whatever tendency to illness there is. Such a flow will work upon *causes* rather than *symptoms*.

Circulations of Energy

There are many ways that this energy can be circulated just as there are many meridians in the body. These are energy circuits, acupuncture meridians, psychic channels, the life that joins the various chakras together—whatever the terms you prefer to use, any mystical system will generally take a limited number of these to deal with in its practical exercises for healing.

One thing is certain though—the Chinese, Indian, and Western systems all agree on there being a central channel although the extent of it varies. It is through this central channel that we draw down into ourselves the healing energy, taking it right down to the very bottom of our physical natures.

Having done this we now circulate it through the meridians. In the Chinese systems, the circulation is performed up the back of the body, down the front of the body, around the waist, up and down the arms and legs and so on. There are also ways of passing the energy around the body developed from Indian sources.

The method used in this pathworking is derived from the Western Esoteric Tradition. We contact the force above the head and bring it down to the feet in an ordered series of changes. Then we bring the force up to the head once more where it spills out like a fountain and falls down on all sides to be gathered up again and recirculated.

In fact, at its center this pathworking uses a variation of a technique that is known as the Middle Pillar exercise. The works of Dr. Israel Regardie should be consulted about this technique, its operations, and its relationship to the Western Tradition and, more particularly, the Tree of Life of the Qabalists, from which it is derived.

The Qabalists deal with a subset of the centers that I have come to know through different practices. The ways I have experienced these leads me to treat those of the group I use as alternating "styles." I sense one group as "radiating" and one as "gathering" with a couple of combined, transitional or pulsing. In the next section, I have laid out how I experience them in terms of a downflow for radiating and pulsing, and an upflow for gathering and pulsing.

The Centers and Their Character

The downflow is the top of the head (pulsing), throat (radiating), solar plexus (radiating), genitals (radiating), feet (pulsing).

The upflow is feet (pulsing), knees (gathering), abdomen (gathering), chest (gathering), throat (gathering), brow (gathering), and back to top of head (pulsing).

These are my own experiences and learning, derived from my time with two magical orders of the Qabalistic style and with three Wiccan groups. I have not looked at how this relates to laya yoga or teachings and practices of other traditions.

This is the symbolism and rationale behind this pathworking. However, prior to this circulation of energy, there is the preparation. We must be prepared and ready to contact or accept the reception of the divine energy. If we are to approach divinity within ourselves, there will always be preparation beforehand. This preparation involves two steps.

First, we must purify ourselves before coming into contact with divinity. We must put away from ourselves all that is "not worthy," as used to be said, or "not appropriate," as we might phrase it today. In the pathworking this is symbolized by bathing beforehand.

Second, we must be open to receive once we have made the contact. It is no good being purified and making the contact if we are not yet able to receive what we meet. We must open the channels. This is symbolized in the pathworking by the drink that is taken after the bath and before we go to the operating theater.

We use a drink because it is an opener—we open the mouth, taking in the liquid essence. All liquids are related to the archetypal element of water, which, as you have already experienced, is associated with receptivity. For example, a lake, when still, reflects like a mirror. It is receptive to all that falls upon it, accepting it without question and without distortion. In the working, we take a drink and thus become open and ready for that which we will contact.

The Circulations

Now let us move on to consider some of the more central aspects of the working. There is a priest and priestess. They appear in this working so that you will realize that you do not work entirely on your own. I have used the terms *priest* and *priestess* deliberately as titles of an office performed, each of the two in its own way. Two complementary styles of doing things. There is no gender implied here at all. In some of the magical lodges where I have participated in proceedings, the roles of priest, magus, or priestess are not gender-fixed and have been performed by anyone of any actual self- or other-defined role in the outer world. There is a role. Any may fill it. One must.

It is not solely by your own conscious efforts that the contact and the circulations are achieved. There is within you the agency to contact the energies and also within you the agency to circulate those energies.

It is a natural thing. It is as natural as breathing but we do not even breathe correctly. How much less then will we employ these natural abilities properly? When we do, however, when we contact the central source and circulate its energies around our bodies, then we become open to life and accepting of life in its fullness. We become vibrant and charged with energy. I have found this; others have reported this. I have no other reference for this but my experience.

It is never too late to do this, by the way, even if our lives have been lived in such a way that it is too late to reverse some of the things that have already overtaken us. We may still make contact, still circulate the energies, still learn to live. Whatsoever span of life remains to us may be lived as abundantly and fully as possible.

You realize that I am saying here that you really have to stop doing in life those things that are known to damage us. The choice, of course, is yours. I am also saying we work from where we now are and within how we are now.

These abilities in ourselves, which are neither male nor female, we symbolize by the priest and priestess. Remember what we said earlier about union between the divine and the human, between, in the Greek case cited, male god and mortal woman. We have a priest, or "send-out" person who stands at our head and a priestess, or "receive and send back" person who stands at our feet as we lie in the theater, ourselves ready to make contact with this energy and receive it into our nature. They are healers.

Now, the important thing about healing and healing via the agency of another person is that it can be carried out at different levels. We can have what is called "psychic healing" and we can have "spiritual healing." Different people use these terms in different ways. I'll define here what I mean by them.

By psychic healing I mean healing that comes to you by the psychic energy that belongs to the healer. In other words, it is energy for healing given to you by another person. You then use that energy to mend whatever it is that is not working correctly.

Spiritual healing, on the other hand, I define as the activation and operation of the healing force by your own contact with it. However, that contact with it is stimulated or intensified by another person—the healer. It is important that you keep this distinction in mind because the priest, the priestess, and all those people present who pull their energy down upon you are at the same time doing both sorts of healing.

You are not going to be given energy by these people. The energy they project your way mediates to you the healing energy, and by sympathetic vibration stimulates in yourself, the activity of your own healing temple.

Your Own Healing Principle

You are in fact paying a visit to your healing temple, the healing principle within yourself. Since this working is built along archetypal principles, it is therefore linked through your personal symbolism to the inner healing principle common to us all. In fact, it becomes linked to the archetype that stood behind the creation of the healing temple we have been discussing, the one built in actuality at Epidaurus. In the last analysis, this archetype stands behind all such healing centers.

You may visit the temple regularly, once a week, say, and you may visit it when you have the need. True healing, however, comes from living a harmonious lifestyle, living in harmony with the life force. This means being open to the life force and then accepting whatever life brings you.

Now, by this I do not mean a passive acceptance, a kind of fatalistic, cynical, existential, pessimistic style of life at all. But, it does mean that you will come to deal with a situation as it occurs.

You don't live in fear before it occurs in case it might hurt you. Neither do you dwell on what has passed. If a situation does bring you distress, minor embarrassment, inconvenience, or frustration, then accept what is, accept the actuality of what life has presented to you—then do something about it.

Acceptance is not lying back and being clobbered. Acceptance is realizing what is the case and dealing with it accordingly and as correctly as you can. It is keeping the valuations and judgments out of the way so that you do not start to say, "I can't do this," or "I can't do that." Life brings to you its opportunities and challenges. Accept them all, and act on them, because this is the only way to have this healing force running through you all the time.

In using this pathworking you are using true healing methods. You are using inner healing principles to harmonize your life. You may find that it requires you to change the way that you live. There may be no other way. We may alleviate symptoms in ourselves but true healing comes from a particular style of living and a particular approach to life. If you do not have this approach, then true inner healing does not occur.

If your life is not already in harmony, then these workings will show you where disharmony lies. You will become more aware of where your life does not let in the healing force. Once you know this, then you have to do something about it. If you ignore these spots where the healing force can't come in, then the healing will not take place. The whole point of workings of this type is to have your whole awareness directed to those spots that need change; then you must change it.

Gradually, by working with this system, you will be led to a way of living, a way of being, which is more and more in harmony with the creative living force, whatever your situation or challenges. It will flow through you all the more. You will be more vibrant, more alive, and feeling life more abundantly. That is what true health is.

Path 6: The Path of Adjustment

✤

In this working, you will once again enter by visiting the crystal cave first and settling into position. Your finer self will step through into a library, but it will not look like it did when you last saw it. When you leave the library and go through the town square, you will be asked to undertake a task. Will you do this? It is entirely up to you whether you do the task right away or wait until another time. The task that you undertake will be an errand. Your task will be to deliver plans for a city that needs to be built and in doing this you are acting at the request of a higher authority. The task will send you traveling over the marches, in the mist, not knowing if it is day or night. It will seem like you are challenged along the way and you will need to find resolve within yourself to continue.

It is entirely up to you if you choose to take on the task or decline and return to take it up again at a later time. You will find in this working links between your normal everyday self and the inner spiritual principle that is a more real you.

The purpose of this path is to realize that we are affected by deep inner forces or drives that spring from deep inner needs. The task is nothing less than accepting and balancing these needs. The task represents what your plan was for this incarnation and, if necessary, will guide you in getting back on track and moving forward. Accepting this may bring challenges—and rewards.

Preamble

Using the method of the earlier workings, make your way to the crystal cave and take up your position in front of the crystal. As you gaze at the design for this working, an ancient circle of standing stones begins to appear upon it.

You keep gazing at the image until it takes on a three-dimensional quality. The image becomes a doorway through which you may step. However, it is only a finer essence of yourself that steps through, leaving the denser portions of your nature in a contemplative sleep within the cave.

———————————— THE PATHWORKING ————————————

Looking around you find yourself in a library. Behind you stands a crystal door by which you entered this working. Upon it stands the design of the circle of ancient standing stones with a broad avenue of stones approaching it.

You turn your attention to the library in which you now stand. This is a place where information is stored, the repository of the learning of all ages. Pass through the library to the front door. Three steps lead up to this door. Each is a different color with the top step also being large enough to form a landing in front of the door. Mount the three steps and approach the door. Examine the door in all its aspects—its texture, shape, and color.

Open the door and pass through.

You are now in a town square, which has a scaffold or gibbet in the center. No one hangs from it at this time. There are many imposing buildings on each side of the square with streets going off at various angles. You notice that one of the buildings is a law court of some kind. Have a look around the square. Are there people here? How are they dressed? How are you dressed? Do not engage in conversation with anyone at this stage.

Suddenly, with a mighty clattering sound, a chariot or cart turns into the square. You see it has one white horse and one black horse. They are wild and panting from the trip. The charioteer is naked to the waist and dark-skinned, glistening with sweat. Tattooed upon his arm is the sign of Cancer, the crab. The horses stop and the charioteer looks around as though searching for someone. He sees you and slowly approaches. Any in his path fall back out of the way. He stops in front of you and addresses you: "I come from She Who Rules this Realm. At Her request I seek out one who will brave the dark and dangerous misty marches and carry Her tokens that I have brought with me. Even now She journeys to the resplendent city to await the one who will take this adventure. Will it be you?"

He holds up a short sword and a balance with its two pans moving slightly up and down. Are you prepared to undertake the task? Think for a moment.

If you choose not to take the journey at this time then you should return through the library and the door back to the cave and thence to normal consciousness.

You give your answer. If it is yes, the charioteer hands the sword to your right hand and the balance to the left. He points out the road you must take and explains that the sword will cleave the mists and the balance will show the path.

After receiving the charioteer's directions, you head out on the indicated road. There are no mists here, just buildings on each side. Gradually though the buildings become further spaced apart and there is more land between each one.

It is getting darker. Night is coming on and you had not realized. Perhaps you should not have taken this on. Still, you can't rely on finding your way back in the dark, so you might as well go on.

The last houses are passed now and peering ahead through the darkness you see something green and luminous. You approach.

It is mist, but no mist you have ever seen before, rather a swirling green clamminess. From within you hear the lone cry of a wolf or jackal. It seems very thick and uninviting, but you remember what the charioteer said and hold up the sword and scales.

The pans on the scales quiver slightly and then settle exactly balanced. The sword hums and sings in your hand for a moment and gleams with an ethereal light.

You advance cautiously and the mist parts before the sword, allowing you to progress. Better keep a tight hand on that sword. As you go on you feel more confident. This isn't so bad after all.

After a short while, you begin to get the impression that you have walked into a ring of standing stones. It is almost as though you can see their shapes through the mist. No matter how far you walk, you cannot shake the feeling that you are still within the same stone circle.

Suddenly, the left pan of the scales dips downward, the right upward. You stop. There are shapes all about you, just out of sight in the mist. You hear voices—threatening, pleading, mocking, proud, and pitiful voices. A step slightly to the right and the scales come back to the balance point. The shapes and voices are still there but lessened somewhat.

You continue, using the sword to cleave the mist and changing your direction as the scales indicate. When the left pan goes down, you step right and when the right pan goes down, you step left. Yet, all the time it seems to you that you are still within the circle of standing stones.

The shapes persist, sometimes swooping in toward you, trying to throw you off course. But, you have a firm grip on the scales and on the sword, too, and it seems they cannot hurt you so long as you keep your attention.

What are these things that would keep you from your task?

The shapes recede. The mists begin to clear. It has been a long journey through the night.

The light of the rising sun catches the domed rooftops of the city ahead, setting them alight with gold and pink. The mist has gone.

Looking back, you see a broad plain. Standing prominently upon the plain is a circle of roughly formed, standing stones, the circle you had been in. What a strange and magical circle it must have been to contain the whole of your night's journey. You turn your attention once more to the city. You approach the gates.

Standing there, you see a lady in a blue robe and a man in a gray robe. Both are of an uncertain age; they are ageless in appearance. You approach. The lady comes forward. Her face is radiant. It is for her that you have brought the sword and scales. She accepts them from you without speaking.

She indicates that you should approach the man, so you do so. He says that he has been appointed to guide you into the city, and, offering his left hand for your right, asks that you follow him through the gates. Can he be trusted? He was with the lady after all so perhaps it's all right. You turn to seek her assurance, but she is gone.

You take the proffered hand and with the sage, go through the gates. You pass along the streets with buildings on each side. The man may speak with you as you walk.

The two of you arrive in the city square. The square consists of two levels with steps down to a lower level. The man points to a building on the lower level. It is a library and he tells you that in it you will find the way back.

Postamble

You take your leave knowing that you may meet this man again someday, and descend to the lower level to the main door of the library. Looking back, you see the man. He waves once and turns away, disappearing into the crowd. You turn back to the door and see upon the step a short flat piece of wood. It looks like an old-school ruler. You pick it up and pass through the door into the library.

It is the same library from which you started this journey. You traveled that journey and did not move from this city at all. Moving through it, you come to the crystal door that leads back into the cave. Pass through it and follow the normal way back to your castle.

Once back in the great hall of your castle, you place the flat piece of ruler-like wood upon the table and think for a while about your experiences. It may be that you also communicate with others at the table at this time.

Finally, you leave the castle and return to normal consciousness in the usual way.

Discussion

The keynote of this whole working is "karma." This much-maligned term is best translated by the word "action" in English. This, however, is a very poor word to tell all that karma means.

When we act, we generate effects of our actions. When these effects are in accord with cosmic law, there is no karma generated. When they are not in accord with cosmic law, karma is generated.

The Eastern philosophies, both of India and of China, espouse the value of "non-action." This does not mean "doing nothing," rather it means acting in a non-karmic way, acting in a way that is not against cosmic law.

The word "action," which is something we are supposed to avoid, relates to those actions that "meddle" in the natural state of things. All other acts are not counted as "action" in this sense, for they are right and proper and in accord with the natural way of the universe.

One misunderstanding that can come from this is that what is in "nature" as opposed to "us," the humans, is natural and right and all that we humans have done is unnatural and wrong.

This is quite incorrect. We are not separate from nature but a part of it, and it is most unnatural for us to deny our humanity and sink to the level of thoughtless animals in an attempt so misguided as to "become one with nature." This has been a popular theme of late. It is only another fanciful cop-out that enables us to avoid responsibility for our own full humanity.

We have many faculties that we may use in our daily life. All of these can be used in unbalanced ways, thereby generating karma, or consequences, with which we will subsequently have to deal. The problem for us in seeking self-knowledge and spiritual development is that these consequences have a tendency to trap us into our usual lifestyle.

We have come along a certain way in our development and those that know us exert subtle pressures upon us to continue to behave in the way that we always have. Trying to change ourselves, we meet incredible resistance. Yet, if we examine that resistance, we see that it has come from the way we have been, from the things that we have already done.

For example, if you have socialized a lot then you will find that as you try to withdraw from socializing to work on more individual pursuits, it may seem like your friends are pressuring you to attend this or that function or gathering. The life you have made surrounds you and can constrain you to continue living in that way.

If, however, the way you live is not along spiritual lines, then one way or another you will be urged to change, to overcome its resistance, and to take off in a new direction, metaphorically speaking.

According to the Western Esoteric Tradition, there is for each one of us a great plan that we have agreed to work into actuality. For one reason or another we usually fail to do this. It may be that we try and then fail through lack of skill or through error. It may be that we dally with enjoyments, unwilling to progress on. Or, it may be that we deliberately distort what is to be, bringing it through in a way that we think most suits our own good.

There are many ways in which we can fail to affect the plan, such is our human ingenuity. Much of this idea has found its way into the Christian teachings that humanity has been given the power of choice and must of its own volition choose the good, the loving, all that is of God. This idea, however, is not confined to Christianity and finds its expression in many other religions. In some religions, it comes out as a requirement to be responsible for our own life and actions.

The first task we have in balancing karma and living the life of non-action is to recognize that we have come by a roundabout and devious way to our present life position. For all we know we could be far from our most desirable place. Yet, the decision to live non-karmically will point us in the right direction immediately.

We still have to cover the ground back to our true path and this will involve some changes and possibly some sacrifice. To deny this is to claim that we are already in accord with cosmic law. This is nonsense. If you believe that you are already at that stage then you would be a virtual Buddha or saint. Have a look around and see if there is a single thing in the world that you are not happy with. If there is, then you have not yet attained.

As soon as we start to make that journey back to our true way, we will encounter the karmic forces in our lives that will press us to deal with them. At this stage we may weaken and drop back into our old ways of being, for these actions of ours have made grooves in the fabric of psychic space and events flow more easily along them than in the ways that we wish to go.

We have to buy a respite. We have to look around and say, "Yes, I acknowledge you. I will deal with you a little later, though." We have to be prepared for some things to pile up a bit and remain unattended if we are to make this change. This can only be done by the recognition of the existence of the karmic effects and the willingness and commitment to deal with them as soon as our new direction is stabilized.

We cannot, after all, walk away from the responsibilities that we have already undertaken. We must discharge them, or at least arrange for their suitable fulfillment. If for example you had agreed to do a certain job for someone, then fulfilling your obligations does not necessarily mean that you must still personally perform that job. Your responsibility is ended if you find someone else who will do it at least as well as you would have yourself. And, similarly for other commitments in your life that may have come about through deviated and unbalanced decisions that you have made in the past.

With this understanding of the underlying theme of the pathworking, let's look at some of the symbols found in this path.

The Library

We begin the working in a library and this symbolizes the idea of knowledge, especially that of the conscious and rational mind. We will also end in this library, thus ensuring that we wish to know and be aware of the forces we invoke.

In this way, the effects of our working will come to us in such a way that we will recognize them in the mind, the conscious rational mind of thought. This will also give us the best way to deal with the effects for if they operated through our subconscious, we would be unaware of what was happening. If the effects operated through our emotions, we would be in danger of becoming too involved with them and not seeing the wood for the trees. It is essential that we understand our experiences and the rational mind is a stepping-stone to understanding.

Law

We leave the library and pass by the adjoining path to a city square containing a law court. The idea here is that we are invoking natural karmic law in a civilized way. We wish to expose ourselves to a law that is conditioned by human values. Raw, natural, impersonal law is too much for us at this stage of our development, although there will come a time when we shall have to stand before its awe-full majesty and face the final Dweller on the Threshold.

The Chariot

We have our task brought to us by a charioteer. According to Qabalistic teachings on the tarot trumps, this chariot is related to the astrological sign of Cancer signifying restriction and boundaries. These are the restrictions and boundaries placed upon us by the effects and consequences today of those things we did yesterday. The crab of Cancer also has claws that can hold on to things in a vice-like grip. We must become aware of the need to let go if our habits and behavior patterns are to be overcome. Only in this way will we be able to cease creating consequences.

The chariot is the vehicle for manifestation of "the plan" and the means by which it is brought to our attention. Here too we encounter the idea that the "Keeper of the Plan" is shown as female. We can look at a plan in two phases: plan/prepare and execute/review. In the same way we can, in later years, look back and see our whole life in these two stages. Looking at segments, we can see lots of units of these two stages: plan/do. One is contained, not yet exposed. One is outgoing and into the fray. In this working, the holder of the plan is symbolically female signifying the womb of preparation and plan for what is to come and what is to be done.

The Plan

The idea of a plan is often referred to by various spiritual, new age, and teaching groups as the "pre-birth plan." It is used in discussions of reincarnation, but in itself it does not require acceptance of reincarnation teachings. Quite simply, the term assumes that there is a "you" before being born and that in some way you create or are given or cocreate a plan of what you wish to achieve for yourself in the incarnation to come. This pathworking is structured to prompt a recall of this.

The Lady and the Tools

Traditionally, that which establishes a protective, encircling boundary within which things may develop, grow, and unfold has been associated with feminine and motherly ideas. That which gives impetus and direction outward, onward, and away is assigned to masculine and fatherly ideas. These principles are far above those of gender as they appear to us and are not in any way modified by our emerging notions of sexual equality or gender fluidity. These are important and valid in their own arena and in our presentation of everyday life to others and to ourselves. In pathworkings we are taking a step back, or inwards, to where terms refer more to principles rather than actuality.

From our point of view in this working, it is the Mother or the Lady who brings us the plan. Later, we meet the man who is the inner world guide for us, thus fulfilling the role of providing us with direction. Similarly, too, the charioteer is male for this reason.

I should add that there are versions of this pathworking that have the sexual roles cast differently. I have only given one version here. It is best to experiment with the one given before introducing other factors. Then you will have a solid basis from which to work in exploring other aspects of the same reality.

Now, at this point in the working you may choose not to proceed further and leave the working by the door through which you entered. There is a sense of timing to be observed in this. It is not always the right time to change direction, as any who have sailed a yacht can tell you. If this is so, accept it and come back to the working at some later time.

However, let us suppose that you intend to go on and complete the working. You receive into your hands the symbols of the plan.

One of these is the balance, the scales that will weigh one thing against another and show the central balance point. The other is the sword, which will cut away all that is not of the plan itself. These you use along the path, for the sword clears the way and the balance shows the correct direction, neither too far to the right, nor too far to the left.

These symbols are archetypal in their association with justice as you will see by studying the traditional statues of the Lady Justice found above, within or around most law courts in some form or another. The tarot card "Justice," number eleven of the trumps in the modern packs but number eight in earlier versions, shows this design and these symbols and this card can also be associated with this particular path.

The path can also be associated with the Hebrew letter *lamed,* the shape of which comes to us from the ancient hieroglyphic designs of an ox goad or scourge.[24] It was this that was used to guide animals in the correct direction and to remove any tendencies to depart from their allotted tasks through its use for discipline.

It is karma that does this for us until we are able to take up the ox goad and apply it to ourselves, modifying our direction and scourging that which is against cosmic law in our actions through self-discipline. It is only when we can apply things to ourselves that we are truly entitled to apply them to other people, and even then not always. Note this well.

Balance

We now must carry the symbols with which we have been presented to our central balance point. This is necessary, for it may be that we do not know what course to take in our own lives to work out the dictates of justice and karma. Experience has probably taught us that if we have been too extreme in

---

24. Hebrew Today, "The Hebrew Alphabet—The Letter Lamed," accessed July 15, 2020,
    https://hebrewtoday.com/alphabet/the-letter-lamed-%D7%9C/.

a certain regard, then the balance point is found by being too extreme in the opposite regard.

This is all very well to experience, but it is not something that we should pursue as a policy. Just because we know that extremities can sometimes lead to balance is no reason that we should seek out and practice such extremities.

It is far better to ask life for balance and have life itself present the course that we must take to achieve that balance. If such a course of action seems extreme, it has nonetheless come about as an appeal to balance.

To pursue merely the extremes in order to bring about balance is to put the cart before the horse. The way to the center cannot be found in this fashion and all extreme action pursued for its own sake will generate more karma. Central and correct action, as the *I Ching* says, is the only action that does not generate consequences.

We seek the balance point and follow its dictates, even if apparently extreme, for while the balance might lead us through extremities, the extremities will never lead us into balance.

The Mists of Ignorance

The way that we must go is shrouded in mists. These represent the ignorance that surrounds us and in which we normally act.

This ignorance is made up of two factors mainly—lack of knowledge and unawareness. In a sense, these amount to the same thing. In one case, however, we might actually know what is required, yet fail to apply the correct action through being unaware of the situation we are in.

We can have insufficient knowledge to apply—remedied by learning—or we can be inattentive to the world failing to apply what is required—remedied by paying attention at all times.

To attempt to find our way back to our true path, we shall have to plunge into and recognize our own ignorance and inattention, or lack of awareness. We enter these mists with only the sword and balance to help us.

We find, however, that the sword will cleave a way through the mists, hence showing that this sword, which cuts away all that is not of the plan, is related to knowledge. It is self-knowledge that dispels these mists of ignorance. Here we see how the application of self-discipline will lead us to self-knowledge.

This sword is a symbol of both, a vital living symbol that can be used in these pathworkings.

The balance, on the other hand, will show us when we are deviating to right or left. By watching this balance, we will see its scales tip to one side or another as we wander off the path. Here is the aspect referred to earlier of paying attention to the situation.

We can see that the balance symbolizes both the operation of justice and the moment-to-moment situation of everyday life. This reminds us that it is at every moment that balanced action must occur and that every moment poses an opportunity for us to begin to live non-karmically.

Within these mists of ignorance we begin to encounter the shades and phantasms of karmic consequences. It is these that will seek to hold us, to delay us, and to set us off course.

These consequences will come to us in many forms in our everyday lives and challenge our values, those codes by which we live. Many such codes operate as defenses against real living and as shields against the confrontation of life in full awareness.

We see many people, for example, pursuing a spiritual path in practicing a form of acceptance. This is all very well until they are required to act in defense of someone else or in defense of one of their own spiritual principles. Then the code of acceptance can excuse them from stepping in to prevent injustices.

Here is where acceptance can become apathy. There are many values that we hide behind to shield us from living life fully. We see this when the phantasms of the mist speak to us, cajole, plead, threaten, and use the many various forms of verbal persuasion that might work upon our own desperate sentimentality. In this mist we will learn, if we have the wit, how it is that we deliberately allow ourselves to be manipulated into deviated actions. This manipulation almost always looks as though it comes from others. But when we examine it more closely, we will invariably see that it comes from our own selves.

The Central City

Through this long night you go, following the way shown by the balance and opened by the sword. Eventually you come to the central city.

It is lit by the sun to remind us that the sun is the central organizing principle of this solar system and holds all planets in their appointed orbits.

Here you meet the lady whose symbols include the sword, balance, and the sun. At one level she is of course the Lady Justice, but at another level she is also the Mother and therefore the Guardian of the Plan. In handing the symbols to her, you reaffirm that you are placing the direction and balance of your actions into the hands of the plan that long ago you agreed to follow. It means that you are giving up the personal will into the hands of the greater.

However, we do not actually give up our own wills. Rather, we come to a state where in our minds will and desire are one. More importantly, you have not given up the tools. By using them, you have internalized them, taken them into your skill set. You can return the outer symbols of the skills and retain the skills themselves.

Here, too, you meet the man, the guide who gives direction to you in these inner realms. Your relationship with such guides is built upon trust and you must seek this trust within your heart. The planning, preparation, and skills with tools have prepared you for tasks ahead. Now, you just need the way pointed out. That is the guidance you are receiving. The woman and the man have, between them, transmuted tools of preparation and practice to a plan of action and the knowledge required to guide that action.

In this way, you will find that your day-to-day actions are prompted by the inner voice that guides you and since you have given the karmic keys back to the Guardian of the Plan, you are able to follow those dictates knowing that all their consequences will operate according to divine law.

The woman does not stay with you, for the dictates of the plan operate from the background of consciousness. The man, however, leads you into the central city and gives you an opportunity to talk with him and to look around. This central guiding principle should remain with you in your normal life and operate in the foreground of your decision making as you go about your daily life.

The Return
Finally, you come once more to a library and in that place you find the door that will lead you back to normal consciousness.

In this library you found these two cities, but the starting point and the finishing point were the same. The difference between deviated and balanced action is very subtle and hinges on the attitude more than any other thing. It follows then that the two are one and the same, conjoined in one and the same place and moment in every second of everyday life. The destination is the starting point and the journey is the process of realizing this.

The journey from one to the other is taken in metaphor rather than in reality. It is said in Taoism that the further you go from yourself, the less you know. All aspects of your nature are to be found in your center and the distance you must travel from one to the other is the distance between attitudes of thought and way of being in your own nature.[25]

At the conclusion of the working, you find that you have blazed a trail cross-country in your mind that has made a groove for your thoughts and actions and feelings to run along. You have mentally modified the world of the dreamtime, and like any skilled shaman, have set in motion forces which will cause life to show you how you come to be where you are and what the karmic factors are that operate in your world. You will also begin to see the direction that you must go.

This does not necessarily mean that you will have to "up anchor" and go to live or work somewhere else, for the lesson that the two-in-one city tells you is that the work can be done right where you currently find yourself.

———

Armed with these insights you will be able to begin anew on the road to self-discovery, remembering that this road leads through self-discipline.

Self-discipline, you will find, is not something to be feared as a tight constraint upon freedom, but is rather the recognition of all that is unnecessary to right living and the ability to gently, but firmly, remove it from your life.

Restriction of this sort removes all the deadwood and leaves only the essentials for you to expend your energy upon. You will have more energy and less indecision. This will lead to a form of contentment and a security in the knowledge that you are at last making some progress.

---

25. Max Kaltenmark, *Lao Tzu and Taosim*, trans. Roger Greaves (Stanford: Stanford University Press, 1969), 52.

Every moment provides the key to redemption, which is the working out of karma, and every moment also provides the opportunity to act without meddling, generating no karma, and working with the full force of cosmic law behind you.

Similarly, every moment harbors the phantasms of ignorance and error. Through the understanding of the lady and the guidance of the lord, you may reach the central balance that is the child of both.

Path 7: The Search for the School

_____ ✦ _____

In this working, you will find a set of steps cut into the wall of the crystal cave, which lead to a large upper area that is a combination of a study and a lecture theater. It is a place that teachers may come to present ideas, skills, or principles. On this occasion, an Egyptian priest will be communicating with you and give you the task of finding the school of the mysteries that is right for you. You will be told this is an individual thing. Preliminary guidance will be given to you, but the search for the school that resonates with you will be your own search. The objective of this working is to find within yourself your own particular "style" of teaching, the teaching that calls to you. The same principles of self-unfoldment are taught all over the world and through different times, cultures, and languages. This working is intended to "prime" your awareness so that something in your life that would pass as inconsequential will instead sound a note for you and indicate a style of esoteric teaching that will be useful to you.

Before setting off, you will share a drink with the priest. The word "wine" is used but the drink itself may vary. If water is intended, then it will be called water in my writings. If the word "wine" is used, it may be wine itself, or mead, ale, or a fruit drink, as required to suit your own preferred principles and the needs of the situation.

While sharing the drink, the priest will tell you that no matter the terrain, you will always leave footprints, and so will easily find your way back. You will be shown the door through which you will leave and return, as well as how to open it from the other side when you return. The priest will also instruct you in what questions to ask if you encounter or make some contact with a particular school.

This working is just a setting. The actual working will all be generated by you. The other side of the door will be bare or rich, as it arises for you.

Preamble

Relax and breathe rhythmically in your work place exactly as in the previous workings. The scene of your work area arises before your eyes. Once more there is one extra door just as before. Rise up in your mind's eye, approach the door, and open it. There is a swirling mist beyond the door. You step through and immediately find yourself, as usual, in the castle courtyard. The door between the realms closes behind you. Make your way to the crystal cave as before. This time, you will not enter the small cave of the crystal but remain for a moment in the main cave.

——————————— THE PATHWORKING ———————————

From the floor of the main cave there is a set of steps cut into the wall that lead upward in a clockwise direction. These steps climb up above the floor of the main cave with its central dark pool and come to a small landing with a plain wooden door. In the center of the door you see a knocker in the form of a lion's head that holds a metal ring in its mouth. However, there is no need to knock. The door is not locked; just use the handle to open the door.

The door opens easily into a small, rectangular lecture theater. You have entered at the back on a long side of the rectangle. To your right there is a low stage with lectern and between you and it stand rows of seats. To your left there is an area with a low table and two comfortable chairs. In the back wall beyond there is a stone fireplace. On the table you see a glass flagon of red wine and two crystal goblets.

Along the two long sides of the room the walls are lined with bookshelves. You look once more at the stage end of the room and see that to the left of the stage there is a curtained entrance. It is through this entrance that teachers may come to address those gathered here in search of knowledge.

As you realize this, the curtain is drawn aside and a man dressed as a priest of Egypt enters the room. He smiles and comes toward you indicating that you should take one of the comfortable seats. He takes the other and says,

"Welcome to the upper room. I am here to show you the entrance to this path. Like you, I have lived many lives and the guise I wear now is just one of them. Like you, I have had many forms and many names.

"In a moment, I will show you the entrance to the path. But first I must tell you what is ahead. The Quest for the School or Teacher is an individual one. Once through the door, you will receive no further instructions because what you find there will be for you and you alone.

"When you go through the door you will follow a short, dark corridor that opens up into a trackless, featureless wasteland. There are no paths to show you the way. You must use whatever skills you have to seek out your school and your teacher.

"As you walk, you will leave footprints. No matter the surface, you will leave a trail behind you, even over solid rock or swampland. Over whatever terrain you find, you cannot help but leave a trail. In this way, you will always be able to find your way back and so can never become lost.

"It is up to you to use whatever wit and wisdom is at your disposal to find the right directions. Let your heart be your compass. If you find your school, and it may take more than one journey to do so, ask questions. Some examples might be:

Who is my teacher?

What school is this?

What path does it follow?

Will you show me the direct route here?

How do members of this school recognize each other?

Is there a password (and what is it)?

Is there a crest or a motto?

Is there anything else I need to know on this occasion?

… and so on.

"The password is sometimes given as a statement and a response. One famous example is 'Do what thou wilt shall be the whole of the law,' which is responded to by 'Love is the law, love under will.'

"But other forms of password and recognition are used by the various schools. If you receive one, it is for your school only and should not be passed on to others, even fellow travelers or supervisors. You can, of course, work the first line into an innocent statement and see if you get the response you expect.

If not, they are not of your school, or not of the same part of the school, for some schools are large and have many departments.

"When you return, you will find your starting point and follow the short corridor back into this room. I will not be here. You will then return in the normal way. Do you have any questions?"

At this point, ask any questions and listen for the replies.

The priest pours two goblets of wine and says, "Your journey may be long or demanding. Drink some wine here with me to fortify you on your quest."

This you do. The priest drinks too.

The priest then gets up and leads you to the last set of bookshelves near the lectern, which are on the same wall as the curtained entrance. He shows you a particular book spine. It is not a book but a lever, and as he tilts it this section of the bookshelf swings toward you to give entry into a dark tunnel.

He shows you the mechanism to work the door from the other side that you will use when you return. Then he gives you some final advice: "The school is somewhere to be found in the wilderness. Be true to yourself and seek it with your heart. It may take time, it may take more than one trip, but the essence is to hold the call within you and the time will come when there is a response."

You thank him and, alone, step through into the dark corridor and the secret door closes softly behind you. You walk along the short corridor and come out into the nighttime scene of a trackless wasteland: the path to the school has begun.

When you return, you will pass once more through this upper room. The priest is not there. On the table there will be a small silver loop of metal, like a link from a silver chain. This you will take with you and place upon the table in the great hall.

Discussion

This is quite an unusual path. Sometimes when a number of people take a pathworking at the same time, they catch glimpses of each other or may have the sense that they are with others without actually seeing anyone. This particular path we usually tread alone.

Occult teachings tell us that each individual self has a certain type of ray with which it is associated. These types or rays can be three, four, seven, nine, ten, or twelve in number, depending on the underlying philosophy of prefer-ence. All of these address, broadly speaking, the one topic of how everything that is came into existence and why there are differences. There is a lot of information on this topic in the literature of the Theosophical Society. That literature is drawn from many sources, but principally from works originally in Sanskrit. Occult tradition also tells us that there is an entity or being who coor-dinates, resonates with, or looks after those of a given ray, which is the same as the one they themselves manifest. In early Theosophical Society days, these beings were called "Masters." We would probably pick a different term today to express the concept.

Within many traditions there is the idea that each of these beings has been responsible for the creation of various "Orders"—magical, mystical, occult—which have been more or less in the public realm over the centuries and that each operate one or more schools on the physical plane. Some traditions teach that inner plane schools are also operated within these orders.

It seems important for a person to find a teaching facility that is working on the same ray as they are themselves. Let's take a look at an example of sport instead of magic. If your "ray" is swimming then you want a swimming school or institute, not a pole vault one. The one similarity across all, however, are the demands of dedication and perseverance.

First Steps

Now, usually when a person starts to search for their corresponding order or school, they do not yet have the information or experience to recognize those of their own group or tribe. Almost all working schools either provide general training or have clear and unmistakable indications of their particular "style" from the beginning.

Most schools offering general training have a high dropout rate, but in many cases this is because while training in such a school the student becomes aware enough of themselves to start sounding their own note much more clearly. When this happens, they come into touch with a school or path that more accurately suits their own inner type or nature. They then leave the orig-inal school and join those of like nature. It is as though the first school acts as an opener of the way for them.

This pathworking series is no different. On this path you have the opportunity to go out on your own with only your personal resources to call upon the contact with the school of your own ray or type. The arrival of this contact in your actual life may take place a short time or a long time after you do the pathworking. This will depend on many factors.

Leo

The sign of Leo is appropriate to this path because it signals the self-absorbed personality par excellence. This is not to say that Leo natives are self-centered. They can be or their sense of self may play out in other ways. But the strong sense of self is what will allow you to call your own to you by sounding your own note, which is not necessarily the same as "blowing your own trumpet." The experiences you will have on this path are purely personal. It is definitely "all about me." Leo is also ruled by the first luminary, the sun, and the sun is often used as a representative of the true or higher self, toward which we all surely strive.

The Man

The Egyptian Mysteries are perhaps the earliest set of rituals of which we have complete and detailed records. Many magical lodges have drawn from these records to define their own magical practices, not least of which was the Order of the Golden Dawn.[26] Some core material from the Old Testament may rely upon a retelling of Egyptian material, the most notable being perhaps the story of "The Flood."[27] And the similarity of colors and posture that exist between representations of Isis with Horus and Mary with Jesus cannot go unmentioned.

---

26. Simon Magus, "A Victorian Gentleman in the Pharaoh's Court: Christian Egyptosophy and Victorian Egyptology in the Romances of H. Rider Haggard," *Open Cultural Studies* 1 (2017): 483–92, accessed December 10, 2019, https://doi.org/10.1515/culture-2017-0045.

27. The Flood is mentioned in E. A. Wallis Budge's book *The Book of the Dead* from the papyrus of Ani. The commentary on Chapter CLXXV (the chapter of not dying a second time) taken from the Naville and the Leyden papyri shows that the god Tem tells Ani of the flood to come and Ani and his wife being saved. Budge notes that it "contains the remains of the Herakleopolitan legend of the flood." E. A. Wallis Budge, *The Book of the Dead* (Secaucus: University Books Inc., 1984), 312.

It is said that the closer the source, the purer the water. In this working, I have chosen to call upon a power from the Egyptian mythos because I see it as one of the oldest Mysteries to have detailed records.

This man in the working is also a priest because it was understood that a priest was concerned with opening people to their own nature and to the nature of the divine, in and out of this world. The priest represents a doorway to the mysteries. In mystical teaching material, we frequently find references to the idea that the doorkeeper and the door are one. It is this door that is the opening, which, therefore, opens the ways for us.

The Wasteland

Once on the other side of the door we find a trackless wasteland. This idea featured in the Egyptian divine pantheon in descriptions of the jackal-headed god Anubis. It was said that this god could, like the jackal, find his way through the trackless wastelands. Another title for Anubis is "The Opener of the Ways." This setting ideally represents the opportunity for the practitioner to unfold into their particular style, ray, path, or way.

If you find a school, then you will proceed to satisfy yourself by using the questions suggested by our upper room guardian.

If you do not find a school within the working, wait a week or so and take the path again. But only do this repeat trip twice, making three trips in all. These workings put forces within you into motion and sometimes it takes time to see results. Just continue on with the next workings. You may get an indication that pops up later, or you may not. Not everyone studies with a school nor is everyone affiliated with a particular stream.

Other Factors

Because this is a highly unstructured working, there is not a lot to be said about the symbolism in the working. More can be said at this stage concerning the structure of these workings, as previously promised.

Each working of the last set of workings was accessed via the cave, either through the crystal or via the upper room of the cave. This means that we worked in the realms of the higher psyche via the medium of the astral consciousness. The work we did on these paths involved abstract principles, which need to be further "clothed" to come into everyday consciousness.

In the workings from the Journeys to Realms Within set, we worked on the settings themselves, establishing a base in the castle, an access to astral consciousness in the cave, an access to knowledge and thought in the tower, and an access to emotional intelligence in the grove.

The next workings will move onto another level and feature a different way of accessing the inner realms. By these techniques we are able to reach higher and higher abstractions using only the active imagination. The technique of the settings dictates the level that we access and the method by which the experiences of that level will be "stepped down": first to the astral level and then normal consciousness.

Pathworkings are more than fantasy journeys in that they are internally structured according to specific, psycho-spiritual principles worked out over the centuries that these techniques have been in use in magical training. They have also more recently been tested, especially those in this current book. This is always done by your author with small groups before offering the work for publication to ensure the workings are correct and safe.

———

Sooner or later in our spiritual journey we reach the point where we can sound out our own note strongly enough to be heard or to resonate with others of similar energies. It will not be long afterward that we will come to know those of a school or training group within our own tradition. This working encourages the process.

Path 8: The World Between Worlds

─────────── ✤ ───────────

In this working, you will be shown another room within your castle, which will be accessed via stone, spiral steps circling around to go up one level. The room will be set up as an alchemist's laboratory with benches, flasks, and other apparatuses. You will meet an alchemist who will show you how to use some kind of a device, a device that will effectively transport you to another realm via an interim realm. In the interim realm, you will encounter the challenge of wandering attention and a desire to just forget everything and remain. You will have to master this challenge, retain concentration. When you do get past this intermediate realm, you will be in a realm of nothingness. The challenge here will be to wait and allow manifestation to unfold. There you will encounter a being and what passes between the two of you will be private. When you are finished, you will return by the same route.

The purpose behind this working is to trigger an appreciation of the cross-over point between two options, states, or conditions. To acknowledge the cross-over point between options is to realize that what first appears to be two options is in reality the two edges of a field spread between. This working helps to foster the ability to see all the options that spread between what first appeared to be two opposites. In these workings we consider the field that stretches between polarities before going on, in the next working, to focus on the role of the polarities themselves.

Preamble

Make your way to the castle courtyard in the usual way. Cross the courtyard and enter the foyer that stands in front of the great hall.

163

Instead of leaving the castle to go to the cave as you've done previously, leave the great hall and look around the foyer that stands between the great hall and the outside courtyard. Here you will find a spiral stairway that leads upwards.

Take this spiral stairway and follow it until you have reached the doorway to an upper room. If your castle has a tower, then it is this tower that you have ascended. The door has the design of a simple empty circle upon it. Open the door and pass through.

THE PATHWORKING

You find yourself in a shadowy and dimly lit archaic laboratory. The exposed walls are made of fitted stone blocks and the floor and ceiling are made of large, gray square flagstones. Around the walls to the left and right are work benches with retorts and stands, burners and furnaces, strange metal boxes gleaming dully and, unless you are very much mistaken, what looks like some electronic bits and pieces.

The only light in this room comes from small windows high in the walls, and despite the fact that you know you have climbed up in the castle to come here, it almost seems that you are in a cellar or basement below ground level.

By the dim light you can see shelves of flasks and strange diagrams inscribed on parchment banners upon the walls. One diagram you might recognize: the Tree of Life diagram of the Qabalists. There's also a chart of the signs of the zodiac and a diagram of the Wheel of the Year. There are various diagrams of the human body showing vital organs, pressure points, meridians, astrological symbols. Other charts show images of animals or writings in other tongues, such as Chinese, Arabic, Sanskrit, Tibetan, or the hieroglyphs of the ancient Egyptians.

The far end of the room is in partial darkness. From these shadows there emerges a man wearing a skullcap and the garb of an alchemist of the Middle Ages. He smiles in welcome and approaches. The alchemist explains he has the means to transfer you to other realms of existence if you wish to go. He indicates a raised dais in the shadows at the end of the room and says that there you must stand to go on your journey.

Alongside the dais is what looks like a control console. The alchemist tells you that this is the power source for his device. He gives you a small metal box.

Look at it closely. It has two colored buttons, one green, one yellow. On the green button there is a diagram of six arrows radiating in to a central point. On the yellow button the arrows are reversed so that they radiate out from the central point. The man tells you that pressing the green button will send you to an intermediate zone called the World Between Worlds. It is an interchange place with many transfer circles, each identified by a unique number. Standing on a circle there, you press the yellow button to enter a parallel realm. To return, the process is reversed.

"But remember," he says, "You will need to check the identification mark of the circle in which you arrive so that you will know which one will return you to this lab." He smiles, raising an eyebrow.

The alchemist leads you to the dais at the end of the room, the control device in your hand. You mount the dais and notice that in the center of the floor there is the design for the astrological sign of Virgo.

The alchemist operates a hidden switch. There is a low hum, which signifies that power is being tapped and channeled. The air between the ceiling and the dais begins to glow like a cylinder of light within which you stand. You watch the man. Finally, he nods that all is ready, and says, "For this first trip, you should look for a circle marked with an equal-sided silver-colored triangle. Remember that, too."

You press the green button. The room about you shimmers and dims. There is a strange buzzing vibration. A dark green light encloses you, obscuring vision, and a feeling in the pit of your stomach tells you that the floor is no longer under your feet.

You do not fall, however, but start to rise. Slowly at first, but ever more rapidly you shoot upwards as though from deep water. The greenness starts to lighten and above you see a shimmering circle of light getting closer and closer. It gets rapidly larger until you seem to pass through it and are suddenly no longer moving.

You pause for breath. There is solid ground once more beneath your feet and you are standing on a light, metal circle surrounded by grass and medium-sized trees. This circle has a design inscribed upon it of a black square. The alchemist told you to remember this design for it is the way back.

Looking around you can see the reason for this as there are countless other metal circles set in the grass among the trees. They stretch into the bright, leafy greenness as far as the eye can see. You were also told which circle to travel on next: a silver triangle. You start looking for it. Remember to bring the control box with you.

As you walk among the discs, looking at their designs, you hear soft relaxing background music. Gentle breezes waft tantalizing perfumes, scents, and smells to you and the dappled green and sunlight overhead provides a restful and lulling light. It would be so nice to stop here. Time has no meaning. It has the feeling of eternity about it. No worries or cares. Just the pleasant dreaminess of rest from your troubles and woes. You will never want for anything here. Somehow you know this. No hunger, no cold, no unpleasant work, no demanding people, no family hassles. You feel a great urge to sit down and stay here, to drift in dreams and memories.

Resist. Resist for all you are worth. If you do not fight the euphoria and press on, you feel you may be trapped here, lost forever. Come. Quickly and urgently now. You must find the circle with the equal-sided silver triangle. Remember. Shake off the pleasantness.

There are all sorts of different designs and colors, but soon you locate the circle with the silver triangle. When you stand upon it, the hypnotic effects of this world start to diminish. You take a last look around and press the yellow button.

Once more the shimmering, vibrating starts as the ground disappears from under your feet and you are falling, very rapidly at first. All around you an impenetrable blackness closes in. Soon your rate of descent slows. It slows until it seems you stop. Yet, there is no ground beneath your feet. You are afloat in an all-engulfing blackness. You wait and wait. You strain to see in the blackness, to hear in the silence.

Nothing.

Perhaps you have made a mistake. You press the yellow button on the control box but it does not have any effect. Perhaps you are trapped in this limbo state. Yet, the alchemist told you that you would be in a parallel realm.

Listen. Did you hear voices singing or chanting softly? Yes, you did, you did.

Overhead, a pinpoint of light. Another. And another. Very quickly in a dome overhead there appears pinhole after pinhole of light until the sky is spangled with what you now see to be brilliant and twinkling stars. The stars are bright and hard in their newness. You feel the ground now under your feet and looking down you see, by the starlight, that you are standing on bare earth.

Look around. It is bare and flat as far as you can see. The sound of the voices continues and the ground begins to shape itself and form into mounds and depressions, hills and dales, and, in the distance of the star-outlined horizons, mountains and valleys.

The melody increases in volume. Listen to the beauty of it.

Suddenly, the notes change and shift to a brighter rhythm and a single deep, rich voice sounds out from the background. Ahead, the sky begins to lighten. You are to witness the first sunrise of this realm. Watch.

The singing continues as the disc of the sun rises quickly and eagerly over the mountains ahead of you. As that first brilliant shaft of light runs across the land from east to west, there springs up in its path a rich green grass. It spreads rapidly to cover the whole world. As the sun climbs higher, the singing intensifies yet again as trees spring up, growing rapidly. Then, shrubs and undergrowth pop up as well. The world is filled with a vast variety of types and profusion of shade and color. An incredibly perfumed breeze plays about you.

Nearby, you hear the silver sound of water running and watch in wonder as a rivulet appears, running its path across the forested land. You know that somewhere creeks and mighty rivers are forming, and far away you can almost hear the sound of the first ocean tumbling against the first shore.

The singing changes again, throwing the rich, deep, beautiful voice into highlight. You look to the east and shield your eyes. Coming toward you is a Golden Radiance, and in the wake of this being all kinds of animals spring into existence. They follow serenely and nobly behind this great Golden Radiance. The sound of the singing increases, louder and louder as the Radiance approaches until the sound is all about you. There is a slight pause as though this whole creation held its breath for a moment, waiting.

In this magic moment it may be that the being before you communicates something to your mind…

The Radiance passes you and the animals follow. Somewhere, sometime, humanity may begin a cycle of existence on this world. You might want to wish them more love, more wisdom than we experience in our normal daily world, although you know that mistakes will still have to be made if the lessons of life are to be learned and understood.

It is time now to return. Take a last look around.

That's odd. There is something strangely familiar about that particular rise in the ground ahead and the nearby forest. And what about those hills beyond the rivulet of water to the right? Don't they remind you of something?

Perhaps not.

Listen for a last moment to the chorus of creation. Then press the button.

The scenery shimmers and vibrates. You are wrapped in the deep sea-green and as you feel yourself float free, you begin to rise. Faster and faster you go, the green getting lighter as you shoot up toward the bright circle overhead.

Once more you find yourself in the World Between Worlds. The disc on which you stand bears the silver-colored triangle. You notice a small circle of woven grass resting on the disc. You pick it up and see that it slips easily onto your finger. You leave it on your finger and look around at the grass, the trees, and the other discs to get your bearings.

Start off in search of your first disc, the one with the black square. It will be fairly easy to find, but as you are tempted with the perfumes, the lights, and the sounds, remember to keep your concentration. Stay awake and resist the hypnotic charm of this realm.

You find this a little easier to do now having once experienced it, and each time you come here you will get better at avoiding the enchantment of this land. However, always be on your guard as this realm may come up with new tricks to distract you from time to time.

You find the disc and stand upon it, pressing the yellow button. The familiar process occurs again so that you find yourself falling, enclosed in blackness.

The descent stops and you feel the floor supporting your feet. Gradually your sight clears and the laboratory comes into view around you. There is a humming sound now dying away as the alchemist looks up from his console. He smiles at you and nods that you may now leave the dais.

As you step down, you hand back the control box to the man and thank him for his assistance. He conducts you to the far door, the one by which you entered, and indicates a large open book on a table. He asks you to sign his visitors' book before you depart and then returns to his work.

You sign the book. Have a quick look to see if there are any names there that you know. Then you return through the doorway and down the spiral stairs to the great hall of the castle. Here you sit down as usual and place the circle of woven grass on the table before reviewing the events of the working. When you're ready, return to normal consciousness in the usual way.

Discussion

This pathworking will take you along the inner tracks of your mind to the source of creativity within your own self. It is based upon chapter 3—"The Wood Between the Worlds"—of *The Magician's Nephew* by C. S. Lewis, which is a part of the author's *The Chronicles of Narnia* series. In this chapter, the main characters find themselves using yellow and green rings to travel via puddles in a forest to other worlds.[28]

The Other World

When C. S. Lewis first wrote *The Lion, The Witch and The Wardrobe* in the 1950s, he put forward the idea of another world that was accessible by magical means to the people of this world. Of course, he was not the first one to do this and we have many stories of magical worlds in the tales of our childhood.

The world of our ordinary senses that we know so well is essentially a world of effects, a world in which we act and in which we see things happen. And yet, the causes for all that we see and experience are to be found in the magical world that exists behind this normal, everyday reality.

It is from this other world, a world I call the "Dreamtime World," that our normal experience arises. It is into this world that all that is gone or outmoded passes away eventually. It is both a world of past and a world of future. It is the world in which myths and legends and fairy tales are true and occurring right at this moment, now as they always have and indeed always will.

I don't know whether C. S. Lewis realized at the beginning of this first book of Narnia the scope that was to follow in the set of chronicles that finally eventuated. What began as a story of the world of Narnia, into which the children of the story pass and enjoy adventures, returning again at a later time, developed into the concept of a whole range of possible worlds that exist independently of this one and of each other.

This idea is found in the mystical philosophies of many lands and times. From the descriptions of the stages of enlightenment of the Buddhists, through

---

28. C. S. Lewis, *The Chronicles of Narnia Volume VI: The Magician's Nephew* (Hong Kong: Enrich Spot Ltd., 2016), 22–31.

the realms of Asgard, to the spheres of the Tree of Life of the Qabalists, there is almost an all-pervading notion among humanity that a number of worlds exist independently: choirs of angels, domains of demons, worlds of fantasy and fairy, worlds of joy, and worlds of horror. Each world having its own order of existence much as one might conceive the orders of angels and archangels so well known in the Christian tradition.

The Box and the Intermediate Zone

Through a mechanism of magical rings, the children in *The Magician's Nephew* are enabled to travel out of the world of normal sense. They do not travel directly into one of the other worlds. Instead, they land in a type of intermediate zone.

This world appears to be an inter-dimensional gateway to a number of different realms. In fact, such a realm does exist, for the power these stories hold depends upon the degree to which they accord with reality. Behind this world there is indeed another world of causes—in fact, several such worlds, each with their own functions, each with their own inhabitants, each with their own type of existence.

If we are to enter any of these worlds and make contact with the realities therein, we must first place ourselves into the correct frame of mind. It is this frame of mind that is the bridge between the worlds. We must induce this special state of consciousness that is itself the world between worlds.

The Role of Attention

To enter this state of consciousness in this world between worlds, the first step is to turn the mind away from the normal world of experience. It's not a turning away that removes our awareness of the normal world, but one in which the emphasis of attention changes.

The second feature of this stage of consciousness is that the attention turned away must be directed to its goal with the fullest concentration possible. From the present day to the times of old, wizards and witches have used their own special ritual of mental techniques to achieve this state of mind, either working alone or in the groups of which they are members. The ritual often involves casting a magical circle to set apart the place in which they work from the world of normal existence around them.

Indeed, this circle becomes the true "magic ring." Once the place in which they work has been set apart, the wizards and the witches are able to bring into their area realities and powers of the other worlds, calling forth demons and gods alike—or so we read in the grimoires and testimonies that have been handed down to us. While these manifestations may very rarely be literally and physically true, effects do occur in magic circles and upon such matters, those who have not experienced the powers and presences for their own selves are not qualified to comment.

The state of mind one is trying to reach in this pathworking is very closely related to the state of mind found in a hypnotic trance, with one important exception. For this pathworking, not only is the attention fully under the control of the operator but also perceptions of both inner and outer realities are heightened rather than dulled.

This bubble in consciousness, mirroring the bubble in a magic circle, is a place where both inner and outer worlds touch and coalesce, where there are more realities than normally experienced, and in this way a gateway is opened to the other realms and communication may pass both ways through this gate.

This magic circle is a world between worlds and the particular world contacted depends upon the keys and symbols used in the magical ritual concerned. However, we may approach the other worlds purely through conscious techniques alone, without the use of ritual, for ritual has only ever been an aid to mental techniques, never the power in itself.

The Role of Symbols

To return again to the story by C. S. Lewis, we find we are presented with the idea of a world that, as yet, does not exist. The children, who are of course the heroes of the story, travel to this world and find themselves with the absence of all sensation, except for a firm footing beneath their feet. From that moment on, they witness the creation of one of these inner realms.

Such an experience is the fountainhead of our own inner creativity and to witness creation among the inner realms is to tap the source of that creativity. In this pathworking, you will pass symbolically from normal existence through the world between worlds, or intermediate zone, to another realm where you will witness creation occurring. This journey is performed through the manipulation of symbols within the visual imagination and this is the way of telling your inner self what you require of it. Having passed through the door of our consciousness to the realm of the visual imagination, we then begin our pathworking.

The Alchemist

The normal consciousness is represented by an alchemist's laboratory. It is here that we meet the alchemist who symbolizes to us the part of ourselves that knows the techniques. This is why the alchemist explains to us the way to travel between the worlds.

Changes in consciousness are often associated with bodily feelings too, especially those of rising or falling. It is these experiences that we encounter in moving from the normal mode of consciousness, represented by the laboratory, to the first intermediate stage of consciousness—the world between worlds.

This world between worlds is a very dangerous place. We must keep our wits about us, for having turned our attention away from the normal world of experience it is very easy for us to lose our bearings. We must stay alert to what is occurring if we are to continue on in the way we intend and not get lost in this limbo state.

Virgo

The sign of Virgo is seen in the alchemist's room as a symbol for fulfilling oneself. One of the titles for Virgo is the "Bountiful Virgin" and the sign has an associated symbol of a cornucopia, spilling out fruits.

There has been much discussion on the real meaning of the word *virgin* among the members of the various groups with which I have engaged in magical work. These vary in the degree of strict scholarship as compared with intuitional recovery of far-knowledge. It is certainly the case that we frequently use the word *virgin* in place of the phrase *virgin intact*. I am saying that the word *virgin* has more than the one meaning in addition to its use as a short form of the full phrase describing the common meaning—someone who has not had sexual intercourse.

The word itself has more to do with completeness and containment than merely related to sexual acts. By appending the word *intact* we indicate that someone is complete by virtue of not having had intercourse. However, there are other ways in which someone may be complete, which relates more to the degree to which one can be fulfilled out of their own self. It is the word *need* on which the meaning hinges. In the more general sense, the idea can apply equally to any gender, the expressing of an archetype through reality.

The idea of the astrological Virgo is one that can fulfill their needs out of themselves alone. All that they need, all that they achieve, can be brought about from their own selves without the help of others.

I am not saying that Virgo natives are like this. The idea of the sun signs is to indicate the task that we have in this incarnation. A fully balanced spiritual being will have the capabilities of all the signs. Indeed, we all have these already in potential. But, the task for this incarnation we live in today is to recognize, develop, and strengthen the qualities of the sun sign under which we are born.

The Same Principle in Different Modes

Each sign has positive and negative characteristics. Well, strictly speaking, they are the same characteristics, but applied differently. Let's take Virgo for example. Many Virgo natives are perceived as overly critical, unfeeling, out of touch with their emotions, pedantic, nit-picking, and so on. However, when the Virgo native realizes that these qualities are for use to help themselves become independently bountiful and not to force onto others, then the skills become positive.

Distinctions and Boundaries

Another idea drawn from the symbolism of Virgo is the ability to draw fine distinctions to enable one to make clear categories. Virgo natives deal similarly in the mental realms. This leads to a clear perception of how things are or how things fit together. All science, logic, and mathematics relies upon the correct application of this skill. From the categories produced, which are sometimes purely mental constructs, patterns can be seen that lead to explanations of life, the universe, and everything else, so to speak. Drawing boundaries of meaning often needs a pedantic approach. For example, when marking the boundary between your property and your neighbor's, it is wise to be precise and exact to prevent misunderstandings and recriminations later.

The Task of the Incarnation

As an aside here, I would like to emphasize that we each have our own tasks for the incarnation we are currently living in. It is through multiple incarnations that we reach balance. Many ideas from popular and popularized psychology do not allow for multiple incarnations and extol the virtues of being balanced in this one life. The last thing a Virgo native wants to get involved in is "getting in touch with their feelings." This would take them away from the task of the incarnation that happens to be at odds with this. The being they are will deal with these skills in other incarnations and indeed may already have done so. We are multidimensional beings showing only a limited part of ourselves in incarnation so that we may work on that part. Each of the sun signs dictates the task of the incarnation to the native of that sign. Anything else is avoidance.

The Magic of the Between

In many circumstances, the in-between state or world has or confers magical powers. For example, I was taught by the head of my Order that the stones for creating runes should be gathered from the shore between the high and low water marks.[29] Many heroes of legend had a curse put upon them concerning their death and this often involved in-between states, such as "neither on land nor on water" or "neither on the ground nor in the air" and so on. Llew of Welsh legend had such a curse and his wife assisted her lover, Goronwy, to construct the circumstances necessary for Llew to be killed.

So at one and the same time, the twixt-state was magical in that it conferred almost invulnerability to some heroes and danger in that it was also the prescription for their demise.

We meet the dangers of the in-between state every day when we attempt to communicate and find ourselves falling into the gap between word and meaning. This gap is large enough to keep an army of philosophers in work for all eternity!

On the more mystical side, Charles Williams in his Arthurian poetry cycle refers to the mystery of the way that, as he sees it, every woman can show forth the goddess by using the expression "the gap between the Queen and the

---

29. By "rune stones" here I am using the term generically for any stones that are marked with particular deigns and then used for meditation or foretelling. Mine are marked with some symbols given to me by my teacher.

Queen's meaning."[30] In Egyptian mythology, Anubis was the Walker between Worlds. This idea of one who can operate in two worlds at once via the in-between state relates to the magical skill of mediation, which is quite different from mediumship.

Mediator and Medium

Let's look at how a medium and mediator differ in how they operate in two worlds at once.

Dion Fortune in her book *Spiritualism in the Light of Occult Science* deals with the subject of mediumship extensively. A general summary of her work describes mediumship as the taking over of the incarnate personality of a medium by the discarnate or non-incarnate entity coming through.[31] The medium usually has no recollection or only vague recollection of what transpires.

With the skill of mediating, so highly regarded in magical orders, the operator maintains consciousness in two states via an in-between state where the mediator and the entity commune. The operator is a conscious and vital participant in the communication process. It is this process that has "brought through" much of the inner teachings of mind and cosmology put out by the orders of the Western Esoteric Tradition.

Stages and Challenges

The study of spiritual pathology concerns itself with the experiences of people who follow a spiritual discipline. Many such people get stuck at a particular stage along their path. They begin to enjoy the experiences they are having in their practices and forget the end result that they originally intended to achieve.

Whatever the technique that they practice, whether it be magical ritual or meditation, transpersonal psychotherapy, or whatever else, they enter an initial euphoric bliss. It is only when awareness and concentration are kept unwaveringly upon the goal that this euphoric state can be transcended and real growth and creativity take place. Zen Buddhists referred to this initial, bubbly state reached by novices by the ungracious term "Zen stink."

---

30. Charles Williams, *Taliessin Through Logres* (London: Oxford University Press,1938), 65.

31. Dion Fortune, *Spiritualism in the Light of Occult Science* (London: Rider, 1931).

It is interesting to note that this state of mind, represented by the world between worlds, can be induced in a number of quite ordinary ways. The taking of some mind-altering substances, for example, can produce this state of mind to some extent.

At the other extreme, you may experience this mode of consciousness by walking for half an hour around a modern city's busy indoor shopping complex. In fact, the next time you are in such a place try this little experiment: keep your attention directed on the people around you, particularly taking note of the expressions on the faces and in the eyes. This attempt at controlling your own attention will highlight for you the factors in the environment that seek to change your consciousness, flipping you unsuspectingly into the euphoric state of the world between worlds.

Disorientation and Suggestibility

Normally, when you unsuspectingly fall into the euphoric state in the world between worlds, this would place you in such an indecisive and wavering state. This allows you to be open to whatever suggestions are put forward to you, which, in the example of the shopping complex, lead you to subscribe to this or that product or store.

Disorientation is a major factor in persuasion. The techniques vary, including, for instance, the common predilection toward placing the interior of shopping complexes at an angle to the outside paths and roadways.

Other Options

The world between worlds in the pathworking consists of a fairly open parkland forest with a number of small discs or circles set into the grass, each of these circles being a gateway to another world. In this particular representation of the pathworking, these circles are numbered so that you may know one from the other and not inadvertently transport yourself to a realm that requires skills beyond your present capabilities.

However, once you have had some experience with pathworkings in general, and this one in particular, it may be possible for you to begin exploring the realms that will open up to you from the world between worlds and to keep track of what sort of realms are found with which numbers and code letters.

I would suggest that a considerable amount of reading of mystical philosophies be required to provide you with the information needed for you to understand what you may experience in exploring these worlds. However, in the euphoric world of this pathworking, we need only keep our attention directed firmly upon the circle we must locate and battle our tendencies to wander off course, seeking only to find that particular circle and to pass through its gateway into the realms of creativity.

Nothingness

Once in the realm of creativity, we encounter the experience of nothingness, dark nothingness, for it is out of apparent nothingness that all is created. An ancient maxim runs *ex nihilo nihil fit*—nothing comes out of nothing. It could not be more untrue, as normally interpreted. The motto is usually taken to mean that if you want something, you can't get it out of nothing. A better interpretation of the motto tells you the origin of nothing or nothingness. It comes out of itself. It is self-sustaining, not created. It does not say that "something" cannot come out of "nothing." It only speaks of where "nothing" comes from. For all of the worlds emerge out of nothingness and will eventually return to nothingness. That of which we are not, at any moment, aware does not, for us, exist, and is nothing.

Music of Creation

The music we hear in the pathworking again relates to the sign of Virgo—the "Bountiful Virgin." The symbol of the cornucopia shows this process of creating out of nothing.

From the pregnant darkness of possibility wherein we find ourselves there begins the creation of a world and we are present to witness that wonderful event. According to occult tradition, the basis for all existence is that of vibration, and the vibration we understand the most of all is the vibration of sound. Magic words spoken by wizards and witches alike are intoned with the proper sonorous vibration of voice if they are to be effective. We can turn to the Christian tradition to see in the gospel of John, a mystical gospel, that "in the beginning was the word." [32]

---

32. King James Bible, John 1:1.

C. S. Lewis has followed the same concept in *The Magician's Nephew* in envisaging a realm that is brought into existence by music, a world that is sung into creation. There is a great power in song. These secrets were known to the bards of old but have been all but lost to our common knowledge, for these people traveled from kingdom to kingdom and from court to court creating through the songs that they sang worlds of fairy tales and myths in the minds of their listeners. They brought alive the stories of old keeping their audience tuned to the heritage of their tradition.

In a similar way, we experience in this pathworking that inner song which brings forth creation in the realms within. Indeed, every facet of our psyche can be brought into activity by some particular keynote or vibration rate. Once we understand this, we begin to understand how to effect creation in the world around us. For if we know the keynote of an idea and can, so to speak, sound it forth, it will indeed become real in the world around us.

Life

Finally, we do not talk here about creation for its own sake, for that is a creation that is devoid of spiritual life. The realms to be brought into being are created on principles, created to be ensouled by divine energies. During this experience of creation you will meet, in some form or other, the principle of divinity—the Golden Radiance—that stands behind creativity from your point of view. This could be any symbol or figure, but it will be the one that has called forth the creation of the world you experience and which, to you, represents the divine life behind all true creations of art and science. Your meeting with this divine principle is a sacred moment of great importance.

Eventually, you take your leave and return again through the world between worlds. For this euphoric non-action state of being is interposed between the pole of creative urge and the pole of action in the world.

There is no end to the great works of art and theories of science that have failed to come into existence through the wavering and indecisive state of mind of those responsible for their manifestation. You, however, will keep your intention upon your destination—the alchemist's laboratory—to which you will return and thereby symbolize the return of your inner creative principle into the normal world around you. Coming once more into the laboratory, you will thank the alchemist for his help and this completes the working.

Each time that you do this working, the world between worlds will have a lesser hold upon you and the inner creativity that you are tapping will become more and more at your disposal in your everyday life. As you do this, you will also become more aware of the tendency to fall into euphoria in your normal everyday existence. Thus, you will be led to resist this destructive state. Once you can avoid this destructive state, creativity will flow once more into your everyday life, enriching it and leading you onward to inner growth and a fuller life.

Interlude: Realms Unknown

$\div$

At this point in our journey we will take a slight sidestep. This interlude marks the boundary between the preparation and consolidation work that have already been done and the character of the workings that are to follow. It represents a boundary between preparatory work and further deeper work.

There is only the one working in this interlude and it takes place within the grounds of the castle. The goal of this pathworking will be to link the current achievements to the earlier workings in preparation for the different style of pathworkings in the final series, Journeys to Realms Beyond.

The realm of this one working is titled "unknown" because it is in consolidation of prior learning and experiences that we find additional meanings unknown and not seen at the time. The unknown becomes known, the previously known is enriched and consolidated, and the way is prepared for learning and experience at a deeper level.

The Nameless Path

---†---

The paths beyond this one will have a different character, as will become clear when you tread them. Every path except this one has a symbolic relationship to a zodiac sign. If those paths were shells of a collection, this path would be the box in which they are kept. If the other paths were different precious gems at a jeweler's shop, this path would be the black velvet on which they are spread for viewing. This path is a container, the background of a painting, the screen upon which static or streamed images appear, the power behind the throne, the ideals rarely mentioned against which you live your life.

At the start of this pathworking, there will be a formal rose garden in the castle grounds tended by a young woman. She will take you around the garden and among the roses using the flowers to suggest teachings and lessons to be learned. She will invite you to go out of the castle and to her cottage where her mother, father, and grandmother live. Along the way there will be a man who is tending sheep and he will ask you a question. You will be invited into the cottage and asked another question. While in the cottage, the woman's grandmother will also ask you a question. However, you won't be required to reply. In the cottage you will see a specific vision within the fire and then finally return to the garden. It is likely that answers to these experiences will not be found until later, possibly in your everyday life.

The purpose of this working is not to provide specific experiences but the sense of a backdrop to all experience.

Preamble

You find yourself in the great hall of the castle. Pause and look around, then make your way outside into the courtyard. Turn left and walk around to the side of the castle where there is a small courtyard and a formal rose garden.

You realize that there is a very young woman crouched down using a trowel on the rich soil. She stands as you walk toward her and you see that she is a young maiden beautifully dressed in fine clothes.

——————————— THE PATHWORKING ———————————

The young woman invites you to walk with her along the paths that run between the beds of the many varieties of rose.

She smiles at you and indicates the roses saying, "These are my teachers. They have a beauty of form, color, and perfume. But, they have their thorns to catch the unwary. I know from them that greatness can come from misery, like a rose ascending a ladder of thorns. The theme of mixed joy and pain is shown by the way they give forth their best when pruned back to almost to nothing in winter. No matter how great their beauty, it will fade and pass. But the next spring it will return."

She tells you that her mother, father, and grandmother live in a small cottage outside the castle, not far away over the hills. She suggests that you go and visit them and she may give you her name by way of introduction.

As you turn to take your leave she asks you to wait a moment. She says, "I am charged to ask you a question. You may find the answer on this path. You may already know the answer from other paths. But the answer is not for me, it is for you."

You wait a moment looking into her fresh, young face. She smiles. "What is transient?" she asks and then turns back to her roses.

You go back to the courtyard and leave the castle. Then turning, you walk around the castle and off through the grassy fields toward the open spaces and rolling hills. It is a lovely day and the walk is pleasant.

After a while, you see some sheep near a stand of shade trees and you walk toward them. As you get closer, you see a shepherd with them. He turns to face you as you approach and you see the face of a mature, strong man who has spent a lot of his life in the open air.

He smiles and comes to greet you. Gesturing to the sheep he says, "These are my teachers. To the uninitiated they seem stupid. But consider this: they are gentle, yet can stand their ground, and if necessary, defend what is theirs. They wander together, taking the grass, sharing the available resources without hoarding. Where one goes, the others follow, yet they have no leader. They produce cloth for our backs, ever-renewing. And in springtime, the lambs revel and play with sheer joy of life. Until I have learned these lessons, I have no need to look elsewhere for instruction."

He smiles again, a full warm smile, and says, "I am going back to the cottage, and I would like you to come with me. But first, I must ask you a question. The answer is not for me, it is for you. What has meaning?"

He walks off over the fields and hills and you go with him. Soon, you see a simple stone cottage with a garden nestled just below the brow of one of the rolling hills.

As you approach, you look at the garden full of flowers, shrubs, shade trees, food crops, and fragrant herbs. A noticeably pregnant woman is working in the garden. She stands to wait your approach.

The shepherd greets the smiling woman with a loving kiss. He introduces her as his partner. She smiles at you from a radiant face and says, "Welcome to our humble home."

She gestures to the gardens and says, "These are my teachers, the flowers, the shrubs, the earth itself. What comes from here feeds us and what we do not use goes back again to the soil. Left to itself, not a lot would come from it. But farmed too hard and it would lose its power of renewal. Working in harmony with it, we produce paradise. And remember that the word 'paradise' comes from the Latin word for garden."

She gestures toward the cottage, "Please, come inside and rest a moment. And, of course I have a question for you." Her eyes twinkle, "What is stability?"

She then turns and leads the way inside.

You duck under the low lintel and enter the simple cottage. Pallets at one side show where the inhabitants sleep. Near another wall there is an eating area. Despite the cool stone, the cottage is warm inside from a wood fire in a large hearth. Near the hearth an old woman sits. She looks up and smiles at you as you stand inside the doorway.

The mother-to-be goes to stand in the center of the room and the man joins her. He says, "Please. Sit by the fire with grandmother."

You do as requested and turn to look at the grandmother. She watches you with a gaze that seems alert and full of wisdom.

"Hello, my child," The grandmother says. "This place is not always easy to find. Nor does it always appear as it does now. But when you have need, you are welcome to come and see us and we will offer what help we can."

She pauses, then continues, "I am going to show you something, but first, as you might guess, I have a question for you to ponder. Take your time thinking over these questions. They may have more than one answer. They may have levels within levels of answers. Use them as a journey of exploration into yourself. You have heard three questions already. Mine is the fourth and last of the set. What is eternal?"

She then indicates the fire with its glowing embers and small flames. She uses a poker to move the logs to the side to let the heat radiate out.

"This fire is my teacher," she says. "It can be yours as well. Look into the fire and let your mind relax and await the vision I have prepared for you. "

You look into the embers and relax. Patterns start to form, patterns of reddish light with black and orange and some blue. Swirling, resolving into outlines of continents, slowly shifting and changing shapes.

A glow begins at one point, grows, and spreads and you realize that you are seeing the spread of humankind across the globe long ago when the continents themselves were still forming.

Other glows begin and rise and spread in the same way on a smaller scale. You realize you are seeing the rise and fall of civilizations, the main center of activity moving from different spots.

You see the blossoming of peoples of power in the islands of what is now the Pacific Ocean. Then you see their eventual destruction by the fire of a thousand volcanoes, ringing the ocean as continents tear apart from each other. You see small dots of bright amid the resulting darkness of the coals and know that human kind has survived, and changed.

You see the crystal palaces and light-powered machines of the peoples of a great Atlantic civilization. Again, you see it all destroyed by inundation as the earth changes once more, whether by nature alone, or with the help of humans. You watch as the remnants of those survivors spread to begin new expanding glows in Africa, the Mediterranean, and in the Americas.

The spread of people continues in larger and smaller waves across land bridges that are covered with water behind them, the Bering Strait, the English Channel, the islands north of Australia.

The Egyptian dynasties pulse as they spread and retract, and you see the spread of different groups across Europe and Asia, across early land bridges and island hopping across the earth. You see the Roman legions spreading over Europe and into Egypt and the hordes of Mongolia being led to their promised land against all obstacles.

Not all of these blossomings are of the sword. You see the spread of learning, fiery strands criss-crossing through Alexandria, through Spain, through Italy.

Then, you see a different type of fire rising and spreading. You watch as the Black Death ravages Europe, syphilis too. Then there's smallpox spreading and being carried to faraway places. You see these things right up to the present day, and you realize that these symbiotic strands have always been rising and spreading and are rising and spreading now and always will. For life of all kinds proceeds like this.

Around and within all of this, there are other spreading patterns: patterns of spiritual light. Rays from Tibet, Stonehenge, Luxor, Tara Hill, Uluru, North India, the Middle East, central China, Japan, and many more. Lights and fires spread by wandering initiates leaving trails behind them that spread in spot fires.

You feel there may be answers to your questions here. Watch the patterns in the fire and ponder them—what is transient, what is stable, what is eternal, what has meaning?

Gradually, the flames expand to full view. They come out of the fire and spread into the room, surrounding you without burning. You turn to look into the room and the grandmother is no longer there.

In the center of the room you see the pregnant woman turning on the spot, counter sunwise. As she turns, she changes from wife and mother to grandmother to daughter and mother again. Slowly the man joins the dance, walking in a sunwise circle with his head turned inwards to constantly face the changing woman

The flames flow out and surround them, circling the same way as the man and rising up toward the ceiling.

The flames become smaller and dance near the ceiling, interweaving and swapping positions, now fast, now slow.

Suddenly, falling like gentle rain, flecks of white fleece and red rose petals fall all around, unceasing. They cover the floor, the people, and you. As this gentle rain falls all around, the red and the white, you are suffused with a pink light that grows and grows to obscure all vision. You are bathed in the pinkness. You feel its gentleness, its strength, its love, its power.

Gradually, it fades and you are back in the fields again with nothing else around. No people, no house, no sheep.

You make your way back over the fields and hills to the castle. When you enter the castle, you look toward the rose garden, but there is no one there. Now you realize, if you have not already done so, that this garden is the very same one you visited at the start of these journeys. It was there all along.

You enter the hall and sit at the round table to ponder the questions, closing your eyes. When you open them, you see in the center of the round table a long-stemmed, red rose with fresh dew on its petals. After a pause, you return by your normal method to your place of working.

Discussion

This is a very special path and somewhat different to others. It is for this reason that this discussion will take a different form from others in the previous series.

Rather than seek directly to elucidate or indirectly to hint at the symbolism on this path, it would be a good idea if you researched these for yourselves. This path is a personal path. The symbols have been experienced personally and their meanings will need to be sought out personally.

The symbols used on this path include a rose garden, maiden, sheep, a shepherd, the cottage garden, the mother, the grandmother or Crone, the fire of scrying, the dance, rose petals, fleece, and a rose. What follows are a few personal notes about some of these symbols.

The Rose Garden

Traditionally, the rose gardens of the English and European style have created a formal setting. If you looked at a rose garden from above, you would see a design that is not unlike a mandala. Like many mandalas, these gardens are often laid out in a four-fold pattern.

A mandala is a diagram that represents an organizing principle. Behind these pathworkings there are a couple of organizing principles, the most obvious of which is the relation each path has with signs of the zodiac. This particular path, however, does not relate to a specific sign and stands more as the central point or idea about which the others revolve.

Rose gardens frequently feature a central bed or item that acts as the pivot for the whole layout. This might be some benches, or a particular and spectacular specimen of rose, or some other focus point. In the same way, this working contains the focus points for the pathworking program as a whole.

The Characters

There are four obvious characters in this working. Three are female and one is male. The female characters are of different ages and represent the threefold goddess in the forms of Maiden, Mother, and Crone. A fifth character is implied because the woman portraying the Mother aspect is pregnant. This is the Child of Promise and together with the man and the mother gives us another Pagan trinity of Lord, Lady, and Child.

The Lady as the goddess is never-changing and ever-changing. The Lord, however, lives a life cycle of youth, manhood, kingship, defeat or sacrifice, and rebirth as the Child of Promise. The hero or sacrificed king drama takes place against a backdrop of the eternal feminine, the goddess ground of all existence. These are all introductions to mystical concepts under the guise of ordinary things. The characters represent principles rather than actual males or females.

The Rose

The rose is the flower par excellence. It buds and blooms on a ladder of thorns.[33] It has been used through the ages to represent spiritual unfoldment out of adversity; the blooming of the inner nature in the material world. The lotus has also been used to symbolize this quality, rising as it does into a beautiful flower rooted in the mire on the bed of the water hole where it occurs.

As a symbol of enfoldment, the rose has appeared in the emblems and doctrines of many magical and spiritual orders. These range from the many flavors of Rosicrucianism, to A. E. Waite's Fellowship of the Rosy Cross, and the Order of the Golden Dawn, which placed emphasis on the tools of the rose cross lamen and the lotus wand. Generally, we can consider most of these as parts of the multistranded Order of the Rose, which traces back through Middle Eastern origins.[34]

---

33. A phrase used by Leonard Cohen in his song "The Window."

34. I use a rose wand, rather than the usual lotus wand.

In China, spiritual groups often combined martial arts into their magical practices and disciplines, such as in the mystical Pavilion of the White Lotus, and at times some of these were behind militant action for social and political change, actions such as the Boxer Rebellion.[35]

Plants and Animals

The references to plants and animals as teachers indicate that the natural world is the best demonstration of how things are. Nature is, if you will, a "given." As such, it is our best teacher not only of the nature of things but also of what lies behind the surface appearances.

The doctrine of signatures, an ancient guide that herbalists used to find plants for various ailments, associated plants that looked liked certain body parts as being able to heal those same body parts. It is the use of this doctrine that leads us to suppose that ginseng, which has a root more or less in the shape of the human body, will work its healing upon the whole person. The Hermetic axiom "That which is above is like that which is below and that which is below is like that which is above, but after another fashion" is another way of proposing the doctrine of signatures, among other things.

From our studies of the natural realm, we can also come to know our own place in the scheme of things for we are all a part of nature, not separate from it. We are no more entitled to regard ourselves as guardians of it than we are entitled to regard ourselves as owners of it. Both views artificially place us outside of it.

Ursula Le Guin said, "But we, insofar as we have power over the world and over one another, we must learn to do what the leaf and the whale and the wind do of their own nature."[36]

The ancient Indian doctrine of *ahimsa*, or *harmlessness*, relates to this idea. Here I mean the doctrine of ahimsa in its more esoteric rather than popular aspects. Indeed this is a very deep study here, which can lead, some say, to enlightenment.

Since nature, which includes us, shows how things are, it can also show us spiritual principles. In the 1970s, there was a lot of work done by some psychol-

---

35. Joseph W. Esherick, "Chapter 2: Sects, Boxers, and Popular Culture," in *The Origins of the Boxer Uprising* (Oakland: University of California Press, 1988), 38–67.

36. Ursula K. Le Guin and Gail Garraty, *The Farthest Shore* (New York: Atheneum, 1972), 75.

ogists of the transpersonal school on the psychological dimensions of spiritual disciplines.

In one such study a Rorschach, or "inkblot" test was administered to different groups of practitioners of a particular Buddhist tradition. The separate groups were made up of students at particular identifiable levels of attainment in the practices, from beginners to masters. In these tests, the subjects described what they saw in the design or what it suggested to them.

All of the subjects reported seeing various things, as would be expected. However, those of the masters group used the perceived item to illustrate principles of Buddhism, in particular transition and the arising and passing away of form and energy.[37]

Reality is similarly ambiguous in that we can see it in many ways. When several people witness a stressful event, they may give quite different accounts of what transpired. Even in everyday life we all notice different things and the difference in focus tells us a lot about the interests of our own selves and others.

If you ask directions from a devout churchgoer, you may receive instructions in terms of religious buildings and landmarks. If you ask someone who recently checked out new cars before buying one, you may get your itinerary in terms of car suppliers. Similarly, when a new student of the Qabalah looks around, they see everything in terms of the Tree of Life.

Because of this quality of the reality as perceived by us, we can also see in it the teachings of the well-known and not-so-well-known teachers of the past— Buddha, Lao-tse, Meng-tse, Jesus, Gurdjieff, Idries Shah, and Baba Ram Dass, for example. There are also the words of Western Esoteric Tradition teachers such as W. B. Yeats, Aleister Crowley, Charles Williams, Dion Fortune, W. E. Butler, Gareth Knight, and Dolores Ashcroft-Nowicki of this branch of the tradition in particular.

The Fire

The essence of divination is the seeing of patterns. Patterns can be seen as structures or patterns in space. They can be seen as cycles or patterns in time. In this pathworking, we view the spread of humanity, the spread of civilization, the

---

37. Daniel P. Brown and Jack Engler, "The Stages of Mindfulness Meditation: A Validation Study," *The Journal of Transpersonal Psychology* 12, no. 2 (1980): 143–92.

spread of learning, and the spread of disease as organic processes having the same pattern. That pattern is life.

In the movie *The Matrix*, the Smith character likens humanity to a virus. The analogy holds not so much because humanity is often a destroyer of its environmental resources, but more because the two are similar as both are life forms that are neither "good" nor "bad" in themselves.

If we understand the organic growth behind all things, we will recognize where the cycle of events is in our own lives—mundane and spiritual. We will come to know what is to come. Then when it does come, we will be ready.

All of these cycles contain phases of expansion and contraction and in this they relate to the "arising and passing away" of the contents of consciousness, as suggested by some Buddhist schools.

The Fleece

There is an old saying, probably based on Saxon lore, which wishes a friend "flags, flax, fodder, and frig." Or, put in more modern terms—shelter, clothing, food, and mating. These four elements of basic survival underpin our social, psychological, and spiritual well-being. In the pathworking, the fleece suggests flax, or clothing, the lamb, fodder. The rose suggests flags, in its use as a symbol of certain magical traditions, and frig in its well-known associations with love. The pink light is the light of spirit tinted by the red and white of these components.

In magical terms, these four elements translate into membership of a like-minded community, empowerment, knowledge, and love—the two-way love between the human and divine, reflected in the higher love that can exist between two people. This four-fold division also relates, as you might guess, to the four elements—earth, air, fire, and water—and the four directions—north, south, east, and west.

The Other Symbols

There are levels of operation in magic. An operation may be intended as work upon the physical plane. Another style of operation may be called "astral." Some operations are mystical in nature. Some rites are multilevel and blend symbols and their meanings. Often across these operations, the same physical symbols are used, resonating with each other and the relevant four-fold divisions.

There are commonalities within a tradition, but across tradition and non-tradition practice the possible symbolic items make a long list. Dealing with Paganism alone, the choices are many and a search on the web will provide numerous sites that show this.[38]

We are the ones who attach meaning to objects, but there are common conventions that are also followed. At multiple levels, which is to say marking differences between natural, magical, mystical, and spiritual workings, the symbolic items may or may not change. I have experienced both with different magical groups.

Different traditions assign different meanings to the symbolic items upon their altars. And within some groups the meanings change or become more refined as the student practitioner proceeds through the group's grades or circles. I studied and worked in more than one order and in different circles within them. In this working, I have incorporated those items and meanings taught to me in my own training and used by me in different groups and situations.

With that said, I have here used a personal set of correspondences I encountered, which I have used and which I particularly like: salt representing the sweat of toil as we express our meaning in the world; water representing the tears of experience gleaned from prior grief overcome; and the wine representing the surging blood of life and its expression in joyous sexual union. I suggest, however, that you make your own connections between outer symbol and inner meanings. I can only offer what I have found useful for me. The experience of them will be personal to you yourself.

---

38. At time of writing, this was a useful site with lots of suggestions for symbols:
    www.groveandgrotto.com/blogs/articles/representing-the-elements-on-a-pagan-altar.

Journeys to Realms Beyond

✛

In this third series of pathworkings, we pass beyond the self and the deeper self and enter into the paths of the great myths and legends of an earlier time. In our quest to delve deeper and deeper into our own inner natures, we have progressed through two levels already to reach this deepest level that borders the Collective Unconscious.

The paths in this series are:

- "The Lost Land of Ys," where we see once again the submerged land appearing in our realm.
- "The Way of the Unicorn," where we meet this legendary being and experience an aspect of its energies.
- "The Crystal Cube," in which we take a journey beyond all others deep into the inner nature of our true self.
- "The Mountains of the Moon," where we mystically realize the true nature of our inner kingdom and of ourselves.

We begin with a journey to the seashore to witness the arising from the depths of the lost land of Ys.

Path 9: The Land of Ys

✧

This working—The Land of Ys[39]—starts in the alchemist's upper room just like it did in path 8. As you enter the pathworking proper, you will journey on horseback to the coast where a "lost land" will arise from the sea. In this lost land, you will seek and find the original plans for your current life. The purpose of this is to reset your life compass, so to speak, to match your current situation with your original plans for this current life. Effectively, this is an inner process to help get you back on track, or if that is not necessary, to more strongly affirm the way you are making in this life. Land rising from the sea is a metaphor for the resurfacing of deep memories, personal or interpersonal.

Preamble

You begin in the great hall of the castle, as usual, and make your way up to the alchemist's room at the top of the tower steps. The room is softly lit now and you are the only one there. You notice a comfortable chair to one side and you sit in this.

You begin to relax and settle and your thoughts drift to all that you have experienced up to this time. You think of all the places you have visited and ponder the meaning that is behind this inner land. As you do so, your surroundings fade.

— THE PATHWORKING —

It is night but there is some moonlight overhead by which you can see. You find yourself at the crossroads facing the castle mound. Behind you stands the

---

39. "Ys" is pronounced "eece" as in "fleece" and as "eese" as in "geese."

forest. To your right the track leads to the cave of crystal. The road to your left leads to the town.

You look down upon the ground and see the sign of Libra set into the ground, the left part pointing toward the road leading to town, the right pointing down the road to the cave, and the bump on top of the sign aligned with the road leading to the castle mound.

Along this last road a young groomsman approaches bringing a horse. You await his arrival. The horse is sleek and well-groomed. You have seen this horse before on an earlier journey in these realms. Its lines betray good breeding. Such a horse would be owned by one of noble birth. The groomsman says to you, "You may use this horse for your journey for there is much ground to cover this night. I shall remain here until you return. Have no fear, for the way is known to her. She will take you to your destination and return you safely again."

You mount the horse and bid farewell to the groomsman. The horse takes the road toward town and soon sets up a fast, but easy pace. You begin to feel more confident, your misgivings falling away in the face of your mount's flowing grace. Although it is the horse that knows the way, you feel its sensitivity to your own needs and desires and this feeling binds you both together as one.

Soon you enter the gates of the town and, passing along the silent streets, make your way to the central market place. All is quiet save for the sound of your horse's hooves striking the hard surface of the street. In the market place there stands an old stone horse trough fed with clear water from the mouth of a lion's face carved into the stone headpiece. At this trough you pause while your horse takes a small drink.

Turning right to leave the market square, you ride out of the town and once again take up a fast insistent pace, racing out over the moonlit downs.

The ground is undulating like a series of frozen sea swells. As you crest one, another appears ahead. You race down into each dip only to climb once more to top another rise.

At the top of one rise, you have a brief chance to see a distant plain upon which stands a circle of standing stones. Then the view is lost as once more you descend to the vale below. Up and down you go until you begin to wonder if these hills will ever end.

At the top of the next rise you pause, for in the valley below there runs a broad river, flowing from right to left. A track runs along the bank of this river and reaching it your mount turns confidently to the left.

The going is a lot easier and soon the valley begins to widen. In the distance you see moonlight glinting from the black waters of a sea and a little while later you hear the soft lapping sound of ocean against rocks. The track you are following leads into some sand hills. You pass over these to the gently sloping and pebbled beach below. At the water's edge stands a white-robed man. He waits for you.

You approach and dismount. He greets you and tells you that the Lost City will soon rise up, and that this only occurs once every sixty years. You must watch the horizon for the rising star that will be the signal. You look out to sea, to the ocean's horizon. A bright reddish star appears there. The man begins his invocation as you listen: "From the ocean's depths and darkness let rise again the Lost City, the city of hopes and dreams, the center of all golden aspiration. Our home was lost to us, yet its essence resides within the waters of the inner self, and times there are when it will rise again to our calling, show us the loving face of its walls and gardens, its trees and streets, its parks and buildings. Arise now lost land of Ys. Arise that we may enter once more and take up the threads that will guide us in our exile."

Your attention is on the rising star. As the man's voice trails away, his words flying winged across the sea, the star flashes silver blue in a brilliant flare. It is the brightest star in the sky. A beam of its brightness shoots toward you along the ocean's surface. It forms a silver path right to your feet. A strange, haunting music hangs in the air as the sea begins to ripple away from you. As the lost land and city rise from the ocean, the water ahead of you recedes, slowly at first, then with increasing speed. The man tells you to go quickly and return quickly as the water will return at a speed that can out-race a rider on horseback.

The retreating waters have left a causeway leading from the shore to the land of Ys. You follow the causeway, leaving the man behind. The ground becomes hard-packed sand and begins, at first imperceptibly, to slope downward.

The land is rising rapidly now and ahead you see the towers of a city emerge. The Lost City has risen above the waters for your visit. You approach it as the ground dries rapidly ahead of you.

Soon, the great unbroken walls of the city are visible. Huge boulders fitted expertly together tower above you. You begin walking around the perimeter looking for an entrance.

After a while, you come to a broad ramp leading upward and running along the wall. This ramp will take you into the city. You begin the ascent, the city wall to one side. Ahead of you is the rectangular opening of the city's main gate. High and broad, it stands with a carving above the lintel. The carving shows two lions facing each other, their front paws resting upon a single, round stone. You feel the great age and grandeur of this place.

You pass though this gate and find yourself at one end of a wide, paved road. It leads to a distant building. To the right and left are other buildings in a park-like setting. There are fountains and statues; there are areas of flowers and trees. It is not orderly and rigid. Neither is it wild and unkempt. It is a pleasing balance of the natural and the planned.

You follow the road. It brings you closer to the imposing building to which it leads. Along the last stretch, the road is lined with statues of sphinxes, winged as in the Greek style. Ahead, the avenue ends in a broad flight of stone steps leading up into the building. You realize that it is a temple of some sort.

Silently, you mount the ancient steps. Before you, untarnished, copper doors stand open framing the dark interior. You enter and find yourself in a large hall, with two rows of pillars, one to the right, one to the left, marching the entire length.

To the right, the wall is hung with rich tapestries. To the left, the wall opens out through a series of porticos onto a balustraded veranda. The floor is set with alternate black and white tiles, and the tiles just inside the doorway bear an intricate, star-shaped design. In the center there is a sunken pool partially covered with water lilies. At the far end of the hall there is a plain, high-backed throne, and upon that throne is a beautiful woman; mature but not old. She smiles in welcome and signals you to approach. As you do, she seems to become more beautiful and more powerful at the same time. She is radiant.

The woman stands before you as the Queen, the High Priestess, representative to us of the Power of the Mother.[40] This is your special audience. For the moment, use it how you will.

After a time, the woman signals to one side and a youth enters, dressed in a plain white tunic and carrying a scroll. The scroll is unrolled and shown to you.

---

40. The use of the term "Mother" here, capitalized, is as an archetypal *role*. There are qualities associated with the role and it is these qualities that are referenced. In outer, real life, these qualities can be provided or displayed by anyone, regardless of gender and, to a large extent, age. Archetypes are exactly that, principles. They find real expression in the outer everyday world in any number of ways.

The woman tells you that here in this city reside the contracts that souls have made for their part in manifestation and the original plans for each individual incarnation. What you are holding is your original design for this incarnation. Study it carefully, be it in diagrams, symbols, picture, words, or some combination of these, for it is time to ensure that it is put into effect.

On a signal from the woman, the youth closes up the scroll and, after bowing to the woman, departs.

You thank her in your own words and the audience is over. It is time for you to return for soon the city will sink once more below the waves. You must hurry.

You leave the temple and descend the steps. Once again, you tread the broad avenue through the night. Soon you reach the lion gate and a slight shudder of the ground under your feet reminds you to make haste.

You descend the ramp and begin the walk back to the shore. The sound of eerie music again fills the air. Looking back, you see the city and land of Ys begin to sink down. The bright star has climbed quite high now.

A lapping sound draws your attention to the approaching waters, lapping and spilling over the causeway. There will be just enough time to reach the shore, if you hurry. You continue on your way.

Soon you reach the man at the shoreline. He has tended your horse for you. You look again and see the last high turrets of the city sink below the incoming waves. Then there is silence. The causeway is gone.

The tidal waters lap at your feet and looking down you see a piece of plain driftwood, about the size of your hand and roughly circular. You pick this up and put it in your pocket.

As you thank the man, take your horse, mount, and begin the long ride back. You leave the sand-hills and follow the river upstream. Soon you come to the turn-off to the right. The way seems shorter now. You enter once more the rolling downs, but this time you seem to come almost at once to the town near where you started. The sun is rising as you enter the town. You reach the central market place. There, waiting to greet you are the town's builders, masons, gardeners, foresters, and beyond them all manner of townsfolk. You tell them what you know of the information shown to you on the scroll and say, "Here is the City. Now is it to be built."

You turn your mount and ride out of the town back toward the crossroad where your adventure began. Here you meet, once more, the groom who brought you the horse. He tells you that he has been instructed to present you with the horse as a gift so that you may more easily travel these realms. The groom also asks if he may stay at the Castle and tend the horse in your stables there. If you agree he will accompany you there. If not, he will depart.

As you ride up to the castle, you realize that the land created in the last working was in fact one and the same as the land in which you now find yourself. You have witnessed two things within—your land's own creation. Herein lies a mystery.

You enter the castle grounds and find a stable for your horse in the courtyard. There are also quarters there for the groomsman if he is with you.

Enter once more the great hall and take a seat at the round table. Place the piece of driftwood on the table with the other objects and close your eyes. When you open them, you are once again in the upper room. You stand up and record your experiences in the book bearing your name, the book that is always kept there. Finally, you depart from the room and descend the stairway. You then return to normal consciousness.

Discussion

Whatever the facts about Atlantis—the fabled city that sank into the Atlantic Ocean—the legends remain and they are with us today very much alive. As with all such legends, it is the meaning that they have for us that is more important today than any of the facts that might be discovered concerning the people and places they describe.

Cultures from all over the world have a legend about a land that sank below the sea, of a mass exodus of their people from some earlier homeland, of a devastating flood. A little bit of symbolism here may help us understand the attractions of such an idea.

This sea can be taken to represent all that of which we are unaware—that part of us that used to be called the unconscious, and before that the subconscious. This part of our being contains all of which we are not yet aware and all of which we are no longer aware.

Our unawareness can be symbolized by the sea as that which is hidden below the surface and that which is clearly visible above in the bright light of the day.

The surface/under sea analogy is not restricted to a discussion on spiritual psychology. It relates to all existence. A wave appears to move but actually does not. It is the result of water rising and falling in place. This could be an analogy for thought. It is also an analogy in physics of the illusion of time created by the behavior of space. Existence as we know it is a surfboard on that wave of illusory time. Further discussion on this is not relevant in this work. Suffice it to say that conscious thought in the Sea of Being follows the same rules.

We can consider all facts we have not yet become aware of as waiting to be born into our conscious awareness, and all that we have forgotten or that has passed from our awareness has, in the same way, left the light of consciousness, dying and returning to the great Sea of Being.

In many philosophies this Sea of Being, this unawareness ocean, is described as the ground of being and it is in this ocean that we live and move and have our being. Indeed from moment to moment our thoughts arise from this ocean of unawareness, and, having passed through our minds, return to it. All events in the world from moment to moment—and everything in our experience—arise out of this sea and then pass away into it again. This sea is then the source of all and it is also that to which all will return. The Indian idea of the day of Brahma—where the universe comes into existence at its dawning and will pass away again at its ending—is another version of the same philosophy on a grander scale.

All these ideas are represented for us in this pathworking by a land that once arose out of the ocean, was populated, and upon which towns and cities appeared where people carried on their existence. Then one day this land of Atlantis, of Ys, disappeared back into the sea. It is a very potent image and can mean everything from the moment-to-moment renewal of thoughts that come into our head and then pass away again, to the great age of existence of the universe and its final passing away.

Our evolutionary history comes from the sea and so too does our personal history, for prior to our birth we float in a sea of amniotic fluid in the womb of our mother.

Indeed, the sea can also be seen as the symbol of the Mother for it is the womb that gave birth to life and when the womb is dark it is the tomb that accepts life back again when it has fulfilled its purpose.

If we follow this idea further, we can see that the purpose of life exists before that life comes forth. Indeed, we must look beyond our normal awareness to seek what the purpose of life and meaning is. We cannot tell from the universe of our normal perceptions what this purpose or meaning might be. We must look beyond these, probe into the areas of which we are not aware, diving deep into the mysteries of our own mind to bring to the light of day some form of plan we are sure existed before we came into this life.

Why are we here? Why are things just so?

Our mission on this planet is hardly known to us. Yet, we came here for a reason. According to teaching of the Western Esoteric Tradition, we each deliberately constructed a personality with which to incarnate into this everyday existence. And if we are to do this, then we have an object in life and an idea of what it is we hope to achieve in this particular incarnation.

Much of the popular interest in past lives can be traced to this desire to find the purpose of our current life and the karmic forces that bear upon it. It is an intention that existed before this incarnation and that guides and directs what we must do now.

We know from those times when we have had a hunch or an intuition that great ideas can arise from the sea of unawareness. We see things in a flash that would take a very long time to explain step-by-step.

The geniuses of history have brought out of the depths of the Collective Unconscious great theories and works of art that have given birth to whole schools and traditions. It is then the task of those who work within these traditions to adequately explain and represent these discoveries—to fully work out in actuality what the genius conceived in a single flash.

The brain and nervous system work in more than one way. On the one hand, we have the network of nerves and neurons, which transmit information along this or that path, spreading out or fanning in and consolidating. This style of working is like the land, with its allocated areas and its pathways and tracks and roads.

The surface of the brain can also be awash with chemicals and thought can take place across the cortex in this non-directional and unbounded way. This method of mentation is like the sea. There are no rigid pathways in the oceans but there are identifiable currents. Water itself is also subject to behaviors dependent on the nature of the land over which it flows.

We all have these two modes of thinking. When, through meditation, we realize this and gain the ability to use these modes at will and to be aware of their individual character and quality, then it is as though we have established a balance point, a "third way," creating in essence a land that is not a land—a point in the ocean where land may appear or submerge. This land can bring knowledge from the depths to the light of day. When it sinks again below the waves, it takes what it has gained or been given from above the horizon back into the depths for it to develop below the light of consciousness.

For this path we use the symbol of Libra, the sign of balance. The symbolism can be seen in the dynamic and never-static balancing between the land and the sea achieved through this land of Ys.

This realm then is the land that, at certain times and under certain conditions, can arise from the sea. It is in this land that, among other things, the plans are kept for every incarnation—our own incarnations and the incarnations of everyone on this planet.

Here too we may find the general plans for the evolution of humanity as a group. If we could only visit this land when conditions were right we could gather the plans, look again at the instructions that show us our forgotten mission, and bring the knowledge back to the solid land of this incarnation. Then we would be able to take a more active role in determining our lives and making sure we followed the path that we ourselves had intended to take.

This idea of being on a mission is in fact very appropriate, for a person on a mission is often away from home. We are all away from home. We are all exiled from our home. The notion of an exile is found in many religions and traditions. It is present in the Christian interpretations of the story of humanity's expulsion form the Garden of Eden. It is also in Judaism where the exile of the Shekhinah became reflected in the exile of the Jews from their own land—a very potent thing.

In the myths and legends that have come down to us, we know that Atlantis went below the sea. Great fleets and armadas of boats left to flee the disaster and landed their cargo of refugees in the Mediterranean, along the coast of

Africa, the continent of the Americas, in Iceland, Greenland and, some have even said, in parts of Australia and parts of Polynesia too.

Many escaped to settle in Britain and coastal Europe. In all of these places, the idea of Atlantis remains in the stories and the memories in the "group mind" of the people. Indeed, in some cases there is still contained in spoken traditions the memory of the people coming to the present country from another land over and above the historical reality of the migrations of humanity in its earliest times.

It is a very basic idea in humanity that somehow we "belong elsewhere," that we are in some sense away from our home. More modern versions of the myth, constructed along theoretical lines, talk about a beautiful planet, in a distant star system from which we originated. Sadly this was a doomed planet and there was mass migration. One group found a suitable planet—the Earth—and landed. It was from this new planet, this new home, that we saw once in the night sky, two million years ago, the super-nova that represented the destruction of our own home. This, too, is a story about Atlantis, but in this case the land is a planet and the sea is the inter-stellar blackness of space—Mother of the Stars. This story also links in with the off-planet "Interventionist" theory that some prefer to the more widespread options of Creationism and Darwinism. From this point of view, those in this modern world who are said to suffer "alienation" are probably the ones who are more in tune with reality than those deemed "normal" who are not so consciously aware of our status as homeless wanderers among the seas and stars.

Whatever the true facts may be, the memory and the myth remain. Psychologically, we carry it in our racial memory and whatever our origins, we carry it physically in our genes, for in our development before birth we recap our growth within the ocean of the mother's womb and our subsequent emergence into the light of day, arising from the sea in the birth process.

It is in that journey into our own mind that we may recover our links with our psychological past, our genetic past, and our prenatal past. Whenever conditions are right, the land rises out of the sea, and we may visit this place and bring back the plans into consciousness.

This, however, is not the sum total of what we must do. Having brought the plans into the light of day, we still have to act on them. We have to marshal our own inner resources to the task that has been set for us. We have to try and coordinate our efforts to act as a whole person and not as lots of individual parts, one part wanting to do this and one part wanting to do something else.

These conflicts and inconsistencies will always be with us and if we are to master or balance them in our relationships with other people, and thereby bring peace to this planet, we must first master and balance them in ourselves and bring peace to our own inner kingdom. This earth will never see the end of wars until we all have resolved the conflicts within.

Each of us has this inner kingdom of self and it is to this realm that we bring the plans. Here, we turn them over to the masons, the master builders of our own inner natures, who can then act behind the scenes of consciousness, bringing into effect what the plans dictate and in that way gathering together whatever resources we have to the task for which they were intended.

We are totally responsible for ourselves. Everything we do and everything that happens to us is fully and totally our own responsibility. We cannot put the blame for anything that befalls us outside of ourselves—not on fate, not on circumstances, not on others.

We trip on an uneven part of the footpath. Shall we sue the council? Or shall we admit that we were not fully aware of our surroundings?

A car comes out of a side street and into ours. We can realize that the reason we were at that point at that moment was a result of our own choices made up to that moment.

Does another constrain us and limit our choices? If so, then before that time our own free choices put us in the position where this person was able to trap us.

But we must also realize that this total responsibility only applies once we are adult enough and capable enough to accept it. As a baby we are zero percent responsible for what happens to us with the 100 percent being at the door of our parents and guardians. In theory, the balance smoothly changes as we grow and develop, with adulthood bringing the full transfer of responsibility to us. This shifting dynamic that must be balanced may remind us of the symbol of Libra.

We would be wise to use those tools at our disposal that enable us to begin acting responsibly and in accordance with our original intention, which we had forgotten and thought lost.

When we have completed our task, we may return once again to the mother, this time to the other aspect, the aspect that receives us back into her arms like the ancient land of Ys sinking once more into the sea until the conditions are right for it to arise again. Just as Atlantis is our true home, so the sea is the true home to the land. So, too, is the space between the galaxies the true home of the stars, whose arising and passing away is in no way different from our own birth and death. Although we are children of earth, our race is of the starry heavens, and although we may not yet return to our homes completely and fully, we can rest there between lives and visit there in our minds.

Undoubtedly, we have strayed from our original intention and taken paths that we had never intended to take. As a result of using this pathworking to find and deliver these original plans, we may discover that we are in the wrong place, at the wrong time, and we will have to do something about it. You may have realized by now that this path is similar to path 6, but on a higher arc.

We will have to take charge of ourselves and take action to move back to where we should be, to be in the right place at the right time, for we are in a sense prodigal children of Atlantis, both sons and daughters.

If we wake up to the discrepancy that exists between our original mission and where we are right now, then we will probably have to do a lot of retracing of steps and backtracking or cross-country trekking before we can even begin our proper task in this incarnation. Do we have enough time to do this? Dare we do it? Dare we face the difference between what should be and what is?

Path 10: The Way of the Unicorn

✛

In this path, you will once again visit the alchemist's room. You will have it to yourself and it is from here you will relax and enter the working.

Out in the open you will see a circle of standing stones. With the assistance of a unicorn and a person acting as moderator, you will participate in a circular dance, weaving with others a ribbon about a vertical pole.

The idea behind this working is to further develop the idea of a field of possibilities woven between two edges or limits. It is intended to stimulate or enhance your ability to see broader possibilities in situations rather than being limited to either/or choices.

Preamble

You begin in the great hall of the castle and make your way up to the alchemist's room at the top of the tower steps. The room is softly lit and you are the only one there. You notice a comfortable chair to one side and you sit in this.

Begin to relax and settle and let your thoughts drift to all the people whom you have met with in these workings. As you do so, your surroundings fade.

─────────── THE PATHWORKING ───────────

You are standing just inside a large circle of tall standing stones, tall, regular, well-finished. You sense it is early afternoon but the sky is a bit dark and there is high sheet lightning. Turning to look back, you see that you have entered the ring along a track through two of the standing stones.

The lightning stops and the sky lightens. You turn your attention back to the center. Over to the left, you see someone is walking into the circle, stopping a short distance from the center, facing to the right. You hear sweet, soft music but cannot locate the source. It seems to be all around you.

Over to the right, you see that a unicorn is entering the circle, moving toward the person near the center to come to a stop a little distance away, giving a slight nod of the head. Clearly, the person standing there is to be the moderator of what is to come.

The music seems to spiral in and you realize it is coming from the unicorn. The moderator joins the song and both moderator and unicorn move toward each other, meeting at the center.

The arms of the moderator open wide to the sides and the unicorn sinks without any fuss into the ground leaving the horn protruding, yet its part of the song continues.

The moderator takes a few steps back opening their arms to the sides. The horn grows, spiraling into a tall vertical pole, at least half the height of an average one-story dwelling.

The music fades and a still silence descends. Waiting. Poised. Ready.

There is the sound of a musical note, from a trumpet or horn, and suddenly lots of people are arriving and running in, brightly clad. They are all dashing and dancing to the center, laughing, and smiling to each other.

They form a ring centered around the central pole. The moderator and others beckon you to join them.

Move to the pole. Walk around, choose a spot that appeals to you and become part of the group. Others will make way for you if necessary.

The music stops. Everyone is waiting.

Then a single, clear note sounds and a profusion of ribbons shoot out from the top of the pole, one end still attached, the other falling to hang down the pole, almost touching the ground and well within reach of the people. The ribbons are all different colors and hues. There are multicolored ribbons as well, some in distinct stripes or patterns, some where pastel colors blend and merge in a random pattern.

Some music of sweet happy sounds in a happy, bouncy rhythm begins. The moderator steps to the pole and takes the end of one streamer. As if this is a signal, all the people approach the pole and select a ribbon. Some run around the pole to view the variety of colors and patterns before choosing. Select one for yourself and take hold of it. As the others are doing, you move out from the pole to take up the slack on your ribbon.

The music swells and all begin moving; some one way, some the opposite. They alternately duck under a ribbon held up coming the opposite way to them and hold up their ribbon in turn for others to duck under. Follow the pattern and the beat of the music. Some coming toward you duck under your streamer and you then duck under the next one that is raised. Sometimes you have to duck under very low and sometimes you have to hold your own streamer very high for others to pass under.

The pace of the music increases and the dance becomes faster.

Suddenly, and quite randomly, some reverse direction while others continue on. There is lots of laughter and variations as some pass under instead of over. Some twirl and untwirl their ribbon about themselves as they go.

You continue as you wish. Under, over, this way, that way. Some are laughing at near collisions You feel happy and put a twirl or two in your own movement around. Just dance your own unique contribution.

As the dance continues, the wrapping of streamers is moving down from the top of the pole as it is covered with color. The dancers are gradually being pulled in to the center. The circle is getting smaller.

Soon you and the others are tightly gathered around the pole and the multiple colors have completely covered the pole from top to bottom. No one can move farther.

The music fades away. You see that the players are tying off the ends against the wrappings on the pole. You do the same and step back as the others do. Many are laughing and exchanging hugs; join in as you wish.

There is the sound of a horn. The moderator stays but everyone else runs off laughing in ones, twos, threes, or more. The person who moderated the event approaches, stands before you and offers a small spiral shard of bone to you. Take this gift and thank the moderator in your own words. There may or may not be a reply.

Then the moderator turns and walks away from you, out of the circle, and into the distance. It is sunny and warm. You are alone in the circle.

You look at the pole of multicolored woven ribbons and recognize your part in this.

There is again the sound of a horn from somewhere and the multicolored pole sinks vertically into the ground, ribbons and all. It is a bright warm day.

You leave the circle, departing through the two standing stones through which you entered. You turn around and look back at the scene. Then you close your eyes. Open your eyes. You are back in the upper room of the castle.

Postamble

First, record your experiences in the book kept for that purpose in the upper room. Descend from the upper room and into the great hall. Place the shard of bone upon the table in one of the few remaining vacant segments and sit quietly, pondering what you have experienced.

Make your way out into the courtyard, return from the working as usual and record all that you have experienced.

Discussion

This pathworking is about sex. But not just about sex, in the same way that Tantric Mysticism is not just about sex.

Among the English-speaking peoples of the world, sex is one of the most misunderstood and maligned aspects of life. I have no idea why this should be when so many other cultures have entirely different attitudes to the subject.

Fortunately, I am mostly addressing more open-minded people here who usually have a more enlightened perspective. How, after all, can we understand the polarities that lie behind creation if we cannot appreciate and approve of the immense attractive power that exists between the God and the Goddess? How can we understand that attraction if we continually misunderstand and misinterpret the reflection of this polarity that we find in human sexual attraction? Of course, Gods and Goddesses are not "male" and "female" as we understand it; the relationship is more important than what the participants are, where significant relationship exists.

Tantric Mysticism teaches us that the essence of sex is energy, the same energy that creates the galaxies and that flows through our bodies. Tantric and other practices encourage us to become aware of these energies and to learn to use them and work with them at will. The essence is to be aware and to be in control. This is also the essence of magic.

Sexual Energy as Creative

The relation between sexual energy and creative energy is hardly worth mentioning. We are mostly aware these days that the same energy is in play whether we are in the act of loving sexual union or creating a work of art. I accept that the process of artistic creation has many stages and aspects. So, too, does the relationship between two lovers. But in the creative act itself, the two applications of energy are one and the same.

Spanish guitarist Andrés Segovia spoke of playing the guitar as being for him akin to making love to a beautiful woman.[41] Sexual preferences aside, he was making the same point that is understood by artists of all types—art arising out of polarity.

Polarity

The writer Charles Williams wrote of the unicorn in his Arthurian poem cycles. His approach was that the archetypal imagery of the maiden and the unicorn was a metaphor for the empowerment of the artist. Speaking in archetypes, he wrote that only a maiden of spotless virtue might call the unicorn to her. Placing his head in the maiden's lap, the unicorn sings. Williams saw this voice of the unicorn as the ability of the artist to create. Only when safe from the world at large can an artist release creative power to the full. The principle can be expressed in many ways. He chose one that he thought might reach his readers.

These are foundation principles of polarity expressed at an earlier time in gender terms. But gender is, of course, a much broader consideration.

In becoming absorbed in the creative act, the artist is vulnerable to the world. Many have labored at their creations for long periods, forgoing sleep and food. The stereotypical artist, "mad" scientist, or other creative person, is seen as careless of the normal tasks of everyday life. They can be seen as unkempt, unable to perform the simplest tasks to look after themselves, their attire, their home, their health. The artist Pablo Picasso burned some of his paintings during one period of his life so that he could keep warm by a fire in the cold winter.

---

41. Described during a September 24, 1964, Adelaide Town Hall concert.

In times past, artists of all sorts had to seek out patrons so that they would be provided with the basics of existence. Even today, arts councils and various government programs fulfill the role of patrons of the arts. The partnership of artist and provider continues as a recognized necessity. In archetypes, we are still talking in terms of two poles: the doer and the one who facilitates it.

I should probably mention at this point that although the tale is of a maiden and a (male) unicorn, this does not mean that it only applies to male artist,-female provider situations. The actual sexes of the players are not relevant to the principle, but it is only cast that way according to medieval understanding.

Polarity is a principle that is only a part of the whole story, a principle not appreciated by many, even today.

Polarity Examined

Let's take a battery with two poles. We call one positive and one negative, a convention. They really only differ in that in the case of a battery one pole has a higher potential than the other at a given time. The difference does not exist in the poles themselves but in the relationship they currently, no pun intended, have with each other. If I could take the positive pole in isolation and introduce it to another pole of higher inherent potential, that positive pole would now be the negative. The positive and negative words we use are relative, not fixed, not attached as attributes of the pole. They are descriptions of different activities in which any "poles" may engage in relation to others.

When we move to look at our household electrical supply it is called "alternating." Now, we have no fixed points of flow directions other than a maximum and minimum. In representational views, the flow goes this way, stops, goes the other way, stops, and so on. This is getting much closer to the field of options and relations possible among human beings. We will return to this reality of options.

Polarity and Creation

A pictorial example for why we talk of polarity might be a loom and the weaving taking place. There are the two parts—the loom itself, with the threads strung, and the mechanism to put one set on top and to switch their positions. The setting alternates. The other component is the shuttle trailing a thread as it goes back and forth. With the loom switching positions and the shuttle going back and forth, these two things with two positions or modes can weave a pattern of almost any design. Wide variety arises out of simple principles working together. Infinite actual creation arises out of limited theoretical conventions of polarity.

Now let's introduce three-phase electricity supply. There is not just a single cycle of a this-way-stop-that-way waveform, but also three of these staggered in time. That is, at any one time there is flow this way, flow that way, and changing over one or other way between the two. Yet, we can still abstract two boundaries, upper and lower, between all the options.

When the magician is defining two poles, the resulting field of play between them is a rich tapestry of not necessarily one or the other, nor set in one state forever. Despite this, we can still refer to the two poles across which the reality fabric is stretched. The pole options make possible a richer variety and more options means more opportunities of application.

The Pole and the Earth

In this working, the horn of the unicorn represents one abstract polarity. The earth into which it descends and out of which the pole rises is the other polarity.

The multicolored strands are the options for manifestation and the weaving is the unique pattern for the individual people in the different ways of dancing, embracing, and displaying a variety of options within the simple two-valued horn-and-earth framework.

In the Holy Grail legends, Arthur had a sword. The sword has been one of many epithets for the male penis through the ages, and even to the present day. Arthur's sword is generally known as Excalibur. However, it had variant names in different versions of the tales. Excalibur draws on Latin *ex calibur* and in one story the sword is called Caliburn. The word *calliban* is another variant and in a Welsh version of the tale the sword is referred to as Caledfwlch.[42] This word can be translated as "hardy in the breach," which seems to refer to its use in

---

42. For details on the Irish and Welsh meanings of calad/caled and bwlch/bolg, see Patrick Sims-Williams, *Irish Influence on Medieval Welsh Literature* (Oxford: Oxford University Press, 2011), page 165 and footnotes 179–183.

battle. However, as "hard in the gap,"[43] it can also refer to sexual prowess in some contexts.

Excalibur had a sheath that was made to match it and this sheath had magical powers, conveying invulnerability upon the owner of the sword. Morgana or Morgaine, the legends tell us, stole this sheath. In so doing she removed his protection into her own care.

Now, the Latin word for sheath, in this case sword sheath, is "vagina" and we also know from the tales that Morgana tricked Arthur, her half-brother, into having sexual intercourse with her. This is also the story of the stolen sheath but under another guise. By cruel fate, just as the magic sword and sheath were a perfect match, so too did Arthur find that he and Morgana were a perfect match and he never overcame that even after accepting Guenevere as his wife and queen.

I must emphasize that these myths are with us today because they espouse abstract, and possibly universal, concepts in the form of symbols. Male and female relationships in myth are about polarities, not about real, physical life. A male figure might be "one pole" and a female "another pole." Abstract myths find their reflections into reality in many different ways. In particular, gender references are not set in concrete as such. They are there as abstract relationships to illustrate a principle one particular way. They might just as well be A and Z. It is not the only way.

I personally know a man and woman who have the same degree of Scorpio rising in their astrological birth charts. In addition, the man has the moon in Scorpio in the first house and the woman has the sun in Scorpio in the first house. Furthermore, the luminaries are at the same degree of Scorpio. This alignment produces a palpably strong attraction between the two of a sexual nature. Yet, the pattern also produces a similarity such that over a period of twenty years, all who have met them have commented that they could almost be twins. These two are a real-world example of the fateful attractions portrayed in the Holy Grail legends: Arthur-Morgana, Merlin-Nimue, Lancelot-Guenevere.

---

43. "Bwlch" is a common term today as a feature in mountain railway lines, like the Ffestiniog and Welsh Highland Railways, and means "gap" in English. The reference is to a point after a steep climb where a deep cutting has been made in the top of the hill so that on approach there is a gap in the skyline. This use of gap is a common term for mountain and hill crossings as, for example, in the famous Cumberland Gap.

It is Scorpio, the astrological representation of sexual energy par excellence, that relates to this path in our journey around the belt of the heavens. Mars traditionally rules Scorpio, although in our present day there are many who prefer to assign Pluto to that role.

Mars is not only a god of war but also a representation of impulse and energy. In fact, war or battle is just one aspect of the application of this energy. It has other uses. The energy can be used for defense. It can be used for protection; it can also be used for sex. The energy of Pluto is very similar but much slower, or long-term in application. If Mars is seen as an acid that eats into rock, Pluto can be seen as the slow erosion by water and wind. Perhaps another way would be to say that Mars is a torrid episode of vigorous and sexual interchange and Pluto is a lifelong commitment of sexual relationship. The two are sometimes seen as the mundane and spiritual aspects of the same force or energy, and in astrological symbolism Scorpio has the two creature correspondences of the scorpion and the eagle.

The power of the scorpion relates more closely with the impulse and sexuality aspects of Scorpio. The eagle shows the same powers at a "higher" or more spiritual level. It can still attack swiftly and without warning, but it can now see much farther and can also vary its sight from wide to a magnified tunnel. The energy has taken wing and so is now much more related to released creativity. The unicorn can be a dangerous, unapproachable animal. Once its voice is released, it is docile, creative, and spiritual.

In terms of the tale of the unicorn, Arthur was the unicorn and Morgana the maiden who held the power of keeping him safe, symbolized by her possession of the matching sheath, the article that conveyed invulnerability. This eventually led to Arthur's downfall at the hands of the son he had with Morgana. The artist was destroyed by his own creation or, rather, creative act.

We can see then that things do not necessarily go well in this tale. Indeed, variants of the unicorn story tell of the maiden being used as bait so that a group of men, sometimes referred to as her brothers, can capture or even kill the unicorn.

The power of the attraction leads us to lower our guard and open up to the other. In this opening of ourselves, of our innermost creative self, we become vulnerable. At that point, we have no protection but what is provided by the other. If that is provided conditionally, temporarily, or by guile, we are lost. If for some reason it is withdrawn, we are equally lost.

While the analogy of these stories can be seen to apply to artists and creative people of possible greatness, we should not lose sight of the fact that they apply to all who share the human condition. Archetypal tales that stand the test of time struggle to the light of day from structures deep within the nervous system that is common to all human beings. The drama of the maiden and unicorn and of the Grail legend characters is played out over and over again in a tapestry of variations wherever humankind gather together. Remember, the symbols, people, and animals in the tales are not fixed in relation to our physical world condition. We humans sometimes act out these principles in any of a thousand different ways, sometimes playing one role, sometimes another. Tales have identifiable themes. We humans act them out, implement them, live them in a wide variety of ways, in any way that we wish and which suits our unique nature.

It is said in the mysteries that we must "know, will, dare, and keep silent." The first three of these relate to the three-fold power of creation—Power, Love, Wisdom. In traditional three-circle training of magicians and witches, knowledge is provided in the first circle by the high priest, the guardian of tradition. In the second circle, the use of power is shown by the high priestess, who controls its ebb and flow. In the third circle, the interplay of high priest and high priestess shows forth the love that exists when we are prepared to be vulnerable.[44] Here we are invited to dare to open ourselves to unconditional love.[45]

Dare we find that other person who will provide the setting we need? Dare we open up and expose ourselves come what may? Ultimately—we must.

---

44. "High Priest" and "High Priestess" are offices, functional titles not necessarily tied to gender. In my training forty years ago, these were not gender-linked offices. I have filled both offices.

45. Beyond this, the three powers combine and of this nothing may be said at this time.

Path 11: The Crystal Cube

✣

There is a change in this working. The starting point is not found in the castle. Instead, this working leads you out of the castle and back into the dark wood that you encountered after your preliminary element work in the village. When you reach the wizard's glass tomb in the dark wood, you will rise up to start the working proper, high into the sky so you see all of the kingdom below. You will travel farther and farther into space from the starting point of the Earth. You will encounter a cube of mirrored walls, floor, and ceiling that will show multiple reflections of yourself and you have an opportunity to make what you will of the experience.

The purpose of this working is to focus upon a little-appreciated aspect of our lives—necessity. It is a symbolic illustration of the way that necessity gives rise to multiple options for its fulfillment. The operation in life of this principle is the idea that every necessity that arises for us in life may have many different ways of being satisfied or put into effect. We just need to pause for a moment and allow those options to arise before embarking on a course to satisfy the necessity, whatever it may be.

Preamble

Begin your working in the usual way as far as entering the courtyard of your castle. This time, do not go into the great hall. Instead, turn and look at the main gates of the castle.

THE PATHWORKING

The gates of the castle are open. You walk over to them and leave the castle. From the castle gates you look out over the wood, which you encountered on your first journey into these realms, then dark and unknown.

Purposefully, you stride down the road toward the wood. You pass the cross-roads and continue straight into the wood. Soon, you come to the shrine of the magic worker's tomb. It is exactly as you first saw it. You gaze once more at the serene face of the one who is entombed within the frosted glass case.

Then you look up and see a patch of sky above you. From this patch among the clouds a beam of light strikes down directly onto the shrine. Its circle of light includes you. You look down and see the bright almost flaming astrological symbol of Sagittarius on the grass.

You begin to feel lighter and lighter. You start to rise in the air and hover above the shrine for a moment. Then you continue your upward flight like a bright arrow into the sky. Up past the tops of the trees you go. Higher and higher. The wood stretches below you, and you can soon see the patterns of fields beyond, each with its own crop or lying fallow. All the different colors form a patchwork below you.

You rise faster now and begin to see the familiar features of this realm in the castle, the towns, the woods, the mountains, the streams, the sea. You see many of the places you have visited and many you have not. The inner landscape is spread below you like a map. Still, you rise higher, faster and faster now.

Still rising, you emerge and see clouds below stretching in all directions like a sea of cotton wool lazily moving. You rise even faster now and the air begins to turn indigo and sparkles with bright points of icy light. Soon there is an indigo blackness all around except below where the hazy blue sphere of Earth hangs in space beneath you.

Look ahead now and see the silver crescent of the moon. It rapidly gets bigger and bigger. It is huge. It has never been seen so large and dark for it is the dark side that you are now approaching.

Strange colors—gray-purple, magenta with green shadows—sharp craggy mountains and plains of craters come into view as you sweep around to the bright side. Harsh edges of contrasts below on the surface of the moon are lit by the sudden brilliant sunrise—sharp, searing white.

Heading toward the sun now, you sweep past the intervening planets. You come closer and closer to the incandescent ball shooting flames far out into space. Its surface, even this far away, can be seen moving, ever restless with shades of brilliant light and the lesser brilliance that looks like shadow by comparison.

You veer away, straight up out of the solar system. Below you is the great disc of the planets in orbit sweeping around their central body, the sun, which you are now leaving behind.

Pause now a little and look upwards. There are the stars with one brighter than the rest. You head toward this one, rapidly picking up speed. It comes closer and as it does there are fewer other stars around until it is the only star visible. There are two darker shapes circling this star, shadowy companions, one very much smaller than the main star and one small, dark and shadowy, appearing to be not quite in existence.

You continue toward the brightness, slowing now. It becomes a point of sheer brilliance, ice cold. You approach and the point of light resolves into a cube shape, a crystal cube of light slowly revolving. You come closer and see it is small, no larger than a person. Its brilliance diminishes as you come closer. You have slowed right down now. Here is your destination.

Reach out and touch its surface. It is as smooth as polished crystal. It is a perfect cube. You work your way around it. Feel its perfection; first one side, then an edge, another edge, around again.

The cube has turned inside out and you are now within it. You reach out to each side and you can just touch the inner surfaces with your fingertips. You see the blackness of space outside the walls.

The walls begin to cloud over. They have become mirrors. You see yourself wherever you turn. Front, rear, left, right, above, below, image after image of yourself stretching off forever in every direction. You move and the thousand images move. You make a sound and the sound echoes to infinity as the images repeat it. Every one of the images has its own infinite set of images too.

Which one is you? Are you one, or many? Are you any?

All the images behave the same. All are the same. You cannot tell image from object. Anyone could be you. Yet you know that *you* are beyond them all.

Self, image, cube—disappear; floating free, dream of light; crystal light of a floating star; yearn to grow, to learn, to express, to *be*. The light is a voice— your voice. Pause a moment and listen

Ahead you see the sun. Approach it. Listen. You hear your name deep in your heart. Ahead you see Earth. Approach it.

Feel. You have sensations. A beautifully balanced self, an identity within, ready for use. Pause and for a moment experience the wonder of this self and identity as you float gently into the atmosphere.

Below you see the clouds. Sink gracefully into them. Feel their cool refreshment. Emerging you see mountains and fields, cities and streams. Gently descend.

Below is the wood. Float feather-like down to it. Land lightly within it. Smell the perfume of flowers, plants, trees, and earth. Acknowledge the ground in welcome.

You are back at the shrine. The tomb is as it was. All is as it was, but brighter, newer somehow. Something at your feet catches your eye. It is a shiny smooth pebble. You pick it up and put it in your pocket or pouch.

Postamble

You close your eyes. You take a deep breath. As you inhale, you breathe the whole inner realm deep within you. Hold your breath for a moment.

This time you will not retrace your steps. When you open your eyes and let out your breath, you will find yourself sitting in the great hall of your castle. In front of you is the round table. Place the smooth pebble on its segment.

Close your eyes and sit at the table for a while, contemplating your adventure and sensing for any others who may have joined you. You open your eyes and look around at the hall with various doors and symbols that have led to your adventures. You acknowledge and perhaps communicate with any you find here or at the table. Look again at the various items you have collected on your journeys and note their positions.

When you are ready, leave the great hall and return to normal consciousness in the usual way. Write up your diary record as usual and review the diagram you have been making of the placement of items on the table. Then, recall the landscape you saw from on high in this working and sketch a map of your inner realm, even if incomplete.

Discussion

Who and what are you? This is something I would like you to consider very carefully.

Have you ever noticed that you sometimes behave differently with different groups of people? Are there certain things that you say to your parents, for example, that you would not say to your intimate friends? Are there things that you would do with your normal friends that you would not do with fellow supermarket customers? Does the way you behave change according to who you are with? If so, it is not really you that changes. Only the behavior patterns change to meet the current needs.

If this describes you, then this pathworking is designed to encourage your knowledge and experience of the core identity behind these different behaviors, used to match up with external needs. You are adopting role-masks to match different situations.

Identity and Mask

If this does not describe you, then you may well already be behaving from your sense of self in varying situations. This pathworking works differently for you. It is intended, in your case, to show that using a different mask, set of behaviors, for a different situation in no way compromises your self-identity. That remains intact directing the proceedings. It is situation driven. I can take up a tennis racket for a game of tennis or a baseball bat for a game of baseball. Neither of these outer sets of tools or clothes alters who I am. It is the same with sets of behaviors and presentations.

The Three-Fold

The pathworking is based on a common mystical theme of essence-self-personality, or Spirit-Soul-Persona, for example. There are different ways of naming and classifying this teaching of the three-fold nature of humans. Well, humans in this context, without meaning to, limit the idea to just human beings. There are teachings that include all creation in such a three-fold set of aspects, but that is not in scope here.

The intention of the pathworking is to symbolically represent to the practitioner three levels of possible expression for an incarnate person. The intention is not to promote one or another but to provide, in symbol, the experience of knowing there is a core identity that is able to choose, from multiple modes of expression, a good one to use for the occasion or time slice at hand.

Context and Behavior

Again, it is easy to see that *where* you are can influence behavior. Contrast for yourself how you act in amusement parks, on the beach, in a cathedral, on a walk in the mountains, driving in heavy traffic, sitting at home.

I want to show you that there is no easy answer to the question of who you are. People, after all, know you only from your words and actions. One set of people knows one "you" while another set knows another "you." These behavior patterns get characterized and labeled by the people around us.

We are a father, a mother, a child, a daughter, a son, a writer, a van driver, a tennis player, a party organizer, an occultist, and so on and so on. These are all labels that we might apply to others and that they might apply to us, according to how we behave with each other.

And, of course, we apply these labels to ourselves too. Often people ask us for identification, not just by name, but also by function, by what pigeonhole we belong in—at least, as far as they might be concerned at the time. People call on us and ask if we are "the owner" of the house, or "the occupant." We might be asked if we were "the driver" of a certain car, "the parent" of a certain child. We might identify ourselves as "the manager" of a business, as a "clerk," "typist," "builder," "home keeper," and so on, when asked what we do for a living. None of this should compromise self-identity.

Identity versus Function

However, none of these labels are the whole story. We are typists when we type, builders when we build, drivers when we drive, gardeners when we garden. Every single one of these labels names a set of actions or behavior patterns, or some sort of relationship between people.

Now, you might think that relationships are different to behavior patterns. Let us try turning some relationship into a pattern of actions. For example, if you are a "mother," then try saying "I mother..." the person it is whom you do mother.

A father may do the same. We find at least two meanings here. On the one hand, you may in fact mother, or father, anyone at all, for it means behaving in a certain way. On the other hand, it relates to a biological and historical event. In this case, it would be better to say, "I fathered..." or "I mothered..." In earlier times, we might have used the terms "sired" or "bore" but these have other connotations now.

Try this out with examples of relationships in your own life. "I child Betty" instead of "I am Betty's child"; "I partner Pat" instead of "I am Pat's partner." Say them a few times to get the feel of them. Try other relationships that you enter into with the various people in your life.

Now in language, relationships are two-way, such as parent-child, husband-wife, landlord-tenant, and such. Yet, in reality this is not necessarily so. You may "mother" someone who does not "child" you. You may "partner" someone who does not "partner" you. You will also discover, if you try these examples, that these behavior patterns are not linked to any one gender. A biological male may mother someone and a biological female may father someone. Think about this, too, and get the feel of it because it is a very important point.

Verbs and Nouns

We see that we have sets of behavior patterns, actions that we perform, that can be described purely and simply using verbs: I drive, I own, I work for. They can also be described by naming: I am the driver, I am the owner, I am the employee of. Actions are fluid, in-the-moment things. Names solidify and confer independent existence. We can be fooled into thinking that we indeed *are* these patterns and habits of action. They can overshadow us, tyrannize us, and restrict us: "I can't do that, I'm only a homemaker"; "I can't authorize that, I'm only a counter clerk."

Even worse, others may incorrectly apply static terms to us when we are merely engaged in an activity. Sometimes it is a useful escape for some; the idea that descriptions of us and our behavior dictate a certain identity. If we accept these identities bestowed on us by some sort of convention in the minds of others, we pay the price eventually. The shield we accept becomes a prison. However, it can be useful when under our control and it really is a case of "need to know."

We do not only do this to ourselves. We might sometimes do it to others too. Think of a time when someone behaved in a way that surprised you. A time when there was a big difference between what you expected and what was observed.

We can carefully observe the way someone behaves and describe it: he drives a van. We can solidify this as a label: he *is* a van driver. However, we can also work the other way around. We can decide that someone *is* a van driver and then have expectations about the way they should behave: "What is he doing on TV, he's only a van driver." And so it goes on. In this case, we are doing to someone else exactly what we might be doing to ourselves—defining a set of "appropriate" actions.

Of course, there *are* sets of appropriate actions to specific relationships and once that set is breached or transgressed then the relationship is no longer in effect. It may even be permanently destroyed as in the breaches of agreed and understood behavior patterns appropriate between partners in a relationship, business, or sport.

Accepting Limitation

Finally, there comes the last possibility of this whole sad story. We can become so used to accepting our own limitations, through self-imposed labeling and pigeon-holing, that we readily accept the defined limits that others place upon us.

We have labeled and fossilized behavior patterns and we have projections, both placed upon others and accepted for ourselves. From this we distinguish three levels.

First, there are the projected expectations and the actual events. These belong to the real world, the earth plane. The actual events are reality, but our perceptions and expectations introduce distortions. Where an action is neutral or ambiguous, we will usually see it as supporting our expectations. Have you ever had the experience with someone that no matter what you did you could not change their beliefs about you? Beliefs and expectations projected on the real world, outside our skins, make up the first level of illusion. The events themselves are real, yet how we see them is usually illusion.

Discrimination and Projection

At this plane of the physical, in the Sphere of Malkuth according to the Qabalistic Tree of Life, we must learn discrimination. We do this by setting aside our outer projections and expectations and then watching what actually happens. We try to "see things as they are." After this we can begin to work on the next level.

On the second level, we have the projections we place upon ourselves and those we accept from others. This is the realm of the astral plane and the Sphere of Yesod of the Qabalists.

It is here that the multiplicity of inner images lies. We may enter this plane through the creative imagination either passively, in order to view what is there, or actively in order to introduce new things. Now, you should realize that what is introduced to this plane will become a reality, for this is the plane of creative action. Indeed, all the systems of "positive-thought" use this plane to work their changes upon our lives and our world. Wishes here become reality, but not always what we expect, for we are not always aware of every part of our nature, and there may well be wishes within us that we dare not admit to the scrutiny of consciousness. Yet, these hidden wishes define our worlds and realities for us. This is why the early students of the Mysteries were admonished, "Know thyself."

The projections we place upon ourselves and those we accept from others find their way naturally into these astral realms. Each self-image accumulates and locks up energy, otherwise it would eventually dissipate. And, sets of similar images associate together by a form of attraction.

This process assists modern advertising techniques. The idea is to identify a common self-image, by desired activity, desired place in life, realistic slice-of-life images, and so forth, and associate a certain product with that image. An "image" in this context, by the way, is not just a single frozen picture but rather a related set of sequenced images that form the behavior fragments and patterns. Needless to say, those who have a strong popular self-image or lifestyle will find a mass of commercial products associated with their ideal self, for the more you espouse popular issues, the more susceptible you are to advertising.

When we become aware of all the options of presentation that are available to us, we can become aware of how we might sometimes appear to different people. We can take control of this. At the supermarket, my presentation is "shopper" and I can share a smile with another shopper as our carts nearly collide turning in and out of an aisle. When I am in the car, I am acting as a "driver" and I would behave quite differently in the same situation with cars and roads instead of carts and aisles.

Masks and Creativity

However, to return to the main topic, what makes these images in the cube creative is that they find expressions through our personalities. They are masks that we wear to play a role and they match our actions. Not only what we say, but also how we say things, how we do things. Each one of the masks is a pattern of stereotyped behaviors that we can hide behind, deliberately take up, use and put down as needed. We can, if we wish, use them as shields to prevent the scrutiny of others and to avoid exposing our supposedly vulnerable selves to the experiences of living in the now. Or, we can deliberately hone the different patterns so they more accurately express our identity in a way that matches the context of the moment.

Levels Leading Inward

This astral realm is the one that we enter by means of pathworkings, and the images we place there will begin to affect our consciousness and the naturalness of the way we deliberately present ourselves in the world. In the working of the crystal cube, we rose up from the ground, leaving the Earth plane behind.

These images, though, cannot be tackled upon their home ground. Introducing new images here, matched to other sets of behavior patterns, could lead us away from integration. We must pass beyond this level and penetrate to our deepest being if we are to bring harmony into our lives.

Therefore, we come to the third level. But, let us first recap the two levels we have already considered.

We first saw the world and our projections upon it. Then we looked at the inner images of the self and the restrictions placed and accepted there. Now we come to the *self* that tries to express itself in the world through these levels. We come to the *you* behind the mask, the sun that illuminates the moon of the astral realms.

Here, we find the principle of integration. It is symbolized throughout all ages by the sun, that vast body which regulates the many planets in their prescribed orbits. We see this idea of wholeness embodied in the monarch, a monarch like King Arthur, who brought all the knights, each a monarch in their own right, to sit at the round table, or like Queen Boudicca who rallied the

Iceni and other tribes against the rule of the Romans in the East Anglia region of England.

In a similar way, we too must bring our many images and behavior patterns to sit at the table of the inner self when this self takes up its rightful ruler-ship of the inner kingdom of our own consciousness.

The self at this level knows itself as *one* and, as one, knowingly finds expression through the multiple selves, the basic stock of behavior patterns, behavior patterns honed to match different situations and challenges in life. Make no mistake about this—you are still behind a mask here, but now you *know* you are doing so. Then you can use the mask, the "persona," the pattern, properly and to better effect.

It is not a fault to have these masks, or even to have a number of them. After all, the ones with more paints in their paint box can create more varied pictures.

Even so, we are still limited by the capacities of all these selves. When we wish to show forth a new aspect of our nature, to realize some newly discovered potential, we have to laboriously construct a set of behaviors, a set of habit patterns, through which we can express this new facet. It is like taking up a new sport or hobby. There is a learning curve and there are errors leading to learning and experience.

New Images of Self

Many people late in life take up some type of formal study. They learn how to be a student. In this way they come to make a new image of themselves. A new knight has come to sit at the round table. Perhaps this one is the knight destined to find the Grail, to restore the wasteland of the self. For the inner kingdom is desolate and it will remain so until the one comes who will sit in the perilous seat, who will undertake the quest of that which lies beyond the community of the table, who will lead you to find that rarest of treasures— yourself.

You now leave the table of the solar system and, soaring on wings of love, come closer to your origin. Now, just as each set of personal behaviors has its own unique existence while we are in incarnation, so too does the total experience of any one life on Earth form an abstract essence that gradually accumulates into what is sometimes called "the Ghost."

Past Life Influence

"The Ghost" can influence us in this life according to some past and outmoded set of behaviors from previous lives. The influence is very subtle for this Ghost, or self-of-the-past, is the essence of the true self, but at its earlier stage of development and while it might be useful to draw upon that vast experience and add perspective to our current situations, it is usually more advisable to steer well clear of it. History abounds with examples where the advisor to a monarch has sought to rule themselves. No less here. In mythology too we have the principle represented. Consider how much damage was done by Mordred, the shadow of King Arthur's past. We must negotiate this difficult intervening space and rise above its level if we are to have a true sense of self.

The Self at the Center

At last we find and enter our crystal cube, the inner diamond body where self and immortality meet. Like Merlin of old, we enter our house of glass. Standing beyond even the harmonizing of the roles, we finally see each role for what it truly is—a reflection of our own true self. Here we cannot hide from the awful truth—we could not project out any role that did not reflect our own self; good points, bad points. Here we face the fact that what we dislike in others is indeed in ourselves. What we demand from others is already in ourselves and what we give to others we give to ourselves.

Yet, we must penetrate beyond this again. We must abandon this multiplicity and penetrate to the essential *one*. We must remove the contamination of self from our perceptions and know things as they truly are. We must drop roles and projections and *be*. Then we shall know what we are.

No Self

The experience at such a time is private and unique. While this pathworking may not necessarily take you straight to that all-encompassing oneness that is a merging with the divine, it can give at this point a deep inner sense of what it might mean or in which direction it may lie for you.

This though is not the whole story, for we realize that we are not able as yet to just *be* the self we have experienced. Having plumbed our depths to the innermost core we find that we must come out into the world again to fulfill our destiny, our "unfinished business." On the return, however, we do not take up the outward roles and projections. Born again through the inter-dimensional cube, we return knowing what we are. Passing our central sun of harmony, we know who we are. Returning to Earth, we know how we are. We bring back, to our daily lives, the knowledge of our link with immortality, a link that inflames the heart and revitalizes our life. The Grail has been seen in Camelot.

Role-Playing and Projection

You will find that this working may make you aware of role-playing and projections in your relationships with others. Being aware of projections enables you to take control over them and see more clearly what is presented by others as-is, rather than through a filter of your own roles. As you move to change things in yourself, to be more direct and rely less on premade roles, you will meet resistance from others. You have changed, or so it seems. This is a part of the learning process. In all your dealings, treat others with a firm kindness. Working magic does not give you the right to trample on all in your way, nor cast suddenly adrift those in your tow. While this might be difficult for you, it is all good experience if you reflect upon the events and seek to understand them.

Anytime you are feeling that you are losing awareness of your role-playing, then settle down and visit your crystal cube again, but directly this time. Not every journey is the same.

One last point: the idea is not to do away with roles and projections, not at all. The whole point is to become aware of these mechanisms by which we manifest ourselves in the world and become the masters of them, rather than their unwitting slaves, and to do it with honesty.

Path 12: The Mountains
of the Moon

✣

This path will give you some surprises. There is a return to your original village and rejection by the people. Your castle and everything is closed to you
so you have no choice but to leave the valley and head up over the mountain
pass. This is rejection. You will leave the realm and climb the mountain, alone,
to find the pass into the next valley. You will meet a priest and priestess at the
summit and share with them what little you have. You descend to the other
valley and what you encounter will be a pleasant surprise.

The purpose of the working is to encourage the realization of the one
identity of yourself at the heart of all changes, all outer representations, and to
know that nothing gained is truly lost, but it may change form.

Preamble

You find yourself in the great hall of the castle. Pause and look around, then
make your way outside into the courtyard. Pause for a moment and remember your village from the very first pathworkings, the village that you left long
ago when you first wandered off into the woods. Time to return and see old
friends once more.

You leave the courtyard and head off back in to the wood where you had
your first adventure.

THE PATHWORKING

After a while of wandering in the wood, you come out at the other side of the
wood into clear country. There, ahead is your village. After all your adventures

you can't wait to get back to welcoming smiles and the chance to tell all that has befallen you.

You walk into the village and head for the village square. Already people have come out of houses and are following behind you. Upon arriving at the square, you see the elders of the village are already gathered. You smile as you approach, ready for the words of greeting.

Something is wrong. There are no smiles but scowls. Some of the villagers look angry. Some look scared and others look on with hatred. The looks of the elders hold nothing but pity and abandoned hope.

You are no longer welcome here. You left your friends. You left the safety of the village life, shunned what they had to offer. You have been gone in other lands and you may have changed. They do not want you back here.

The elders nod. You are banished. You must leave.

The villagers act at once on this pronouncement, crowding in on you, grabbing at your clothes, your hair, your things. They rip your fine clothes; strip you of your possessions. Somewhere along the way you lose your footwear.

Dejected, hurt, sad, and angry, you turn and leave the village, chased out by the yells and taunts of those who were once your friends.

Ragged and barefoot, you head back through the wood toward your castle. When you arrive, the gates are closed and locked. You have no key. You cannot get back in and no one responds to your calls.

You head off to the crystal cave. Perhaps there you will find a vision that will guide you. When you arrive at the entrance to the cave, a huge boulder blocks the way. There is no way in.

At this point, you realize that no matter where you go, everything will be closed to you. You have lost all that you had. It has all gone.

Think for a moment. If all the places you have been are closed to you, where can you go? Is there anywhere that you have not yet been?

You look beyond the cave entrance, up into the mountain beyond. You seem to know that it is part of a range separating this land from others, the Mountains of the Moon that form a natural barrier to this realm. Perhaps your new adventures will be found in a new land, perhaps new friends. Perhaps a way to start again now that all has been lost.

You see the feint traces of a track leading up and curving around. This must be the way. You follow for a while and as the path turns, there ahead of you stands one of the village elders. The elder says, "Take this, you may need it."

A piece of dry bread and a half-full wineskin are thrown down on the ground. You bend to pick them up and stand to thank your benefactor, but there is no one there.

You continue on the path for a ways, climbing higher and higher. At first the path winds back and forth and the going is easy, but soon the path gets steeper and heads nearly straight up the steep mountain. You pass a large rock and you see that the astrological sign of Capricorn is clearly carved deeply into it.

At times you look behind and get glimpses of the land you have left. You see the forests, the downs, the ocean, and the rivers. From the shadows that begin to spread across the land, you know that the clouds are rolling in on the mountain. Eventually, you pass into the clouds and in the silent wetness, you continue on.

Eventually, you come out above the clouds and see a pale blue sky with a wintry sun that gives little warmth. You have reached a point where the path become less steep and you see that it leads up through a saddle to the higher ridges beyond. You pause for a moment and take a little of the bread. You only take a little, as you do not yet know how far you still have to go. You are also feeling a little chilled so you take a couple of small sips of the warming wine.

You continue on, climbing ever higher, up into the saddle point and then on to the ridge ahead that marks the borders of your world. As you climb, you look down and see only an ocean of white cloud with your mountains as the only islands to be seen.

Soon you reach the flatter area that marks the summit and highest point in the pass. On that summit there stands a priest and a priestess who look vaguely familiar. Behind them there is a stone altar with a golden plate and crystal chalice upon it. They smile and you approach. It is the priest who speaks.

"You have with you bread and wine. Are you willing to share that which sustains life and that which brings joy? For only so may you pass on beyond."

To pass you will have to share what little you have, to give up what you may well need in the journey ahead. Are you willing to do so? There is nothing for you behind. Your only choice is onwards. What was has gone. The choice is yours. Go back to nothing or share what you have. If you feel you cannot share wholeheartedly, leave the path now and return to normal consciousness.

Deciding to continue, you hand the bread and the wine to the priest who takes them to the altar. The priestess beckons you to come closer. You see that there is salt on the plate and some clear water in the chalice. The priestess speaks, "You have brought us the bread that sustains life. It is also the teaching that sustains spiritual life, grains of truth leavened with experience. It is as vital as the air we breathe. On this platter is salt. As we work though our incarnations in Earthy planes, we perspire and in our perspiration there is the salt of our toil. It is of the earth."

The priest says, "You have also brought us the wine that brings us joy as it runs its fiery course through our blood. It signals all the passions and the energies that they call forth and hence we deem it spiritual fire. In the chalice is pure water, the water of the ocean of birth, the water of the mother, and the water of the sorrows the mother suffers at the hands of her children, by what they do and by what is done to them. We see that water is also the tears of sorrow that are part of life and renewal."

The priestess breaks the bread into small pieces onto the platter with the salt saying, "Toil and teaching mingled."

The priest pours the wine into the chalice with the water and you see the swirling red and white as they mix.

"Joy and Sorrow intertwined, the priest says.

The priestess turns to face the sky beyond the altar and raises the platter saying, "Let all joy be to she who is the grain and to we the children of that grain."

The priest turns likewise, raising the chalice and says, "Let all joy be to he who is the vine and to we the children of that vine."

It seems that a light beam strikes down onto the platter and chalice and you know that the offerings have been accepted. The priestess turns, picks up a piece of the salted bread and presents it to you. You open your mouth and she feeds it to you. She then turns to the priest and gives him a piece of the bread. Finally, she takes a piece for herself.

The priest turns and offers you the chalice with both hands. You place your hands on his and drink from the chalice. The priest then offers to the priestess in the same way before taking a drink himself. The priest and priestess embrace and kiss and then both come to you for the exchange of an embrace with each and, if appropriate, a kiss.

The priest speaks again. "You have shown that you are prepared to share your knowledge and your joy. You have shown that you are prepared to receive toil and sorrow in return. Only such may pass to the lands beyond and you have earned that right. Pass on now and enjoy what may come."

You take your leave from here, beginning your descent on the other side of the mountain ridge. Below you spreads again the carpet of cloud and soon you enter its cool damp world.

You continue the steep descent with care, and you come clear of the clouds that are already dispersing. Below, there spreads the features of your new land. You see forests and rolling hills. You see rivers and the sea. Not really a lot different here than the other side of the range. You look back and can now see the peaks of the Mountains of the Moon, no longer shrouded from view.

You continue on and the path becomes easier, less steep, and winding more, back and forth. Feeling happy and light of foot, you come to the lower reaches of the mountain and enter a forest, still following a path that now becomes clearer and more worn.

As you walk through this mighty forest, you begin to think that it is not that much different from the one you entered, so long ago, on your first journey into this realm. As if to lend weight to this idea, you see a clearing ahead and in the clearing there stand some stone columns surrounding a glass-like coffin. As you move closer you see that in this new land the lid is off the coffin, propped to one side, and the coffin is empty except for a pair of golden sandals.

You lean down and pick up the sandals. These will come in handy on your bare feet. You put them on and as you stand upright again you catch sight of your reflection in the glass lid. You are dressed as the wizard. You are the wizard, the wandering person of power and the carrier of tradition.

The wizard in the tomb of your first journey was yourself, part of your nature entombed and imprisoned. Now it is free. You have regained your knowledge and power.

If the land this side of the ridge is the same as the land on the other side, then you know where the castle should be. You head in that direction. Soon you leave the forest and there as expected is the castle. You walk confidently up to the gates and call out.

A guard appears at the top of the gateway and asks, "Who calls for admittance?"

You reply in your own words to the effect that this is your castle and you have returned from your adventures.

"How do we know it is you?" asks the guard.

You cup your hands and hold them out. When you open them again, a blood red rose is there glistening with fresh dew. The gates open and you are welcomed into the courtyard. There are people going about the business of running a castle, looking after animals, gardens, making alterations and repairs. You enter the great hall with the rose still in your hand and you sit at the round table with only its empty segments.

You close your eyes and think on what has occurred in this path. When you open them, you see several items laid out in a circle on the table. This is what you see:

A rough block of quartz, previously your stone or rock, representing your first path and your unrefined inner nature at that time.

A black mirror of scrying, previously the crystal shard, representing your visions in the crystal cave.

A master key to all gates, previously a flat piece of rusted metal, representing the power of knowledge learned in the library tower.

An oak chalice, previously the small acorn cup, representing in its material the Lord of the Forest, in its shape the Lady of Light and in its contents the Child of Promise, all met in the grove.

A short staff with a single carved serpent twining around it, previously the gnarled and twisted stick, from the healing temple of Asclepius.

A short sword, previously the flat piece of wood, having balance in its grip to give you the powers of discernment from the path of adjustment.

A silver chain, previously the single silver link, with a pendant bearing the mystical emblem of most significance to your path, representing the path you found at the school of the wisdom.

A magical ring, previously the loop of grass, giving the power to observe in other realms of mind and spirit and pass between them, as you experienced in the world between worlds.

A pentacle, previously the small piece of driftwood, with a design on it representing for you the nature of the universe, a plan for the builders from the land of Ys.

A horn wand of will, previously the shard of bone, giving the creativity to give birth to your desires, your hopes, your dreams, being a gift from the unicorn.

A polished crystal cube, previously the smooth pebble, representing the other pole of the rough block, the refined nature of the person of inner knowledge, of magical power, of spiritual love.

These are your new gifts from many of the paths. You realize, too, that the wizard's robes and the sandals you wear, represent this path, the journey that you took into the unknown, to find yourself when all was lost, to cross over to the other way of seeing the same reality, by sharing gains and accepting loss.

Finally, you place the red rose that is in your hands, and originally from the Nameless path, in the center of all, and the center of your original gifts from the elemental monarchs, for here all gods are one god, all goddesses one goddess, all paths are one path, on which we are all fellow travelers and there is but one initiator.

Ponder these thoughts and your gifts. When you are ready, return to normal consciousness.

Discussion

This working begins with an important point. No matter what we may wish about the results of our spiritual training, change cannot be avoided. By this I do not mean external change, the kind of change that comes from abstaining from habits or addictions, following healthier eating regimes, and such. Some who make these changes then endure a daily battle to stay away from past addictions. For some the changes are in behavior without inner restructuring of the individual. The behaviors change but the feelings of dependency remain.

The Use of Experience

As we grow from birth, we structure our inner nature according to our experiences of the outer world in which we find ourselves. All of the sense inputs that go into the inner building of ourselves, according to our basic genetic makeup, come from a variety of sources.

First, there are the events themselves—events of the outer world. These are seen, heard, smelled, felt, and so on. With these we have our own inner reactions and valuations. These, too, are taken as building blocks for our inner structure. Two people will evaluate similar experiences in quite different ways, so the external events are in no way determinants of the style our inner building will take. There are statistics on this of course and researchers tell us that a child who experiences certain things will have a high chance of growing up a certain way.

But, the choice is always there to evaluate the events in our own way. These predictions can only be statistical and no one can say in any one given case how that child will develop, even if it were possible to control or know the external events at all times.

Effects of Magical Work

But, to return to the theme, once we have worked magically, we have begun to alter the inner structure of our being. While the learning of new skills or changing our diet may only marginally alienate us from our fellows in close society, the one thing all animals seem to know is when there is an inner difference. Once you have made changes to your inner self, you will be detected as being no longer of your group, family, or tribe. The fundamental differences are sensed and at very low levels of consciousness, difference is perceived as a threat. This is a natural response, yet we can work with it and tone down its effects if we are aware of it. If not, we behave like the maddened mob.

The Setting Apart

The pathworking program you undertook provided you with an alternate set of events to help you bring your inner structure into harmony with archetypal principles. Since you and the rest of your tribe had previously lived with a structure built haphazardly from events and value systems shared among you, this harmonizing of your own inner structure sets you apart from those who were your peers.

At best, they drive you away. They may also blame you for any mishaps that have befallen them. They may, in fact, become a danger to you.

Thus, it is said that a prophet is not without honor—except in their own home. We are not allowed to change so significantly.

This principle is represented by the expulsion from the village. Naturally, you will, in such circumstance, end up leaving stuff behind you. Things that were once of value and part of your life are suddenly deemed "owned" by others. You are stripped of them. There are many people who have experienced change when within a relationship with a partner. And, many have stories to tell about what they lost in the breakup. People, when threatened, can make claims on things that you believe belonged to you.

Loss

This loss from the expulsion is part of the process of spiritual growth. You must leave things, ideas, and values of the past. You have psychically moved on and outgrown those old forms but you do not yet realize this. Because of this, you experience loss.

Such is the extent of the loss that even those new experiences of your life that led to this situation are no longer of use to you. In fact, they, too, are closed to you.

There is a French expression, "Reculer pour mieux sauter," which can be translated, "To step back in order better to leap." This is very descriptive of the process of spiritual advancement.

The Dark Night

Many processes of development consist of a series of upward developments punctuated with a series of plateau consolidations. Not so for spiritual development, because spiritual development is a movement not of levels within a mode of being, but a change of the entire mode of being.

We cannot just continue to climb. It is no longer the same mountain. We must descend to the valley to tackle the next height. The higher the next peak, the lower it seems we must descend.

This spiritual experience is often called " the dark night of the soul" and despite the fact it says "the" it is a process we can go through many times in our lives. If you look at things from a mystical point of view, you will probably realize that this "dark night" is the other side of depression.

Feelings of depression are something many of us experience at one time or another. I am not talking here of clinical depression, a diagnosable and serious condition. We can feel down, disappointed for a while, and later it passes. What is happening is that inner changes are taking place and closing off things in the outside world that were previously available to us. We experience this as loss rather than as stepping back to leap better. This temporary feeling that leads to a positive change of direction is not *in itself* a disease or disorder, it is a natural process of the soul, but can be intense or overpowering. Although it signals not the end but the opportunity for a new beginning for a better path, we still have to face it to get the power needed to leap forward again. If that challenge is at the wrong time or seemingly too big at the time, it can sometimes overpower us, hampering our abilities, darkening our perceptions.

This is like drawing a bow. The arrow thinks, "What's wrong with me? I seem to be going backward" and it is sometimes called situational depression.[46] Wrongly evaluated, it can be fatal.

Entry of a Helper

It is perhaps, at this point, that you find a helper. This person has probably been available all along through your situation. You just were so deeply into yourself that you did not see it. I know from experience that we can be so down that we push away the very people who could help us, if only they knew just to *be* and not *do*.

But then, the drawstring fully back and going no further, we look forward again, the drawstring is released, and we see the next height to be scaled. Another peak of the mountains of the moon beckons to us. Another land lies beyond. Maybe Shangri-La, Shamballa, or the Grail Realm.

After the breakup of a marriage, I had friends who were ready to help me through the following period with emotional support and comfort. I knew that only later. At the time, I was not open to seeing it and even in one particular case actively rejected any attempt that person made to get close enough. She was there not to help me out of where I was but just to be there, with me. It meant a lot when I realized this later.

---

46. Timothy J. Legg, "Situational depression or clinical depression?" *Medical News Today*, September 28, 2018, https://www.medicalnewstoday.com/articles/314698.php.

The moment comes when we see who will help us and they are standing at the side of the track with something to help us on our way. This is a person who loves us with the pure love that will allow them to speed us on our way, even if it means they will never see us again.

We represent the help here with bread and wine, recognized across cultures as the foundations of sustenance.

Capricorn and Other Symbols

It is this act of climbing the unknown heights that brings us into line with the sign of Capricorn, the mountain goat. If you have ever seen mountain goats in their habitat, you will know that not only can they safely stand on bare smooth rock inclined at a ridiculous angle, but also they can unerringly leap from rock to rock. For us they are a symbol of confident progress in a difficult terrain.

In addition, the mountain has been used in many cultures to represent matters of the spirit or the divine. The Greek gods and goddesses lived on Mount Olympus, for example, but this is a common theme through many of humanity's cultures.

While climbing, in this working, you occasionally look back. This is a natural process where even though you have begun your new life after the dark night you still have throwback memories of the prior time. This, again, is not an aberration but a perfectly natural process. It can be observed in the removal of any conditioned behavior.

Someone may give up smoking and feel that they have mastered it when the desire no longer exists after three weeks. A week later—bang—the desire hits out of the blue. This can go on for many months, the desire becoming less and less each time. In classical psychological conditioning terms, this is part of "extinction" of the conditioned response.

The End of Before

In the working you eventually come to the clouds, and from this point on you no longer get glimpses of the before time. The changes you were going through have now "set" in place. The past has no further hold on you. It is here where you can begin to use the help that the loved ones have given you, taking a little of the bread and the wine, allowing their support to carry you on without being too needy for it.

What a wonderful sight it is to be high on a mountain range, above the clouds and to see the cloud as an ocean among islands. It is at such a time that we can realize that although, at some levels, things appear separate, below the surface they are joined—the mountains are parts of a single range. Maybe we can come to see people like this. Maybe we realize that each peak may at times feel all alone among others, alone but yet all are connected, even with the deep valleys below.

Priest and Priestess

The valley of rejection is far below and you now stand at the peak or crossover point where the possibility of bliss and love and acceptance exist. In this heightened awareness, may there not be a hint of the divine? Or at least, we can recognize those who can mediate that love and bliss and acceptance to us. These are represented by the priest and priestess, figures who traditionally act as contact points between humanity and divinity. But of course, they seem familiar. They have been with you all along, more or less visible from time to time. Did you recall them from other pathworkings?

But all is not freely given. You need to give something in return. The knights on their Holy Grail quest met challenges and tests where they had to do something or give something to prove themselves for the next stage in their adventure.

In this case, you need to give what had been given to you. One who loved you gave you the means to move out of your prior state. At this point you are in a state and frame of mind to be a helper to others, to freely give your love and support to others.

The Symbolic Offerings

The wine, water, bread, and salt represent the four elements of the wise. These are fire, water, air, and earth, respectively. Bread is the staff of life exactly as the air we breathe. Wine puts fire in the veins. The meanings of each of these four has been given in the working itself and will not be repeated here. It might be a good idea though to meditate on those meanings and plumb their greater depth. These four are used in the Pagan "sacrament."

The pathworking then presents a tableau where the priest and priestess bless the bread and wine and offer it to divinity. This particular form of this practice is the same form used in the rites of my Pagan groups.

In some traditions, the essence of divinity is deemed to enter the bread and wine. In consuming it, that essence enters us and in the consuming of it we feed each other. In this way we become on some level children of the gods and goddesses, a Child of the Lord and Lady. The embrace and kiss seal this.

With some essence of divinity within you, you have shouldered the style of the divine in some measure. In the Judeo-Christian mystery tradition, it is said that God gave humans free will because He wanted them to turn to him out of choice, not compulsion. How this differs from the exoteric Old Testament god who comes across as vengeful, punitive, authoritarian and, well, petulant.

Discovering Love

To love someone is to let them make their own choices, go their own way, make their own mistakes, even hurt you, and all of this making no difference to the love you have for them. I guess the closest we get to this at times is in the love we have for our children. Through that experience we can sometimes get glimpses of what such a divine love would be like.

It is that here you are asking yourself, through the working, to be prepared to give freely of your love and knowledge and joy even if the return will only be toil and sorrow. This is a deep mystery.

You continue your progress of return from these rarefied heights of spiritual consciousness. You pass below the cloud and can now see ordinary things again, features of your future landscape. In the dark night of the soul you came to meet the divine and as you emerge you see new possibilities and a brand-new future.

After a while you realize that you have not lost anything at all because where you are is like where you had been, only now you can see its possibilities for the future that you did not see before because you find yourself in the same realm that you left.

The Start and the End

What does this mean?

In one of the Holy Grail adventures, a group of knights come to a gorge or river across which there is half a bridge. That is, the bridge spans half the gap and then stops.

When the knights ride on to the bridge and come to the end of it at the midpoint of the gap, there is a creaking sound. The whole half-bridge pivots across from one bank to the other. By turning around and leaving the bridge, they find themselves on the other bank and in the Holy Grail realm.

But the mystery of this is that this Grail realm is not a separate realm at all. There is no other bank. There is no pivot on the bridge. The land in which they ride and experience mysteries is no other than the land they were always in. They see it differently as they now see the reality of it, not just the mundane exterior.

There is a similar tale about being led by a jackal across a trackless waste to the other side, which is yet the same side. There are references in Buddhist text to "the other shore" which once reached is "this shore." The message of the mystics is ever the same when we seek to cross the abyss. They have entered through the door by which they left and know the place for the first time.

And another change has taken place. Because of your experiences you have released locked-up energies within your own nature. The restructuring—I hesitate to use the worn-out term re-programming—that the images and experiences of the pathworkings encouraged has given you access to powers and resources you always had. It is just that they could not be accessed or would not flow.

Owning the Realm

In this realm that you have traveled and lived over the past twelve months, you are indeed the wizard and the owner of the castle. Your control over the events in this realm is symbolized by your production of the glistening rose.

This vignette is taken from a story about the Sufi Poet Jalaluddin Rumi. It is how he proved who he was to gain access to a town after curfew after walking out of the desert. Now, in this realm, you can do it too.

Not only that, but you have more obvious helpers in your castle now, running things. You can accept these various people as symbolic personifications of skills and talents within your own nature that are now available and empowered to get on with whatever is required.

And ... the Tools

At first you do not see the gifts you had received on the other paths and it is for a moment as though you have also lost these. But, in fact, you then see those same gifts differently. You see their inner reality. Rocks may dream to be quartz and every circle is a ring of power. With these, your magical tools for this realm, you can start defining your own practices and adventures. For this realm is truly your own. Use it wisely.

Conclusion

✛

You have come on quite a journey through novel experiences and helpful realizations. You have established the inner kingdom of your own personal nature and the places in that realm are linked to meanings that are important and relevant to you. It is a place you can visit at any time.

When you have traveled in the outer world as a tourist, you may later encounter sights, sounds, people, incidents, or more in everyday life that evoke memories of your travels or bring incidents from your travels to mind again. Perhaps there is a smile for a fond memory.

It is very similar with pathworkings.

After you have made your travels in the inner realm, you may well find that events in the outer world resonate with your inner experiences. This can be very interesting and provide opportunities for further realizations and personal unfoldment. You could jot notes in your diary when such experiences occur.

Now that you have established your inner world and made your place in it, you have opportunities for further learning and inner experiences.

This book has provided a groundwork experience for the technique of pathworking for self-unfoldment. You have established an inner realm that you can revisit and use at any time. Your inner realm can sometimes give you answers to outer world problems or can simply be a container of favorite places to visit. It can also be the starting realm for even more adventures in self-unfoldment.

May you be blessed in all your traveling. Good journey.

—Simon Court

Appendix A: Relaxation, Breathing, and Seed Thought Meditation

─────────── ╬ ───────────

This appendix is included to give some instruction on relaxation and breathing for those who have not had experience of such exercises before. It also provides details on a method of meditation well-suited to partner pathworking experiences. The relaxation and breathing should be used prior to pathworkings. In between workings, it can be used to prepare for meditation.

Certainly there should be an initial period of rhythmic breathing and physical relaxation, with an attendant sharpening of the inner senses, before beginning any serious inner work.

Here, then, are some suggestions in case you require them.

Relaxation

One of the simplest ways to relax is to start at one end of the body, say the head, or the feet, and consider each set of muscles one at a time. By contracting those muscles momentarily and then suddenly relaxing, that group of muscles will usually be left in a more relaxed state than before you started.

By progressing steadily along the body from one end to the other, you will find that your body is noticeably more relaxed at the end than at the beginning of the practice.

One should be careful not to relax too much and fall asleep! Relaxation while lying down may lead to sleep more easily than when relaxing while seated in a chair.

As the body relaxes, the mind or inner senses should become sharper and more finely concentrated, in a sort of seesaw effect.

One area worth particular attention has been found to be the muscles around the eyes—top of cheeks, side of eyes, forehead—all those come into play when one narrows the eyes.[47] Relaxation of these groups is worth a considerable amount of work.

Breathing

One of the best breathing systems in use is one that in the Western Esoteric Tradition is called "The Four-Fold Breath," although it is known in other traditions. Paraphrasing Shiva's instructions to Devi, recorded four thousand years ago:

> The Breath turns from in to out, and it also swings from out to in. At both these time, realize! Or when in-breath and out-breath become one, touch the empty, all-creative center. Or when the breath is all out and stopped, or all in and stopped, pause, and the small self disappears.[48]

In this procedure you breathe in to an arbitrary count of four, hold, without stopping the throat, for a count of two, breathe out for four and then hold again for two before repeating the cycle.

In magical terms, we have the In Breath of the Mother, the Out Breath of the Father and the Non Breath of the Androgynous Child split between the two. In the change from one to the other, we, the Child, may hear.

When performing any breathing exercise, the diaphragm should be used. Expanding the abdomen pulls down the diaphragm and draws air into the lower lungs. This should form the first half of the in breath with the second half filling the upper lungs through expansion of the chest.

Breathing out should reverse this process by first pulling in the abdomen to push up the air in the lower lungs—displacing that in the upper lungs—before contracting the chest to expel it.

---

47. H. Syz, "Reflections on Group- or Phylo-Analysis," *Acta Psychotherapa* 11, supplement (1963): 37–88.

48. Paul Reps and Nyogen Senzaki, comps., *Zen Flesh, Zen Bones* (New York: Anchor Books, 1967), 214.

Seed Thought Meditation

This is the form of meditation you should perform during the four weeks between pathworkings. It will expand and enhance your inner world experiences and help anchor them in consciousness.

Pick an idea, a correspondence, a symbol, a thought, either from the experience of the working, the details of the working itself, or one or other aspect of the symbolism and explanations in the associated discussion.

Dwell in a relaxed way on the chosen seed thought. Something associated with it will come into mind, usually. Dwell on that for a while, turning it this way and that in examination, metaphorically. Another idea related to the new one will arise. Ponder that one. You are following an association chain. Keep allowing associated ideas to arise and be considered until you think that you have traveled too far from the original seed thought.

Return to the seed thought and follow a new chain of associations. Continue this until you feel you have extracted enough or until the further associations just stop.

Then, return you attention to your breathing pattern briefly, note your relaxation, and then open your eyes, stretch your arms, legs, and so on, and return to normal consciousness.

Finally, write down your chosen seed thought and the realization chains that arose. If nothing arose, that is fine. Just note that down.

This meditation method can be a powerful tool in unlocking your potential for creative thought.

Appendix B: A Note on the Structure of the Paths of the New Moon

✣

This appendix provides some additional notes about this pathworking series. These notes are snippets that may provide you with additional insights into the series and the experiences you have had.

The Tree of Life

Although the structure of the series maps beautifully onto the signs of the zodiac, the series was originally conceived with a different framework. The framework was the Tree of Life of the Qabalists. This structure shows spheres of form function and consciousness in relationship to each other. The system is used to show the descent of original essence into manifestation by a series of stages or transitions "down the tree." It also is used to show the way back as our spiritual nature evolves "up the tree."

Malkuth

The first working was intended to represent the sudden awakening in the world of Malkuth, the bottom-most sphere of manifest existence, the world, the body, and so on. The spiritual experience of this sphere in Qabalistic teaching is discrimination. It is this discrimination that allows us to "wake up" and make a difference between living the reflected or unreflected life. That is, to just live or to take direction in our living. If we just live, we get lost, spiritually speaking. To take charge, we need to discriminate between the real and the unreal, the permanent and the transient, and so on.

What I have just written may appear at odds with some methods of spiritual unfoldment. If so, let me add that moving from the unreflected life to a life lived in consciousness is an appropriate *first* step for the particular method used in this series. I will mention this again later.

Yesod

The next sphere on the Tree of Life is Yesod—the treasure house of images. It is for this sphere that I devised the idea of the crystal cave, borrowing from Mary Stewart's books about Merlin and from certain symbols in use in some magical orders.

The sphere of Yesod is causal toward the sphere of Malkuth, the plane of effects. Although it is the plane of effects it is the one we are normally conscious of and the one in which we believe all cause and effect takes place.

The magical experience received on making contact with the sphere of Yesod is "vision of the machinery of the universe." You will have to see this for yourself, of course, but consider this—Yesod contains the causes and Malkuth the effects.

If we act in Yesod, the effects will be seen in Malkuth. How else is it that Rumi could make a fresh rose appear in his cupped hands? To work magic, we work in Yesod and Yesod is the sphere of the visual imagination.

Hod

The next sphere on the tree is Hod. This is the sphere of form, of logical thought and mentation. It is the image-making faculty that feeds into the active images used in Yesod. It is ruled by Mercury, who governs all forms of communication. I chose a town and a library to symbolize this experience.

Netzach

The next sphere is Netzach, representing force, often in the form of nature. In other words, it is the life force that moves and ensouls the sterile forms made in Hod, called by more than one Qabalist "cosmic emptiness." This animates those forms making them usable in Yesod. This life force, the power of nature, I chose to represent with the grove and because this force has a strong fertility and sexual element; you meet a god and goddess, who may just as well be Pan and Aphrodite as any other. You also meet the Radiant Child.

It is we who are the children of the gods and goddesses, but we do not yet see it and the radiant child is externalized as their child of love and of the woods.

Tiphereth

In Tiphereth we can find all the healing gods who are also sacrificed, and often resurrected, gods. Because of this, I placed the healing temple here in the series. However, the healing temple working came out of my mystical experience while at the Temple of Epidaurus in Greece.

It was there that I "saw" the reverse idea where rather than sound coming out, it was healing energy focusing into and at the center. It was also there that I "heard" the chanting and knew how the temple had been used.

Geburah

The next sphere on the ascent is Geburah, ruled by Mars. This is the force that breaks down things either drastically, caustically, or by slow erosion. Its power dismantles. This is where I chose to place the pathworking relating to karma and karmic adjustment.

The trumps of the tarot are placed on the twenty-two "paths" that link the ten spheres of the tree of life. One of the paths connected to this sphere of Geburah has the card "the Chariot" associated with it and this is another reason it is in the working, basically as a "place marker." This is sometimes useful in a series of items.

Chesed

The next sphere of Chesed is the sphere of building up, which balances Geburah. It is also associated with Jupiter and the benevolent constructive nature is often associated with the great teachers of humanity, some of whom are humans who have "gone before." It is for this reason that I placed the experience of the school here where all paths are one and where each may find their own way, their own path, their own teacher, their own teaching.

Da'ath

Normally the next path would be the third sphere of Binah but in later Qabalistic teachings (which nevertheless were long ago) a sphere was added that exists in another dimension. This is the sphere of Da'ath or knowledge. As it straddles the abyss—a sort of "rift" between the realms of spirit and those of existence, referred to as a "fall" in many religions—it is related to all things inter-dimensional.

For this reason I placed the working the World Between Worlds at this point. The style of the working came to me from two sources. One was a reference in a book by science-fiction writer A. E. van Vogt that had the hero temporarily trapped in an in-between world. The second was the creation of Narnia in one of the books of the *Chronicles* by C. S. Lewis. This sphere has much to do with the mysteries of making and unmaking.

Binah

We come to the next sphere proper. This is Binah, understanding, the great mother from whom all proceeds. It is also a form sphere like Hod. Out of these ideas and the legends of Lyoness and Ys, I built the idea of a submerged city that had a plan. This would then be the primordial plan of existence for each one of us, just as Binah has the submerged plan of all existence. The magical grade associated in Lodges of the Golden Dawn Tradition with Binah is Magister Templi—Master of the Temple. The temple could be thought of as our own self.

Chockmah

Next in order comes Chockmah. On the downward path it is the point where duality first appears. It is a sphere of power and that power comes out of the tension between two poles. Hence the way of the unicorn is a polarity working. Into it I drew on many tales of unicorns. I chose the unicorn because of references made by Charles Williams in several of his writings to the unicorn as the giver of voice to creation, only when he had the partnership of a suitable maiden, who setting aside the dangers allowed him to rest in her lap. I have converted this to the horn of the unicorn's generative nature that becomes the central pole and the multicolored streamers. The music represents the voice of the unicorn in song and the dance and the weaving of one creation out of the infinite number of possibilities that potentially exist between the two polarities of impetus and background.

In human terms it is the one partner who so loves the other partner that they willingly become the background against which that partner's creativity can blossom forth.

Nature could not create the perfect being and so made types who share the skills needed to be the perfect natural being—"man" and "woman" in character, but not necessarily in physicality. That is, I use these terms to refer to function, not physical gender. The brain can be wired this way or that way or a bit of both but cannot be wired both ways at once. Even so, one partner may be plus sometimes, minus others, and midpoint at others. The other partner will be likewise. Energy is created when the poles are separated, statically or dynamically changing.

Kether

The final sphere on the Tree is the topmost sphere of Kether. This is the supreme sphere, the first appearance of "something" out of the Great Unmanifest. In our terms, it is the "Big Bang" that began the universe, put crudely. It is all possibilities and none. It is pure necessity with no other reason for existence.

For this working I wanted to recap the theme of ascending the Tree to that point. Hence we begin at Earth (Malkuth), ascend the Middle Pillar to the Moon (Yesod), then the sun (Tiphereth), then the star / cube (Da'ath), and finally the disappearance into essence (Kether).

The Unmanifest and Return

In the Mountains of the Moon I envisaged the theme of "passing beyond." To do this I borrowed heavily from many mystical texts and teachings and from the idea I learned within the magical school in which I initially trained, The Society of the Inner Light. You see, beyond Kether there is only the Unmanifest. The only way we can understand anything is if it is manifest, no matter in how rarefied a manner. Therefore, it has to be for us that as we pass beyond Kether we find ourselves manifest again.

We ascend the mountain, "walk with god and are not,"[49] and return—changed.

---

49. King James Bible, Genesis 5:24.

As I mentioned at the beginning, some systems of mystical unfoldment teach that removing the involvement of mind and ego and taking life as it comes is the method to use. In the Western Mystery Tradition we take a roundabout rather than a direct route. The only purpose of building structures and symbol systems during the practice of the way of magic is to reach the point where we transcend them.

You may well come to a point where you can say of life, "Everything is as it needs to be." The roundabout route is to bring you to that realization for yourself and in yourself. At the start of the journey, it is just something you believe from what someone else has said.

The Nameless Path

The thirteenth working, the Nameless Path, is taken from one of the poems in the Arthuriad of Charles Williams.[50] In the poem the images of rose and wool appear very powerful. However, I wanted to combine this idea with the underlying background of all. This is why I chose to represent the three-fold goddess in this path who acts at all levels as the background to the god and to all existence. In a sense it could be said that it is an attempt to represent the Great Unmanifest in its nature of standing behind all manifestation.

Because it represents what stands behind, we may not always be aware of it. We see the subject of the painting primarily and the background of the painting provides context for the subject. We tend not to see backgrounds in their own right. But from time to time, when circumstances happen to be suitable, we can be suddenly hit by the background itself, as though the subject and setting switch places. It takes us by surprise and is not something we consciously do as a rule. For this reason, I gave this path no particular place in the sequence, assigning it to whichever lunation happened to be the second in a zodiac sign. This varies from year to year.

The thirteenth path also indicates the Order that stands behind these teachings as I present them. It is an old Order and from time to time withdrawn. Many known Orders have derived from it. It has been known as a mystical Order though all traditions. It is the Order of the Rose. The theme of the Order is not to provide a specific teaching, take it or leave it, but by standing

---

50. Charles Williams, *Taliessin Through Logres* (1938) and *The Region of the Summer Stars* (1944) (London: Oxford University Press, 1954).

behind outer schools its theme is to provide the training necessary for those who study in it to find their own path and school that suits them. In doing this we will "bring Cedar from Lebanon and Gold from Ophir."[51]

Finally, an onion has many skins and the journey within may take many ascents of the Tree of Life until we become one with the center. Even these simple pathworkings can be used sequence after sequence, taking you to places where your understanding of the nature of being unfolds at deeper and deeper levels.

In a sense, the journey has no goal. In this it is not lacking because the whole idea of a goal is flawed. There is never a destination in the unfolding of life. There is only the journey itself.

---

51. Taken from the materials used in the building of the Temple of Solomon, I Kings 10, 11. Also often used by Dion Fortune in her works on magical training and the Western Mystery Tradition.

.

Appendix C: Magical and Training Organizations
✧

This appendix is about magical and training organizations. The previous appendix lists works of some of the people mentioned here. When we humans decide to take up training of any sort, there are those who prefer to work alone, those who prefer to work in groups, and those who like a bit of both. The guidance of the developmental work usually comes from a person with prior skills and experience in those skills, whether the teaching is presented in person, via audiovisual media, in print, or some other medium. These are not mutually exclusive.

My early training in the mysteries began with books and solo practices. I then joined a group where I received direct information and guidance from some already skilled in the areas of magic and mysticism. Later, I began setting up and working with groups of individuals who wanted to study and work with what some call "The Mysteries." This last was more informal, and in learning and practicing we had fun.

Of these options, you may have your own preferences. If you prefer to work alone from written materials, then use this book as an introduction and there are the books in the bibliography, some of which have been referenced in this book and some I can recommend on the basis of my knowledge of the authors. This is just my personal list from my knowledge and experience. There are, however, many training groups and plenty of opportunities to find a match to your own personal preferences in material and instruction method. An internet search will provide plenty of options for further study in this aspect of the tradition.

First in the list is the main school in which I trained, **The Servants of the Light.** This school offers a comprehensive training course in the Western Esoteric Tradition. It was initially started as The Helios Course by Gareth

Knight, who wrote the introductory lessons. W. E. Butler wrote the main training material. For several decades the director of studies was Dolores Ashcroft-Nowicki. From mid-June 2018, Dr. Steven Critchely assumed the role of director of studies. I had a lot of help and guidance from this organization. More information can be found at www.servantsofthelight.org.

The Society of the Inner Light was my first and brief encounter with a magical order. It was founded in 1924 by Dion Fortune (Violet M. Firth). Many have been through its training course in the Western Mysteries, of which studies in Qabalah are only one part. Today, it still offers training, supervised for United Kingdom and European residents and unsupervised for others. Check the website www.innerlight.org/uk for more details. At the time of my first studies with them, by mail and solo practice, the guidance was professional and matter-of-fact. That suited me fine. I have no information on their current methods of training, but I have every reason to believe that the organization is just as professional and dedicated in their training as they ever were.

Quest is run by Marian Green and offers workshops in formal and natural magic. The reason I recommend this organization is that I have attended group workshops and know Marian to be a skilled and dedicated worker and instructor in the Western Mysteries, formal and natural. Her work and teachings include formal Qabalistic magic. However, I believe the main focus to be the less formal but none-the-less structured and effective Natural Magic. Find out more at www.magicalquest.co.uk or from Quest magazine.

You can also write to: BCM-SCL, **Quest,** London, WC1N 3XX. Last I checked in 2019, this address is still correct and has remained the same for at least forty years. BM/BCM is a London-based commercial re-mailing service I have used myself, being nomadic by birth and upbringing. On that basis, I feel confident providing it for those who still enjoy letter-writing.

The Order of the Golden Dawn. There are a number of Golden Dawn groups continuing in various ways the work and teachings of that Order. A lot of training and source material is available online. In addition, some of the training schools in the Western Esoteric Tradition run sub-groups along the lines of the Golden Dawn. These are usually only open to members and invited members of other "sister" groups.

Bibliography

Alighieri, Dante. *The Comedy of Dante Alighieri*. Translated by Dorothy L. Sayers, Harmondsworth: Penguin Books, 1982.

Allen, Richard Hinckley. *Star Names and Their Meanings*. Mineola, NY: Dover Publications, 2000.

The American Heritage Dictionary. "The American Heritage Dictionary Indo-European Roots Appendix." The American Heritage Dictionary of the English Language. Accessed December 10, 2019. https://www.ahdictionary.com/word/indoeurop.html#IR091000.

Ashcroft-Nowicki, Dolores. *Highways of the Mind*. Wellingborough: The Aquarian Press, 1987.

———. *Inner Landscapes*. Wellingborough: The Aquarian Press, 1989.

Benchley, Robert. "The Most Popular Book of the Month," in *Of All Things*. New York: Henry Holt and Company, 1921.

Brown, Daniel P., and Jack Engler, "The Stages of Mindfulness Meditation: A Validation Study," *The Journal of Transpersonal Psychology*, Vol, 12, No. 2, (1980): 143–192.

Budge, E. A. Wallis. *The Book of the Dead*. Secaucus: University Books Inc., 1984.

Butler, Walter Ernest. "Esoteric Government." Servants of the Light. Accessed December 10, 2019. https://www.servantsofthelight.org/knowledge/esoteric-government/.

Chesterton, G. K. *The Autobiography of G. K. Chesterton*. Edited by George J. Marlin, Richard P. Rabatin, John L. Swan, Joseph Sobran, Patricia Azar, Randall Paine and Barbara D. Marlin. San Francisco: Ignatius Press, 2006.

Crowley, Aleister. *The Book of the Law*. York Beach, ME: Red Wheel/Weiser, 2004.

Denning, Melita, and Osborne Phillips. *Magical States of Consciousness*. St Paul: Llewellyn Publications, 1985.

Drioton, Etienne, Georges Contenau, and J. Duchesne-Guillemin. Translated by M.B. Loraine. *Religions of the Ancient East*. London: Burns & Oates, 1959.

Esherick, Joseph W. "Chapter 2: Sects, Boxers, and Popular Culture." In *The Origins of the Boxer Uprising*. Oakland: University of California Press, 1988.

Farrar, Janet and Stewart. *The Witches' Way: Principles, Rituals and Beliefs of Modern Witchcraft*. London: Guild Publishing/Robert Hale, 1984.

Fortune, Dion. *Practical Occultism in Daily Life*. Wellingborough, UK: The Aquarian Press, 1935.

———. *The Sea Priestess*. London: The Aquarian Press, 1957.

———. *Spiritualism in the Light of Occult Science*. London: Rider, 1931.

Gruben, Michelle. "Representing the Elements on a Pagan Altar." Grove and Grotto. August 11, 2017. https://www.groveandgrotto.com/blogs/articles/representing-the-elements-on-a-pagan-altar.

Hebrew Today. "The Hebrew Alphabet - The Letter Lamed." Accessed July 15, 2020. https://hebrewtoday.com/alphabet/the-letter-lamed-%D7%9C/.

Homer. *The Odyssey*. Translated by Alexander Pope. London: J. Walker, and J. Harris, 1811.

Johnson, Kenneth, and Marguerite Elsbeth. *The Grail Castle*. St. Paul: Llewellyn Publications, 1995.

Jung, Emma, and Marie-Louise von Franz. *The Grail Legend*. Princeton: 2nd revised edition, Princeton University Press, 1998.

Kaltenmark, Max. *Lao Tzu and Taosim*. Translated by Roger Greaves. Stanford: Stanford University Press, 1969.

Knight, Gareth. *The Magical World of the Inklings*. Longmead: Element Books, 1990.

———. *The Rose Cross and the Goddess*. Wellingborough: The Aquarian Press, 1985.

———. *The Treasure House of Images*. Massachusetts: Destiny Books, 1986.

Kotansky, Roy, translator. *Lamella Orphica*. Mid-fourth century BCE. Gold, 2.2 x 3.7 x 0.1 cm (⅞ x 1 ⁷⁄₁₆ x ¹⁄₁₆ in). The J. Paul Getty Museum, Los Angeles. http://www.getty.edu/art/collection/objects/7194/unknown -maker-lamella-orphica-greek-mid-fourth-century-bc/.

Le Guin, Ursula K., and Garraty Gail. *The Farthest Shore*. New York: Atheneum, 1972.

Legg, Timothy J. "Situational Depression or Clinical Depression?" Medical News Today. September 28, 2018. https://www.medicalnewstoday.com /articles/314698.php.

Lewis, C. S. *The Chronicles of Narnia Volume VI: The Magician's Nephew*. Hong Kong: Enrich Spot Ltd., 2016.

Luke, Helen M. *Dark Wood to White Rose*. Pecos: Dove Publications, 1975.

Lupton, Hugh, and McGowan, Liz. *A Norfolk Songline*. Norwich: Hickathrift Press, 2000.

Magus, Simon, "A Victorian Gentleman in the Pharaoh's Court: Christian Egyptosophy and Victorian Egyptology in the Romances of H. Rider Haggard." *Open Cultural Studies* 1 (2017): 483–92. Accessed December 10, 2019. https://doi.org/10.1515/culture-2017-0045.

Matthews, Caitlín. *Arthur and the Sovereignty of Britain*. London: Arkana, 1989.

Matthews, John, and Caitlín Matthews. *The Arthurian Book of Days*. Hemel Hempstead: Prentice Hall, 1990.

Moen, Larry. *Guided Imagery*. Florida: United States Publishing, 1992.

Online Etymology Dictionary. "Origin and Meaning of Root *reg-." Online Etymology Dictionary. Accessed December 10, 2019. https://www .etymonline.com/word/*reg-.

Orpheus. *The Hymns of Orpheus*. Translated by R. C. Hoggart, Grand Rapids, Michigan: Phanes Press, 1993.

Reps, Paul and Nyogen Senzaki, comps. *Zen Flesh, Zen Bones*. New York: Anchor Books, 1967.

Roselli, C. E. "Neurobiology of Gender Identity and Sexual Orientation." *Journal of Neuroendocrinology* 30, no.7 (December 6, 2017). https://doi .org/10.1111/jne.12562.

Sims-Williams, Patrick. *Irish Influence on Medieval Welsh Literature*. Oxford: Oxford University Press, 2011.

Steinbrecher, Edwin C. *The Inner Guide Meditation*. Wellingborough: The Aquarian Press, 1983.

Stewart, Mary. *The Crystal Cave*. Hachette, UK: Hodder & Stoughton, 1970.

Syz, H. "Reflections on Group- or Phylo-Analysis." *Acta Psychotherapa* 11, supplement (1963): 37–88.

Waite, Arthur Edward. *The Hermetic Museum Volumes 1 and 2*. Loschberg 9, Germany: Jazzybee Verlag Jürgen Beck, 2017.

Williams, Charles. *The Figure of Beatrice*. Cambridge: D. S. Brewer, 1994.

———. *Taliessin Through Logres*. London: Oxford University Press, 1938.

———. *Taliessin Through Logres* (1938) and *The Region of the Summer Stars* (1944). London: Oxford University Press. 1954.

Williams, Charles. and C. S. Lewis. *Taliesin through Logres, The Region of the Summer Stars, Arthurian Torso*. Grand Rapids: William B. Eerdmans Publishing, 1974.

Wrightson, Patricia. *The Nargun and the Stars*. Sydney: Hutchison, 1973.

To Write to the Author

If you wish to contact the author or would like more information about this book, please write to the author in care of Llewellyn Worldwide Ltd. and we will forward your request. Both the author and publisher appreciate hearing from you and learning of your enjoyment of this book and how it has helped you. Llewellyn Worldwide Ltd. cannot guarantee that every letter written to the author can be answered, but all will be forwarded. Please write to:

Simon Court
℅ Llewellyn Worldwide
2143 Wooddale Drive
Woodbury, MN 55125-2989

Please enclose a self-addressed stamped envelope for reply,
or $1.00 to cover costs. If outside the U.S.A., enclose
an international postal reply coupon.

Many of Llewellyn's authors have websites with additional
information and resources. For more information,
please visit our website at http://www.llewellyn.com

Notes

Notes

Notes

Notes

Notes